The Welfare State in Competition for Global Talent

Mika Raunio/Annika Forsander

The Welfare State in Competition for Global Talent

From National Protectionism to Regional Connectivity – the Case of Finland

Foreign ICT and Bioscience Experts in Finland

PETER LANG
Frankfurt am Main · Berlin · Bern · Bruxelles · New York · Oxford · Wien

Bibliographic Information published by the Deutsche Nationalbibliothek
The Deutsche Nationalbibliothek lists this publication in the Deutsche Nationalbibliografie; detailed bibliographic data is available in the internet at <http://www.d-nb.de>.

ISBN 978-3-631-59725-5

www.peterlang.de

Preface

We hope that this book adds some new insights to the increasing discussion about labour migration. Although the literature of the field is already rather substantial, it most often deals with South-North brain drain or issues concerning the traditional talent magnet countries like the USA and Australia, or other major migrant destinations like Germany or the UK. The dynamics and special features of small, competitive, welfare states are rarely discussed in detail. Regional economic development and development policies also acquire a new flavour when individuals and human talent, instead of firms and investments, are attracted. The consequences of this are not only economic, but also social and political in various ways. One stimulant to this book was the observation that the policies focusing on the regional development and migration of highly skilled people are converging in the global innovation economy.

The empirical focus of the book lies in the Finland of the early 3rd millennium. This period of time is significant, because it provides a view to the phase in which Finland as a welfare state with its highly competitive economy and a leading-edge ICT sector seemed to be a bystander in terms of global talent flows. While global labour flows, including highly-skilled people, always follow the economic development to some extent, there are also countries, or rather regions within countries, that have created rather strong transnational or global networks and communities between them and a global pool of talent. There are negative and positive aspects in these relations, but especially interesting is the scarcity of those networks and communities from a region where cutting-edge research, world-leading ICT technology, welfare state and a competitive economy locate.

The authors would like to thank all their colleagues who have been involved in the process during the years. Especially we would like to thank Perttu Salmenhaara and Mika Helander, who participated in the writing of the Finnish-language book "Sykettä ja suvaitsevaisuutta" (Edita 2004), which offers the basic body for this English-language version as well. Maija Mäkinen, who (partially) translated the text helped us to find the right words. Institute for Social Research and Unit for Science, Technology and Innovation Studies (University of Tampere) and The Centre for Research on Ethnic Relations and Nationalism in Swedish School of Social Science (University of Helsinki) made it financially possible to produce this book.

This book is result of the two major research projects and years of studies concerning labour migration, immigration and mobility of highly-skilled individuals. We would also like to thank the leaders of the key projects “Should I Stay or Should I Go?” (2001–2002) headed by Professor Markku Sotarauta (University of Tampere) and “Regional Brain Gain” (2003–2004) led by Dr. Pia Mero (SITRA).

Mika Raunio & Annika Forsander, Tampere and Helsinki, 4 June 2009

Table of contents

1 Connecting to global brain circulation

Nobel Prize winner Chen Ning Yang received his degree from the University of Tsinghua in northeast China in 1944. In spite of his young age, the talented and highly motivated physicist had long dreamed of working alongside the top scientists in the field of atomic physics, which attracted him particularly. But the most important research in the field was being done in the West, mostly in the United States. At the same time, Japan's ongoing war created instability in China as well. Hence, obtaining a research grant in 1945 for travel to the West seemed like a dream come true. Yang was particularly excited about the prospect of meeting the top scientists in the field, including his own inspirers Enrico Fermi and Eugene Wigner. That year, Yang's ship sailed into the New York harbour and headed toward University of Chicago. In 1957 he was rewarded for his work with the Nobel Prize in Physics (Hakala 2003, 293-295). Today he holds professorships at the Chinese University of Hong-Kong, the University of Tsinghua (China) and the New York University in the United States.

According to Guellec and Cervantes (2002), from the beginning of civilisation, intellectual capital has responded to demand by moving. During the Renaissance, Spain hired officers of the Italian navy, and Italian architects and painters were sought after in France and Northern Europe. In the 1600s England used the expertise of Danish makers of instruments and measuring devices to gain status as the world leader in the field. In the early years of the 21st century the demand for information and communications experts has increased particularly in the United States and the European nations of the OECD (ibid. 2002, 79).

The global migration of talent thus represents rather the rule than some kind of historical anomaly. Often it knits two places together over time, as professor Yang's case indicates. Thus, the key message of this book is that in a global knowledge economy that depends on innovation and talent, policies should aim to connect regional and national agents with global brain circulation rather than bolster protection for national systems. Migration of talent has been the historical sideline during economies based on mass production and strong nation-states, but has gained importance along with the strengthening of the global and knowledge-based economy.

The story of Chen Yang and other historical examples illustrate the phenomenon that the book at hand scrutinizes: The global competition for talent from an individual knowledge holder's point of view. The migration of talent has always included two elements; for regions and nations, it is a strategy to increase their competitiveness, and for talented persons, a way to find creative and inspiring environments where they can develop their expertise and enjoy the use of it. The international migration of experts is an ancient phenomenon, but more significant and topical at the moment than ever before, because of the shift towards a global, knowledge-focused economy.

Finland seems to be one of the winners in the global knowledge economy. The explanations for this often point to the combination of a highly developed innovation system that is able to utilise the knowledge economy, with a welfare state that offers citizens good services, high-quality education and a safe, equal society to live in (Castells & Himanen 2001). For the same reasons, Richard Florida (2005) lists Finland as one of the most likely winners in the competition for global talent. According to him, Finland is one of the challengers who will successfully compete for the best brains with the traditional, giant talent magnet, the United States (ibid. 2005). It seems, however, that it takes more than a competitive knowledge economy and the welfare state to connect with global brain circulation. Old policies do not work in the new environment. This book discusses in detail what the roles of an advanced knowledge economy and welfare state are in attracting global talent, and what other cultural and societal traits have to be considered in this context. The above-described circumstances make Finland an excellent "laboratory for social science" to elaborate on these questions. The discussion will lead us to point out, where it is evident, that not just national, but especially regional conditions and policies have a crucial role in the process.

The results obtained from the "Finnish laboratory" have great significance also in a wider context. Novel conditions for producing, utilising and supplying human capital are the most essential factors in succeeding in the global economy for all advanced nations. The shift brings the dynamic and globalisation to the labour market as well (Castells 1996; Nonaka & Takeuchi 1995, 42). The formation of a labour market sector that operates over and across national boundaries and cultures – but that is still in many ways regulated by national governments and influenced by local cultures – has a critical impact on the dynamic of development in urban areas and nation-states. The rise of such a "marginal" phenomenon – global migration of talent – to the centre of the economic vortex and mainstream has an impact on the way labour markets operate. It presents new challenges for policy makers, employers and for experts themselves.

Beyond the illustrative case study of Finland, this book will examine the shifting of the global economy's dynamic to the global labour market, the global economy's institutionalisation into a structure that permanently shapes society, and the impact of these factors on the way skilled labour is distributed globally from the perspective of an individual expert. The basic generic question, i.e., *what factors steer individuals to a particular region in the global field of choices,* is approached in a situation where the operating environment is global rather than national and the key resource is the individual knowledge holder, a human being, rather than a faceless labour force. In order to understand this phenomenon, the new roles of both nation-states and individuals need to be scrutinized.

If nation-states should be seen as more open and less exclusive, the extreme interpretation of the new individual is as a member of (a) "global tribe(s)" rather than just a citizen. The "tribes of experts" that operate in the global economy are said to form around shared traits such as ethnic and cultural background, common ideology, a particular narrowly defined area of professional expertise, or an academic discipline. What is common to all of these groupings is that they view global networking and the resulting diversity as well as changing identity as a solution to the new environment and modes of operation, which they find themselves facing (see Florida 2002; Kotkin 1992, 4-5; Lash 2002, 43; Mafessoli 1996, 6). The members of these groupings have a global view toward issues – they recognise the local and national qualities and place them in wider context.

1.1 Key questions, structure and research approach

Both regional competitiveness and the survival of the welfare state are closely connected to job growth and to where companies are located, but they are also driven by the location of expertise and individual experts. In terms of competitiveness, where the occupations of the experts are concerned, the availability of the best skills and knowledge are extremely important. Employers should be able to choose their key employees from the global, not just the local pool of talent. If an employer cannot recruit globally because of whatever social, economic or institutional attributes in its surroundings, this represents a competitive handicap. This logic seems to have been applicable lately at the national and regional level in the context of the global competition for talent (Florida 2005; Kuznetsov 2006; Kuptch & Pang 2006; Saxenian 2006).

The need for regions and nation-states to be competitive is a consequence of the globalisation of the economy. In recent years, this development has bred several well-publicised competitiveness comparisons between nation-states. Often, Finland appears in the top league of these rankings. For example, two well-known ranking systems, the World Economic Forum (WEF) and the International Institute for Management Development (IMD), have ranked Finland among the most competitive nations in 21st century ratings, ranging from first-place to eighth-place, with slightly different placements in different lists (see Ali-Yrkkö et al. 2004, 45)[1] At the same time, Finland has been referred to as a laboratory for the information society, and has reached top billing also in studies that measure the level of the information society.

Although competitiveness comparisons have been criticised (Rouvinen 2004) for their poor ability to predict economic development, from the point of view of social change, they deliver an interesting message. They do show that economic competitiveness is not connected to a particular social model or operational cul-

1 WEF; www.weforum.org/gcp and IMD; www.imd.ch/wcy

ture. Each country forges its competitiveness on the basis of its social model, and difference can be the very thing that provides a strategic edge. In these comparisons, for example Finland, Singapore and the United States have been ranked at the world's top. Thus, three very different social models have appeared at the top of competitiveness and information society comparisons. Finland has been used as an example of an information economy success that is built on the foundation of an open welfare society. Based on this, Castells and Himanen (2001) have created the following division between the different information societies:

- The Silicon Valley model – a market-driven, open society
- The Singapore model – authoritarian information society
- The Finnish model – open information society based on the equal distribution of welfare.

The ability to compete is not dependent on ideological differences between different social models (of market economies). More important is the quality and efficiency of the policies that steer social and economic life in societies that are founded on different models, as well as other cultural or societal traits. Finland has been able to develop technologically and economically in the global information era, and still retain the ideological foundation of the Nordic welfare state with its emphasis on equality. An information society can be a Nordic welfare state, and vice versa, even while the globalisation of the economy places pressure on the Nordic ideal of an equal society. The social system itself is not essential; rather, what makes the difference is the adaptability and credibility of its institutions in the global operating environment (Friedman 1999). In other words, pursuing global competitiveness does not necessarily mean a transformation toward a more neo-liberal society, but it may in fact be possible to find a competitive edge in new interpretations of the Nordic welfare state.

Having said this, the results of the present study suggest that this logic works the other way around as well: a welfare state regime and global competitiveness with an advanced knowledge economy may not be enough in the competition for top talent. The first key message of this book includes the idea that *a globally competitive welfare state is not a self-evidently attractive destination for human talent, since local conditions are interpreted through an individual's eyes in much more detailed form than in a macro-level definition.* Macro-level interpretations of societal models leave so much room for variation, that when evaluating the opportunities from the perspective of a "global individual", much more detailed and regionally embedded analysis is required within the same loose frameworks. Human resources are a rather distinct form of resource and need profound micro-level analysis to be understood.

The need for more detailed analyses may be illustrated through the pros and cons of the welfare state in the case of Finland. The attracting and deterring factors are often different sides of the same coin. This dilemma of attractiveness may be defined in simplified form as follows: 1) Low income disparities provide a stable and equal society, but also low income for highly skilled professionals in a global comparison. 2) A high level of social capital and trust may ease interaction among natives, but provides rather closed networks and culture, to which foreigners rarely gain entry. 3) Safe and well-functioning "small town" living environments may also translate to a low level of diversity and rather "dull" inhabitants. 4) Well-established welfare services may be of a high-quality in national macro-level comparisons and a valued sign of a humane society, but through the eyes of wealthy individuals, the benefits of concrete welfare services may be marginal or even non-existent. 5) Innovation environments are of a high-quality and highly developed, but due to their small size and an abundant number of highly educated natives, the saturated job markets are not available to most specialists.

These ambivalent or even contradictory factors make Finland a rather uninteresting alternative for some experts, whereas they are at the very core of attractiveness for others. Looking at these kinds of push and pull factors does make it possible to examine the question of the location dynamics of global talent, but does not provide a deeper understanding of the phenomena. Consequently, the second key message of this book *is that a detailed study of push and pull factors is needed, but it must be carefully placed in the local, national and global contexts, so that we may discover what steers the movement of talent. Our claim is that several forms of "openness" are required on multiple levels of society and the economy.*

In the Finnish case, globally operating companies and individual scientists – i.e. advocates of global knowledge society – were the main attractors for foreign experts, as opposed to the nation-state itself, or its city regions. In order to attract more foreign talent, high-quality creative innovation environments should be developed further while bearing in mind the above-mentioned problems. A creative innovation environment combines elements of business and human environments to provide a sustainable way to utilise and support human intelligence as a source of wealth. For this, the combination of the welfare state and an advanced knowledge economy can offer an appropriate platform, provided that the specific traits – pros and cons – of the location are recognised and adjusted in relation to the global environment from individuals' point of view.

To understand the specific characteristics of Finland beyond the competitive welfare state framework, in this study we look for answers to the following key questions:

1. *How does immigration policy, at a national and EU level, prevent or support the flow of international knowledge holders into regions?*

   1a) What are the historical and social factors that contribute to attitudes and practices toward immigration?

1b) How do national regulatory systems regulate and channel mobility in the globalising labour market?

2. *How do experts choose their location in a global field of choices?*
   2a) What is the role of globally operating organisations as channels and as providers of information and images for skilled labour in a globalising, information-saturated world?
   2b) How does the universalist welfare state treat foreign experts in terms of national culture and institutional structures?

3. *How do foreign experts experience the impact of national and "global cultures" within corporations(=workplaces) and in regions(=places to live)?*
   3a) What are the specific strengths and weaknesses of urban areas and employer corporations emerging from the interfacing of national and global cultures, that enhance or erode their attractiveness in the eyes of experts in the global labour market?
   3b) What factors give corporations and urban areas a competitive edge in being able to retain skilled labour?

The book contains ten chapters that aim to answer these questions. Chapter 1 introduces the key messages, research questions and the framework of the study. The rest of the book may be divided into three thematic parts: chapters 2 to 5 draw a picture of the globalising world, Chapters 6 to 9 focus on the migration dynamics of experts, based on the results of case studies from Finland, and Chapter 10 concludes and integrates the issues.

In the first thematic part, Chapter 2 places Finland on the global map in terms of labour migration policies and migration history. The cases of Ireland and Denmark are used as points of comparison. Chapters 3 and 4 describe the global environment that provides the new dynamic and the institutional settings for the international migration of highly skilled labour. Chapter 3 also illustrates some key sources behind the new dynamics and logic at work in the globalising labour market. Chapter 4 focuses on the incarnations of this global dynamic: institutions, organisational structures, commodities and ownership questions. Chapter 5 provides a more focused description of how the national boundaries of Finland are reshaped by the European Union, its own government as well as corporate decision making. The role of the nation-state is in no way disappearing in terms of international labour migration; rather, it is significantly changing while at the same time adjusting its social system and national culture to the global environment.

In the second thematic part, Chapter 6 opens the discussion by considering the attractiveness of Finland in the global field of choices of experts. The roles of "life-style", global connectivity and official gate-keepers are scrutinised in the creation of "globally attractive images and brands". Chapter 7 goes to the core of the global movement of experts to look at working environments and career development. How can regional innovation environments acquire the characteristics that appeal to creative individuals at the global level? In Chapter 8, the focus shifts away from work environment to living environment. The key question is the dilemma of the welfare state, i.e., how appealing is a nationally organised welfare and social system from a global point of view? The question is not easy to answer, but crucial to ask. Chapter 9 focuses on the physical, functional and social aspects of the living environment. These aspects, as elements of attractiveness in a global context, have been the subject of debate, not just recently, but throughout the history of migration studies. From an individual's perspective, not just work environment but also qualities of the living environment at large define the quality of a creative innovation environment.

Finally, Chapter 10 concludes the discussion and sums up the key thesis of the book. Some policy recommendations are made in order to illustrate the interdependence of labour migration with other policies. The framework and the key elements of attractiveness are illustrated in Figure 1. At the core is the creative innovation environment as a combination of the work and living environments that are moulded by national culture and the social system. Images and "brands" are reflections that transmit the messages for those who are still potential immigrants.

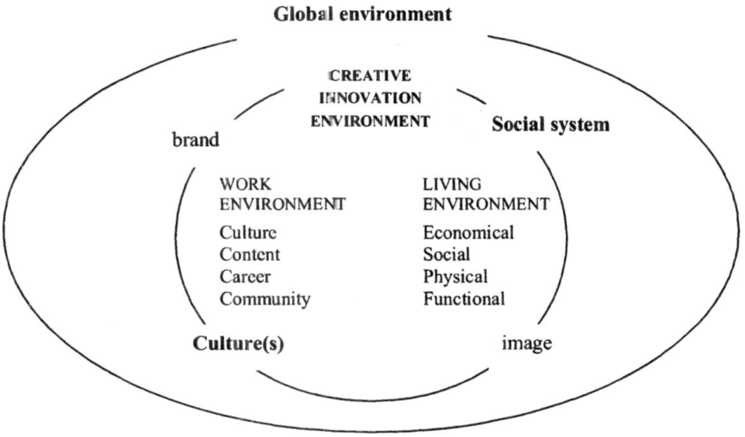

Figure 1. Framework of the study and the generic elements of the attractiveness

Research process and data

The answers to research questions were sought from multiple, abundant sources. The study's main voice is given to foreign experts working in Finland. The data consists of 149 thematic interviews of foreign experts in the ICT and biotech industries as well as key individuals connected to their recruitment, including managers, relocation consultants and officials. Foreign spouses of ICT experts were also interviewed. ICT experts were additionally subjected to an internet survey. The following list describes the data that is used[2]:

- Reference sources – for example, various documents, research reports and published articles
- Telephone survey on the proportion of foreign employees in corporations and universities
- Research survey conducted among immigrants employed in the ICT industry (N = 556)
- Personal interviews with immigrants employed in the ICT industry (N=66) and their spouses (N = 31)
- Personal interviews with foreign researchers in university biosciences (N = 22)
- Personal interviews with managers and human resource personnel who recruit foreign experts, relocation consultants who ease the adaptation process, and civil servants (N = 30)

The regional context used in our research consists of Finland and its four main city regions; Helsinki, Tampere, Turku and Oulu (Figure 2.). The operational context is made up of globally operating individuals, the organisations that employ them and organisations that regulate international migration. The movement of experts across national boundaries is a global phenomenon that uses the nation-states and their urban areas as platforms. The interplay between local and global in a particular geographic area – from a nation-state to a city – creates social and cultural encounters that continually remake the content and rules of operation within each. The examination of the individual's role in this context also helps render visible the changing function of the nation-state in the field of choices that individuals face.

2 For ICT experts, the empiric data used in this study utilises data that was gathered for the Research Unit for Urban and Regional Development Studies, Sente, (University of Tampere) by Mika Raunio in the project "Should I Stay or Should I Go" (2002). For the biotechnology experts, additional, new data was collected by Annika Forsander (University of Helsinki) in the "Brain Gain through migration" project (2003). Empirical material and methodology are described in more detail in Appendix 1.

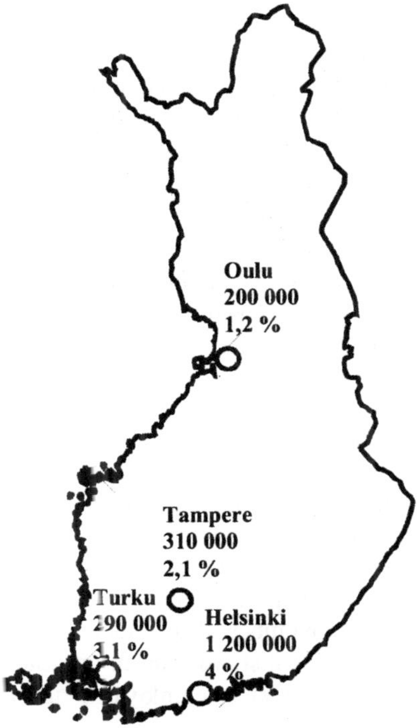

Figure 2. City regions used in the study, number of inhabitants and proportion of foreigners (%) 2002 (Statistics Finland)

The experts in our study work in the core fields of the knowledge economy – biosciences (or biotechnology) and ICT. This selection was determined to some extent by the availability of empirical research targets – foreign experts – as well as the necessity of selecting a sector with a global labour market already present in Finland. In addition, these sectors are named in the strategies of both nation-states and city regions in Finland and around the world as fields of the future, upon which the welfare of societies and the competitiveness of regions are being secured.

For four decades, the human capital theory has postulated that people and their professional skills form a key resource from the standpoint of economic activity, and that they are not merely economic capital or tools of production. The most commonly used definition of highly skilled labour, or more precisely, human resources in science and technology (HRST), can be found in the "Canberra Manual" prepared by Eurostat and OECD. According to the manual, human resources devoted to science and technology must have successfully completed education at the tertiary level in an S&T field of study and/or have been employed in an S&T occupation, where the above-mentioned qualifications are normally required (Auriol & Sexton 2002, 15). In this study, most experts not only possess a university-level degree (over 90 %) and an occupation where new information is both created and applied, but also a skill set that is in high demand and, because of its scarcity, provides a competitive advantage. By "foreigner" we mean a person who is not a citizen of the country in which he or she resides. "Immigrant' is a broader concept and refers to people who reside outside of their country of origin, regardless of whether or not they are citizens of the new country.

Beyond their foreignness, the target group is defined through their expertise as follows: they are experts who work in positions of demanding management skills, and they create new knowledge or apply existing knowledge in novel ways. Experts may also work in other types of positions that require the application of special expertise in a way that is significant to key business operations. Most experts are relatively highly educated (Raunio 2001a). The definitions cannot be rigid, because different companies have vastly different needs. In this study, an expert may be a research and development (R&D) manager, researcher or other team member in a research and development unit, a marketing director or professional with special qualifications, a member of a production team who creates specifically tailored products, or a scientist working in an academic department. When referring to the target group, the study employs the term "expert"[3]. When interpreting the results, it is worth remembering that the target group works for organisations and multicultural work environments that operate globally and that, in a Finnish context, represent highly internationalised work environments.

The study used the triangulation method – an appropriate choice when combining perspectives from migration research, regional studies, and economic and globalisation research, all of which are multi-disciplinary by nature. The concept of triangulation in its original meaning emerges from navigation and refers to defining the location of an object as accurately as possible through the use of several reference points. The same idea is applied when using triangulation in the social sciences.

In the social sciences, triangulation was originally seen as a method of source critique and quality control, adding to the validity of the research. Similarly, in the present study, it is possible to view triangulation as a method of quality control. When data from one source is inconsistent with data from another data set, examining the discrepancy can either reveal a mistake or help understand the multiplicity of the issue. In approaching a new area of study, as is the case here, it is good

3 Experts and professionals who work in yhe service of the public sector (for example, physicians and teachers) comprise an important source of human capital. However, in this book, we have chosen to focus on lines of business that are the most critical to the competitiveness of urban areas and the employed foreign experts.

to use the broadest possible approach and the greatest possible number of data sets, methods and researchers to map out the phenomenon under study. None of the research data or theoretical perspectives would have been sufficient alone to illuminate the phenomenon, but working together, they were able to produce a broader perspective. Mapping out a new area of research also introduces questions regarding the sufficiency and scope of the data, which can be complemented by using various types of material and data.

Because our target group had not been studied before, it is difficult to evaluate representativeness or the effect of attrition on the findings. The target companies were carefully selected to be useful from the point of view of the study's outline and objectives, and the experts working therein can be said to comprehensively represent the opinions of foreign ICT and biotech experts working in Finland. In spite of attrition, the study's validity is improved by the fact that, when the data was analysed, quantitative data was being used mainly as background for qualitative data, instead of running an independent statistical analysis of the profile and values of foreign experts working in Finland.

Finally, special efforts were made to guarantee anonymity to prevent respondents from being identifiable. The respondents' anonymity was ensured by eliminating and modifying identifying details in reporting. For purposes of interpreting the data, it is important to name the line of business and country of origin of a respondent, but other identifying details (age, gender, place of residence, occupation etc.) are omitted in that context. The elimination of personal information was very important for many respondents, because it would be easy to identify an individual on the basis of occupation and nationality in a small country such as Finland. For most people, career development matters and opinions related to them are personal information that they do not want publicly examined.

Context of the study: globalising knowledge economy

It is important to place the key questions of the research into a wider context. Globalisation is the key issue in the attractiveness of regions and the international migration of experts. Thus, it is appropriate to evaluate globalisation's various dimensions, its impact on labour markets, and through them, numerous social issues. 'Globalisation' has spawned a swarm of buzz words – global nomads, free flow of capital, people and trends, and has obscured the boundaries of place and of the nation-state. The globalisation of economies has obliterated the boundaries that define individuals, corporations and the society that surrounds them, and the relationships between these operators is continually redefined.

In an economy driven by knowledge, creativity and worldwide networks, individuals and corporations are bound to their operating environments in complex ways. When highly skilled labour is the key resource and the labour markets of experts are global, what kind of dynamic and operational logic should a nation-state or urban centre embrace in order to be successful? In regional development, the answer has often been to develop an innovation system (or environment) (Cooke et al. 2004). But how can these innovation environments, focused on the development of business environments and supporting local interaction, move toward more human and international aspects? Should we add in immigration questions, or the development of multicultural work environments, or the emergence transnational networks?

In the case of migration policy, the intensifying collaboration among EU nations has a significant impact on the forms that globalisation takes. EU cooperation transforms the meaning of nation-state boundaries so that the flow of certain capitals, products, trends and people can occur with more ease than previously. Nations and national economies, however, remain important units in EU cooperation. Mobility in the global labour market is restricted by the nation-states' regulatory systems, such as visa and residency requirements, that place a value not only on expertise but also on an individual's nationality. Nation-states impose various "legalised attitudes" on different individuals. Regardless of his or her level of expertise, it is significantly easier for an EU citizen than someone from a "third country" to cross national borders within the EU.

It is particularly in regulating immigration that EU cooperation is critical – and much of national immigration laws and administrative strategies reflect back to nations through EU policies. The expansion of the EU in the 1990s, and more recently in 2004 and 2007, with the addition of twelve new member nations, has had some impact on the volume and directions of migration within the EU and from outside it, but it has had a particular effect on administrative mechanisms. For that reason, this book examines not only the impact of national regulatory systems on foreign labour, but also the mechanisms employed by the EU to regulate immigration, and the connections between the two.

It is noteworthy that the EU strategy for immigration is to create a counterpoint for traditionally attractive North America, so that skilled labour would choose Europe instead. This objective has been set in a situation of rapid change, where a comprehensive viewpoint or a transnational management system for the relocation of skilled labour is only in the process of being debated. The issue has received attention, and transnational agreements along the lines of GATT have been proposed for regulating the movement of experts (Ghosh 2000; Straubhaar 2000), but the competition for expertise is settling into one waged between nations and continents.

New changes seem on the way as indicated by the weakening – in some business sectors, dramatically so – draw of the United States and the simultaneously growing attraction of technologically and economically renewing Asian locations. The debate has also encompassed the increasingly important role of developing giants, i.e. the so-called BRICS countries (Brazil, Russia, India, China, South Africa) in the world economy, which cannot be separated from the global redistribution of skilled labour (Florida 2004a; Rutanen 2003; Ali-Yrkkö et al. 2004). In this situation, the EU and its member countries will shift positions, thus further emphasising the interconnectedness of political and economic systems.

Operating models that have reacted to the effects of globalisation have helped create "islands of global economy", reinforcing the development of a global labour market. It is probable that labour markets that operate according to conditions set by the global economy will continue to proliferate, and that mobility across the boundaries of nation-states to these labour markets will increasingly become the norm. In many professions, people's résumés will reflect work experience from several countries. The internationalisation of the labour market and the cultural diversification of work environments that are tightly connected to globalisation will create their own, special by-line in this change. For example, in the case of Finland, multi-ethnicity does not yet permeate all of society, but sensitivity to ethnic diversity is a daily part of many work environments and organisations brought together by globalisation. It should be acknowledged that divorcing organisations from society is highly artificial and thus, changes that are taking place within organisations are also connected to social change. The interdependent and reciprocal nature of organisational and societal changes emerges as a crucial issue also in the present volume (see Casey 2002).

The global dynamic of the labour market is in many ways a result of changes in the organisations that employ experts. When organisations recruit beyond national borders, and careers consist of temporary assignments in different countries, the global labour market opens up not just to future Nobel laureates, but to other experts as well. It is true that the global labour market often affects only certain, specialised lines of business, and that it has come about in part – but only in part – as a result of corporations becoming multinational. We claim that global mobility is occurring in lines of business that require highly skilled labour and value expertise, possessing cultural and social expertise, including proficiency in the local language, is not as crucial a success factor as are other skills that are connected to the job itself.

Industries that genuinely deal in global mobility and employ from a labour market that transcends national boundaries are mostly in the areas of ICT, academic research and business management. The lines of business we examine in this book represent ones that have recently experienced the globalisation of their labour markets: the ICT industry and the foreign experts in university biosciences. According to Iredale (2001), the ICT industry constitutes a precedent that anticipates the creation of a transnational labour market that operates outside of national regulation. Factors that have contributed to the transnational trend in the ICT industry include the following:

- Rapid growth created strong demand and opened up the field to experts globally.
- The industry is characterised by the applicability of expertise outside of any cultural context and by the use of English as working language.
- Learning on the job makes it possible to acquire and update skills.
- High labour mobility within and among companies both regionally and globally.
- The industry is largely unregulated by trade unions or other mechanisms.
  (Iredale 2001)

The framework of our study provides an excellent setting for examining the rendezvous of global talent and the nation-state. A voice is given to individual experts working in two of the most global lines of business, in a foreign country (Finland) that has a reputation as one of the most competitive economies and egalitarian welfare states, but still has an extremely modest foreign population and restricted immigration policies. Our social science laboratory is thus well equipped for the experiment.

1.2 Challenges for the welfare state

Unavoidably, profound changes are emerging. The new structures of the global economy are forcing the Nordic model to undergo changes. The situation is driven by the three above-mentioned long-term trends guiding economic development. The challenge of expertise arises from the increased role of technology in production and the growing importance of research and development in competition between corporations. The challenge of internationalisation translates into the globalisation of the economy and the internationalisation of individuals and labour markets. The challenge of limited resources means that there is less labour available in industrialised countries as a result of the ageing population and structural unemployment.

Economic, social and cultural changes are tightly interwoven in the great wave of change, and the modes of operation that are stipulated by globalisation and internationalisation present new challenges. Some expertise-intensive occupations already look quite international: English may be the working language, the teams multiethnic, and they may be spread out in different parts of the world. In such contexts it is considered normal for employees to change countries of residence every few years. Traditionally, universities and research institutions have been international and expertise focused. The rise of the new economy and new media sent IT professionals wandering from country to country to work in various incarnations of Silicon Valley and in technology parks. The flow of capital, not attached to any one country, has had the effect that not only new technology companies, but also older technology companies have switched to English as the administrative corporate language. The internationalisation of corporations requires that, as geographic unity declines, the organisation shares a common language.

Box 1. Innovation environment as an answer to competing in the global knowledge economy – the case of Finland

In Finland, a strong regional emphasis and especially the role of city regions are visible in development approaches such as the "Center of Expertise Program" or "Regional Centres Program (RCP)". The aim of the Regional Centre Program (RCP) is the development of a network of regional centres that is based on the particular strengths, expertise and specialisation of each region. Regional development based on a network of regional centres results in a more balanced regional structure for Finland and enhanced international competitiveness. In the future, the resources of national regional policy are intended to be specifically targeted at regional centres, and the enhancement of the network consisting of them. RCP is a government special programme in accordance with the Regional Development Act. RCP was implemented in 34 regions between 2001 and 2006 (www.intermin.fi).

A more innovation-oriented programme is "The Center of Expertise Program", which was launched in 1994 in eight different Centers of Expertise. Due to its subsequent success, the government decided to extend the programme in 1998 and 2002 by appointing new centres of expertise and by increasing the number of fields of expertise in the existing centres. Then 22 centres of expertise covering 45 fields were appointed for the period of 2003–2006. The task of the centres of expertise is to use internationally competitive knowledge and skills as a resource for business activities, the creation of new jobs and regional development. It is a fixed-term special programme that, in accordance with the Regional Development Act, aims to pool local, regional and national resources to utilise high-level expertise (http://www.oske.net/in_english/). In 2006, the concept of "Strategic centres for top-expertise" were introduced, financial investments substantially increased and aims re-focused. Still, the basic approach – efficient utilisation and production of knowledge within certain key regions – remains and is being strengthened.

As with the development of Finnish immigration policy, the development of a regional dimension in Finnish technology and innovation policy was also motivated by the regional policy of the European Union (EU), which Finland joined in 1995. The fundamental transformation of the Finnish economy, however, opened up new opportunities of economic restructuring also at the regional level. The Center of Expertise Program and the introduction of polytechnic universities in Finnish education system with a strong regional orientation underlined the regional focus of Finnish innovation policy. The establishment of Employment and Economic Development Centres, whose main task is to develop their regional economies in a systemic way, has also strengthened the regional dimension of the innovation system (Schienstock, Kautonen & Koski 2004, 128). The production of human capital and support for new company formation are thus implemented as a part of existing innovation systems, whereas attracting creative and talented individuals is still an often discussed but rarely implemented part of the process. This pattern can be found in most Northern European nations.

In most advanced economies, especially in Nordic countries and in northern Europe, national and regional strategies view innovation systems and expertise as the foundation on which economic competitiveness and the welfare of citizens are built. In recent years, concepts such as 'cluster', 'learning economy', 'learning region', 'innovation system', 'innovation environment', and most recently, 'creative city', have been repeated whenever strategies for regional or national competitiveness are being forged (Schienstock & Kuusi 1999; Cooke 2004; Porter 1989; Florida 2002). The role of city regions as social operators becomes central, because they are seen as the engines behind this development. Often reliance on expertise is supported by government programmes, and by embracing a number of social strategies, such as an information society strategy (See Box 1).

More broadly, when competitiveness and welfare are both built upon the power of knowledge, a country needs doers and payers: individuals who, with their expertise, are able to respond to the challenges set by increasingly demanding work tasks and who, as tax payers, pay for the services provided by the welfare state. Also needed are corporations that employ these experts and the knowledge to convert their expertise into economic wellbeing through wage development and tax payments. Research and development jobs have been estimated to produce approximately 2.5 new jobs for each initial R&D position in the region through subcontracting and services, and in this way, knowledge-based industries support regional employment also indirectly, by increasing the demand even for less highly skilled labour.

At a regional level, the availability of expertise is increasingly a precondition for competitiveness. Knowledge and expertise are scarce resources, because of the dynamic of the knowledge economy, which centralises knowledge and expertise regionally as a result of increased demand, and because of increasingly specific skill requirements. This is especially true in science based and research and development (R&D) intensive innovation environments that form the backbone of Finnish innovation system. From the point of view of distribution of expertise, competitiveness is a reciprocal process of attraction in which the choice of location made by an employer prompts the relocation of experts, and where the availability of experts, conversely, often determines the choice of business address. Florida (2002:2005) even claimed that "in creative economy" jobs follow people rather than people follow the jobs. (ibid. 2002; 2005)

One example of this dynamic is the Swedish mobile phone and network manufacturer Ericsson, which announced the move of its headquarters from Stockholm to London, because high income taxes scared off potential, highly skilled employees. In response, Sweden's government announced a plan for targeted tax breaks to attract top experts. Ericsson, however, had already made the decision, and moved its headquarters to London in 1998 (Kotler, Asplund, Rein & Haider 1999, 24).

The availability of highly skilled labour not only influences where corporations operate, but determines the possibilities of starting or developing projects within corporations in a given region, because most international trade and export occurs internally within corporate conglomerates. A similar phenomenon is also reflected in workforce mobility – corporations abound with groups of temporary and project-based staff, who are hired to carry out a particular project, as well as projects that take the teams responsible for them from location to location, because their expertise is crucial to the project. Even when a corporation remains in a particular location, certain operations and the employees associated with them may be transferred to regions that offer better resources and efficiency for that operational area. Hence, it is not enough that city region is able to offer workforce and provide higher education; it must also appear sufficiently attractive to experts on the international labour market – including potential arrivals and those already in the region.

Reflecting the dynamic of globalisation in general, there are already numerous examples of HQs recently moved abroad in traditionally Finnish-owned firms as a result of new ownership: Sonera, Salcomp and Tamrock to Sweden, Sinebrychoff and Cultor to Denmark, Timberjack, Metsä-Serla Chemicals and Nokia Paperi to the United States, and so on (Ali-Yrkkö, et al. 2004, 29). In addition, Nokia, for example, has transferred some HQ operations abroad at the same time as its traditionally Finnish top management is becoming increasingly international. Global employers are truly becoming global.

A broader, related question in terms of the future of the welfare state is labour shortage. As diminishing numbers of new labour enter the labour market due to shrinking generations and low birth rates, discussions have recently abounded all over Europe about the changing age structure. One concern is how to retain the structure of the welfare state, as the economic dependency ratio declines and pensions use up a growing portion of the welfare state's purse. Another concern is the labour shortage brought about by demographic change, particularly its qualitative consequences: who will do the jobs that are left over, when the number of pensioners exceeds the number of people entering the labour force? According to Keeley (2007), in 2000, about 15 % of the population in OECD countries was aged over 65 years, whereas by 2030 the number is estimated to reach 25 %. From 1950 to 2000, the size of the working-age population in OECD countries rose by 76 %. The projected growth from 2000 to 2050 is just 4 % (ibid. 2007, 12).

Thus, the need for expertise and the internationalising labour market are both connected to a broader social shift, where the labour force is growing only beyond industrialised nations, in countries with cheap labour. Low-skilled production has long been flowing into these countries, but in recent years even jobs that require increasingly specialised skills are being done in Asia. Simultaneously, industrialised nations compete with each other for these jobs with increasing fervour. Together with this issue of social debate arises the *need for tax payers* who ensure a solid funding base for the welfare state, so that it can continue paying benefits; and the need for labour to replace the retiring workforce, whose annual volume exceeds the number of new workforce in most developed nations. It has been estimated that in Western Europe, up to 40 percent of the current workforce will retire by 2010. This will have the greatest impact on manual labour jobs, because a large proportion of those soon to retire currently work in such jobs. According to one view, the situation has been made worse by the ever-climbing level of education in most European countries. Who will work in the continually expanding service sector – in jobs that require muscle, but not advanced education, and that cannot be transferred to countries of cheap labour? This introduces the question of the global division of labour and its impact on different societies. What roles will different regions acquire in this global and national division of labour?

The labour market may divide internationally and nationally. At a national level, division means that low-skill service jobs will increasingly be handled by immigrants. At the international level, low-skill manufacturing jobs are concentrating in countries with low production costs, where suitable labour is available and corporations can operate under conditions that are favourable to them. The egalitarian ideal of the Nordic welfare state is in opposition to the idea of the active immigration model implemented in many Central and Southern European nations, where low-skill, low-wage jobs are filled with foreign labour – either legally or illegally (Forsander 2004, 212). All of the Nordic countries have balked at granting work permits for cleaning or construction jobs. This policy is intended to fight a deeper segmentation of the labour force into low-skill jobs that are held by immigrants and the "better" jobs of the original population – a situation that is already a fact in many European nations with far greater immigration volumes than Finland, where only intimations of such segmentation are visible. The retention of low-skill jobs in industrial nations or, conversely, their transfer to countries with low production costs, will deepen the labour market divide between high- and low-skill jobs.

The globalisation of the economy has altered operating conditions in every country. Competition for wages, the productivity of labour, and taxation all occur globally and evoke a situation where regional or national differences in the productivity of certain lines of business are more visible. Differences between generations, education levels and operating sectors are also more pronounced in the labour market, causing tensions between various interest groups. In addition, the weakening tax base, decline of employed workforce, and availability of skilled labour all represent threats to Nordic welfare states engaged in global competition. Together, all of these factors have introduced a strained relationship between the goals of productivity, employment and equality. This tension cannot be resolved merely through more education or innovation-promoting policies – a more broad-scoped social approach is needed.

Financing an equal welfare and information society requires that a solid tax base be maintained. Yet it seems that the kind of welfare state we now have cannot be supported merely by taxing people and organisations. Alternatives include cutting public services, reorganising through privatisation, or expanding the tax base. Rather than struggle between the supporters of welfare state and the promoters of global competitiveness, in other words, the search for an ideologically defined social model à la the Cold War, there should be a unified effort to improve the institutional quality of existing society in order to cope in a changing operating environment. Part of the solution could be a more extensive use of immigrants as labour, tax-payers, consumers and talent in a multicultural society. This requires the merging of the ideologies and practices that support the ideals of the welfare state and global competitiveness.

In many advanced national economies, the global economy and its associated phenomena have been recognised as the starting point for economic success. Nevertheless, cross-border migration continues to be an emotional issue and a seeming threat to existing identity more than, for example, the flow of investments and goods that cross the same national borders. In part, the explanation may lie in the fact that opening national borders and institutionalising transnational operating methods are a sensitive topic – they can be seen as fundamental challenges to existing national identity. In the abstract, the concept of national identity incarnates on organisational and individual levels, when encounters with foreigners suggest that there is more than one right way to think, behave and do the job. According to Schein (1992), individuals and organisations often resist change because of a fear of excessive change to existing identity. Identity as obstruction for change may be bypassed when a sufficiently credible way to change the operational model can be presented or when existing identity does not change too quickly or too radically. Learning new things becomes acceptable, provided one is able to retain one's identity for the most part. There is a desire to protect an identity that has brought success, even if it results in failure when operating in a new system (Schein 1992, 300).

As part of the expanding life sphere of individuals, the globalising labour market affects the development of urban centres and regions differently than the flow of consumer goods or capital. The centre is no longer only in the physical or operational environment, but also in methods of operation and culture. Nobel Prize winner John Cornforth (Chemistry) said, "I think that we should not focus on the personality of the inventor as much as on the scientific atmospheres that allowed the inventor's ideas to take root" (Hakala 2003, 303). What kind of culture and what ways of operating create an atmosphere in which the transnational labour market can grow and develop? What kind of culture and ways of operating will help benefit from the global pool of experts that the transnational labour market places at the disposal of organisations and regions? Facing the new circumstances will change the attitudes and operating practices to which society and its organisations and individuals have become accustomed. Thus, agents of innovation environments confront challenges that require the understanding of surrounding society's cultural traits, institutions and values more profoundly than before, to be able to position themselves among their global rivals in the eyes of the transnational expert.

1.3 Fuelling innovation systems through brain circulation

Along with challenges, the globalisation offers opportunities in terms of connecting to global talent pool. Successfully connecting to the global labour market of experts can be broken down into three necessary factors: a rapidly reacting immigration policy that also guides the experts, the creation of attractive and individual-oriented centres of expertise, and the recognition and utilisation of cultural difference as a resource rather than a threat. In a society based on the development of high-skill sectors, in the best scenario, immigrants do not form an additional labour resource for labour-deficient industries or a mere complement to domestic labour, but are instead a resource for innovative industries to renew creative capital. The innovative process requires chaos. Diversity and difference of opinions and approaches – even contradictions – are fuel for the innovation. Someone has to rock the boat in order to avoid the consensus that prohibits innovation. Changing information on interfaces where different views converge creates the most fruitful conditions for the innovative process (Sthåle & Grönroos 1999, 110-112). Thus, multicultural and diverse networks or teams of professionals are valuable assets for an organisation, region or nation aiming to utilise innovativeness and creativity in pursuing economic success. The most profound example of the vast impact of talent flows on the regional economic development of knowledge intensive regions may be found in the migration and return-migration of both students and experts between the United States and Asia.

At the end of the 1980s, Michael Porter observed that the competitive advantage of the United States depends on its ability to benefit from the foreign labour in its labour market. In the future, growth will originate in minority and immigrant groups (Porter 1989, 705 and 779). Indeed, the United States serves as an example of attracting foreign expertise through work permit practices and taking advantage of foreign expertise in the labour market and as fodder for universities, at the same time as creating centres of expertise that appeal to both employees and students. In addition, the United States is an example of how exclusivity and intolerance can quickly quash the attractiveness of even areas with a long tradition of attracting foreigners.

Largely, the question is whether European nations are able to compete for the global pools of experts, and also what the role of emerging economies will be in the redistribution of skilled labour. From an economic standpoint, China, India and Brazil may be counted among developing nations, but viewed in terms of region, the picture is not as simple. The developed urban areas of China and the technological centres they accommodate, or Bangalore in India, challenge western urban areas to compete for the same resources of expertise (Kiander 2004). Internationally, the most significant flow of experts in recent decades travelled from Asia to the United States. Changes in this migration flow reflect future challenges in the relocation of talent, offer a picture of the dynamic of such redistribution and of the policies required to steer the process, as well as its effects on the development of relevant regions.

First of all, the recruitment of foreign labour has clearly become an institutional part of the U.S. labour market and immigration practices. Apart from expertise-based immigration, temporary visas such as H-1B visas[4] have been available for skilled labour since the early 1990s. One goal has been to hasten the processing of immigration applications and expand opportunities for employers who wish to recruit from other countries (Martin 2002; Rollason 2002). The institutionalisation that has taken place, however, stemming from the needs of the economy and the labour market, has been forced to adapt to recent shifts in political attitudes and values.

Second, the impact of immigrant experts, particularly those from Asia, has been critical to the growth and success of the world's largest technology centre and regional innovation system. In 1998, 24 percent of all technology companies in Silicon Valley had an Indian or Chinese director or CEO, and employed 14 percent of the region's workforce. In 1980–1984, 12 percent of high-tech companies had been founded by an Indian or Chinese immigrant, and by 1995–1998 the figure was already 29 percent. All in all, around 40 percent of all new companies had a foreign director or founder (Saxenian 1999; Saxenian 2002). A similar but even more pronounced trend can be seen in the numbers of foreign students. In 1995, foreign students earned 39 percent of natural science degrees granted at the doctoral level, 50 percent of the mathematics and computer science degrees, and 58 percent of engineering degrees. Students from China, India, South Korea and Taiwan accounted for over half of these S&E doctorates (Johnson & Regets 1998, 1-2). Ongoing and future technological development and innovation are thus strongly correlated with the human capital of experts from other countries.

---

4 The main visa programme to attract skilled labour to the United States as part of the 1990 immigration laws. Requirements include at least a Bachelor's Degree for jobs that match qualifications. The employer files for the visa, which allowes hirins a foreigner. The Ministry of Labour need not be separately notified, and the spouse of the hired immigrant receives a visa that grants temporary residence and allows children to attend school, but no work permit. In 2001, the number of visas was increased from 115,000 to 195,000 (Martin 2002, 278).

Third, the system of innovation that relies on a global pool of experts is being threatened by the attitude shift and closing-off toward the rest of the world occurring in the United States. Policies toward foreigners have been tightened, on the one hand because of the war on terror, but also as a result of the protectionist attitudes of a government that wants to shield national industries. The declining draw of the United States among science and technology experts can be seen only in part as a consequence of the increased appeal of other countries. The United States granted a total of 166,000 work permits to science and technology experts in 2001, but in 2002, only 74,000 – a drop of 55 percent. A related, though less sharp, decline in the number of work visas granted has occurred in other industries as well – for example, in entertainment and in economic fields. Part of the drop can be explained with terrorism-related, tightened immigration practices, but also with the country's new, aggressive and exclusionary attitudes toward "outsiders". The U.S. has gone from an era of favouring immigration, funding research and development, investing in education, and spearheading international free-trade agreements, to protectionism and inversion, which drive science and technology experts to other countries (Florida 2004a; 2004b). The immigration policies are not merely a matter of administration, but also of a new political ideology that represents an institutional attitude toward foreigners and immigration itself.

For Europe, it is essential to be able to vie for experts and to ensure that administrative changes and appropriate development measures do in fact positively affect the direction and volume of foreign experts. As the United States closes its doors, China, which as a traditional sending country loses people, has been highly active in persuading the experts who left to return from Silicon Valley and other centres. The dulled sheen of the United States may in fact be seen in part as a result of the growing appeal of Asia and China. An active policy of development has brought results, and China has succeeded in bringing back 130,000 of the 580,000 students who left to study abroad, mainly to the U.S., and currently the annual returning rate is 20,000 – 30,000 students per year. Such a shift is also lodged in the identities of individuals: for many Chinese young people, being Chinese has become a source of pride. The fact that China has opened up politically and become an active participant in world politics and the global economy (for example, the WTO) has been essential in this process (Rutanen 2003, 60).

The roots of the development process, as of all important processes that affect regional development, can be found in earlier decades. One factor that helped launch the process was the number of students in the 1970s who left to study abroad, most of whom graduated abroad and never returned – in 1979, the proportion of returnees dipped below ten percent. The Chinese government established, in 1980, a science and technology park in Hsinchu and put forth several other initiatives to build up the high-tech industry. The park began as 17 companies in an area of 605 hectares (about 1,500 acres) and offered returning migrants good economic benefits and services and a high-quality living environment that corresponded to what they had become accustomed to. Career development was supported by the area's two universities. In addition, the forming of a transnational community received support from government-sponsored conferences and meetings, where experts from China and the rest of the world were brought together. By the late 1980s, the technology park featured 121 companies, many founded by returning migrants, who also actively recruited friends and acquaintances from Silicon Valley. This determinant developing of regional innovation system perhaps partly explains the rapid increase in immigrants between 1999 and 2000, apart from a general economic boom in the industry. In 1983, there were 27 residents in the technology park who were mostly highly educated and with foreign work experience, but by 2000 that number had exploded to 4,108 people. In the case of Hsinchu, it was an active policy and the development work of 20 years that spawned a centre of expertise with 289 companies and 102,775 employees, 14,865 of whom work in research and development (Luo & Wang 2002, 255-257). The returning migrants with professional expertise and business networks created mostly in Silicon Valley were the key source for the development of Hsinchu, partly created in order to attract them as lost talent back to the country of origin.

The phenomenon as a whole has been affected by development measures, but also by the new political openness, and the effect of these two combined on the identities of individuals. Conversely, the change in identity further supports the development measures and political openness. A short-term adjustment tactic to a period of rapid economic growth was a programme of "professional personnel building" in 2002–2005, intended to attract new technology professionals (IT, aerospace engineering, biotechnology etc.) who were long-term or even permanent residents of other countries, and for whom there was a demand. The government offered foreign experts a high salary, special laboratory conditions and tools, and the opportunity to realise professional skills in a unique and individual manner (China Daily 2002). The professional personnel building programme also indicates an adjustment to the way in which to attract experts – returning migrants are no longer the only focus; rather, the goal is to attract foreign experts in particular.

In sum, the global relocation process of talent can be steered through developing regional innovation environments, migration policies and global relations. In recent years, the debate about increasing economically driven immigration and the need for a new kind of proactive immigration policy has, however, been inspired as part of a general European discussion about the ageing workforce and improving competitive advantage. Consequently, immigration policy should not be separated from other globalisation-related policies.

1.4 Connecting regional innovation environments with the global pool of experts

In dealing with the global network of experts, and its social and institutional structures, it is useful to emphasise the dual nature of globalisation. The sociological study of globalisation uses the concept globalisation above, meaning the freeing of capital flows and the creation, reinforcement and spread of transnational institutions – including political alliances and corporations. The counterpoint to *globalisation above* is globalisation below, which refers to the growth of immigrant communities at a local level and the strengthening of hybrid, multicultural spaces in urban environments (Portes 1997). If the above-mentioned Silicon Valley example represents development along the lines of *globalisation below*, there are several regions, where the situation is reversed. In this context, Finnish regions are used as a case in point to illustrate the challenges of those formerly rather isolated regions, which try to connect to the global pool of talent without a heritage that connects them "from below".

The Finnish economy actively joined the global flow of capital and transnational structures, including the EU, in the 1990s. The volume of immigrants increased rapidly and simultaneously, although still with less intensity than in most European countries. In the case of the target group in our research, R&D professionals, the volume is lower still: in this comparison, Finland is at the same level as countries in Southern Europe. Indeed, it is probable that a notable obstacle to Finnish globalisation development and attractiveness on the global labour market may become the lack of globalisation below. In the Finnish labour market, too, globalisation above is a strong trend, and, for example, the presence of the ICT cluster and the internationalisation of the field are more a result of Nokia's globalisation than the reverse (see Steinbock 2004). The threat to development is the lack of an international atmosphere and transnational social environment as factors that attract skilled individuals to Finland and keep them there. Finland has connected to the global regime that moves experts from "above", so the danger is that a short immigration tradition and lack of immigrant communities discourage people from anchoring to Finnish society, particularly if the key representatives of globalisation above, i.e. globally operating multinational corporations, dilute their connections to the country. Networks created by individuals through globalisation below may have their roots even deeper in a region's social and institutional structure than "foot-loose" high-tech companies without strong social or cultural bonds with the surrounding region.

The networks and cooperative relationships created by immigrants have brought about concrete benefits to the operators who participate in them. For example, immigrants from the same country have formed trade guilds that are rooted in close-knit social networks based in a common background and familiarity with one another's modes of operation, and that function as financiers, for example. An instance of such collaborative financing are the globally operated, so-called credit rotation associations established by Chinese businessmen, which collect money among their members and function as a kind of cross between an insurer and a bank. The associations finance corporate investments as well as new businesses (Light & Gold 2000).

The financing of spin-off companies that are expected to grow and of other new businesses is not just charity work to help out one's countrymen, but activity that aims for financial gain and is built upon shared *social capital*, i.e. networking and trust. Already in the 1960s, the Indians and Chinese who arrived in Silicon Valley and even Europe's major immigration countries functioned not only as financiers but also as role models and tutors for new entrepreneurs. Ethnic networks also work transnationally back in the direction of countries of origin: many originally Indian or Chinese companies doing development work in Silicon Valley have transferred areas of development or production to their countries of origin through contacts maintained there. Transnational activity is also promoted through familiarity with the language, culture and operating environment of the country of origin (for example, Saxenian 1999; 2002; 2006; Barré et al. 2003).

Global experts use social networks, whether acting as individuals or as representatives of their organisations. In terms of regional development, it is useful to anchor such key persons in locations where their knowledge capital can be used directly or indirectly through networks. In this sense, it is not a case of mere brain importation but real brain circulation, which must be facilitated by regulatory officials and other channels that must react quickly to capture the benefit.

The process to anchor global experts – both native and foreign – should not be viewed merely as the process by which the experts adopt the ways of the country where they operate. It may be an opportunity for various agents in a city region to join the network of global experts and even an opportunity to benefit from the global social capital, to strengthen and internationalise an agent's or an entire region's innovative capacity. When experts leave, it is not just a loss – it is also an opportunity to view the experts as potential resources as cooperation partners or entrepreneurs, who may invest in an area where they forged relationships and made cultural and community attachments while in-country.

By anchoring individuals as fully as possible to their operating environment, their expertise may contribute to a region's future needs. The goal must be to connect them to networks and communities of experts that offer interesting collaborative opportunities and competitive partners in an environment that has been found functional. From nations' and cities' perspective, the movement of global experts need not only contribute to brain drain or brain gain, but brain circulation. To reap the benefits of brain circulation in the form of expert networks, there needs to be a concrete connecting point that binds the experts together. This can take the shape of certain concentrations of expertise that are central to the network, such as various organisations that fuse new information. Changes in social practises are thus part of the societal change required when plugging into a global pool of knowledge.

From this point of view it is not only the social realm that has to obtain new practices; also our understanding of symbolic realms has to be "tuned to the frequency of a global environment". In terms of image making, too, experts' impressions of a region's quality of life and availability of opportunity are important. Those who leave the region spread their experiences effectively through global networks to exactly the right target group. Thus, foreign experts offer a possibility to connect a particular urban environment to the global network as an interesting and attractive connecting point, if professional communities, high-quality jobs and opportunities for professional development are available. This strategy must be actively developed, however (Raunio 2002). Until now, the situation in Finland can be characterised through the words of a manager who recruits experts for a living: *attracting highly skilled labour to Finland is a challenge.*

Diversity management has been one of the most popular forms of business consulting during the last ten years, as organisations have tried to adapt their management practices and personnel to the multicultural and global environment. Yet the findings here show that Finland, and particularly its expert organisations, are a long way away from making diversity management a part of everyday working life (e.g. Prasad et al. 1997; Flood & Romm 1996). Exceptions exist in units run by globally operating businesses, where the manager or managers emphasise the role of diversity management as one of the tools in the innovative process. However, diversity management has recently been the target of much criticism, and lack of it is rather indicator of indifference and avoidance of the issue in general, than something we should crave for in order to really plug into global pool of talent and then cope with all the new situations the process provide.

When implementing personnel strategies, a central question for organisations is whether they are consistent with other operating strategies. For this to occur, personnel recruitment and welfare should be improved in such a way that they support the organisation's other goals, including efficiency and profits. The same strategy synchronisation is also applicable at the national or urban level, where the focus is on developing human resources and synchronising development strategies with immigration policies. The human resources strategies of corporations are intended to bring about the best possible work environment for employees, and at the same time encourage professional development among employees so that it supports the organisation's business strategies. Really connecting to the global pool of experts requires, in other words, changes in organisational operating cultures and institutions of the nation-state. European Union and national legislation and global competition have all contributed to the greater role of urban areas as engines behind regional development. This requires that countries and their urban areas operate in synchronicity. At a national level, this is manifested in legislative issues, in urban areas as the creation of hubs for development activity and in organisations, as changes in operating culture – learning how to function as part of the global economy.

Behind the expertise-based transnational operating methods, a broader, common network society structure looms, with its own rules of operation, and its stereotypical roles and institutions. This institutional structure is not homogenous – neither are the "tribes" – and nor was the structure consciously created for particular target groups. Instead, it formed from a multitude of goals. According to the arguments presented in this book, the most important resource of the knowledge economy, expertise, is dislodging from the reality of the nation-state and creating its own invisible dynamic and network society, to function as a foundation on which to operate and also as a platform for the transnationally mobile individual.

Institutional change, in order to "take", needs to be politically legitimised. As the operating methods of the global economy become legitimised in the institutions that run society, this represents a shift from the nation-state toward a transnational constellation of "knowledge-based communities or tribes". The operational dynamic is accommodated by constantly grounding it more and more in institutions and in culture, which indicates that it will be around for a long time and that it is being rooted into society's structures and processes. The question is, how deep will the roots of globalisation extend, and what geographic locations will receive it – of where and how the transnational culture of the global economy will influence and manifest itself. Or will the adjustment be overwhelming and resistance become too intense, to the point that that the process collapses, as was the case with the first globalisation process before the First World War? (see Friedman 1999; Hobsbawm 1994).

On some level, we have to be able to analyze the entity to which the phenomenon connects. For example, in terms of the globalising labour market, decision making about issues such as immigration, the labour market, security and economy have widely varying starting points. If development measures are expected to have an impact, we need to leave behind the sectorally structured institutions of the industrial era and re-examine the phenomenon as a whole in light of the new dynamic. It is not merely important to attract experts, but also to embrace a global dynamic that is directed at brain circulation. The phenomenon has been seen in several variations, from the remigration of the Chinese and the closing doors of the United States, to Germany's desire to steer its experts abroad to acquire job experience, and Finland's tentative intention to utilise foreign expertise in its own labour market. But everyone is incorporating into their institutions the same global labour market. Supply and demand in different regions and the ability of regions to attract experts determine in the end how intensively the transnational labour market of experts becomes utilised. As transnational mobility settles into different social layers, however, it sends a clear message about regional development: the competition is genuinely transnational, and the rules and objects of competition must be identified more carefully than before. From the perspective of development and policy, one must recognise the dynamic, use it to gain benefit, and know how to work with it. To understand this dynamic, also the individual and regional levels have to be carefully scrutinised along with more traditional organisational and national levels.

2 Finland in the global field – Ireland and Denmark as points of comparison

2.1 Immigration histories

It is useful to provide a brief introduction of the situation and historical process of Finland in the global field of economy and migration, in order to understand recent and current developments. To make the case more illustrative, Ireland and Denmark are used as points of comparison. Both are small EU countries like Finland, but with some important differences. Ireland is a country with a history of substantial emigration that, still in 1980s, was referred to as "the poor man of Europe" because of its underdeveloped economy. Then, in the 1990s, it underwent a sudden change to a country of immigration and began to experience rapid economic growth. Beyond these similarities with Finland, Ireland is a liberal market economy and an English-speaking country, i.e. profoundly different in its economic and cultural base from Finland, which is a co-ordinated market economy with a unique language. Denmark, again, represents a Nordic welfare state, also with a unique language, but differs from Finland in having a traditionally strong position in international and European communities and, until recently, being an open and tolerant country. By using Ireland and Denmark as illustrative examples, the aim is to understand the rather unique situation of each country in terms of immigration, although certain similarities in macro-level structures and historical processes may be recognised.

Ireland was the last EU country to become a country of net immigration. This only happened in 1996, and the main causes were rapid economic growth and an unprecedented demand for labour. Unemployment declined from 16 % in 1993 to less than 6 % in 1999 (Ruhs 2006, 2). Declining unemployment was the case in Finland as well during the same period, but Finland had already become a country of net immigration at the end of the 1980s. The difference is that the net flow of migrants has been about the one-third of that in Ireland, and outflow of natives has been much lower in Finland than in Ireland. In addition, of late, the net flow has been mostly labour-based in Ireland, but family-based in Finland. In both countries, the balance in the flow of citizens is negative and net growth is a result of the strong positive flow of foreign nationals.

However, Finland's position as a small and remote, albeit developed nation is in transition. In a post-war economy built on nationally organised mass production, the international attractiveness of a particular region or organisation in the eyes of global experts was not a key factor in financial success. The situation allowed Finland to attain an astouncing rate of growth in the status of living in the space of three decades. Without the ability to utilise previous international experience and with a quiet existence alongside the Soviet Union, Finland's contacts with the outside world were few, creating a situation in which the internationalisation that came with the new global era was a real surprise. Many of the connections that link individuals and organisations to the global operating field were quite weak. At least following reasons explain the lack of connections and the low numbers of foreign labour in Finland:

- Finland changed from a country of emigration to a country of immigration only during the 1980s.
- Immigrants have not been necessary from an economic standpoint, neither experts nor manual labour, because the country was poor and became industrialised late.
- Female labour has been utilised effectively and women are highly educated. For example, women occupy up to 55 percent of expert occupations – the highest figure among all of the OECD countries.
- Broad social mobility has brought people from all social strata to expert occupations and thus guaranteed a "homespun" diversity in the workforce. Nowadays social mobility seems to have slowed down.
- The small population and its homogeneity have created close social networks that can be exclusionary toward those coming from the outside.
- Attitudes have not favoured immigration, which has been viewed as a threat to the country's internal security.

It should be acknowledged that immigrants are strongly overrepresented in a few sectors and are concentrated in a few geographic regions. This is particularly visible in the area of the capital region, Helsinki, which accommodates about 50 percent of the nation's foreign-born population (Ministry of Interior 2006). Not surprisingly, sectors where immigrants are overrepresented offer mostly low-paid and low-skill service jobs. According to cleaning, construction and bus transportation companies operating in the Helsinki area, about 25 to 50 percent of their workforce is foreign born. The proportion of restaurant workers is also many times higher among immigrants than is their share in the total population. In other words, immigrants have been distributed unevenly across the Finnish labour market, much like in other European immigration countries. It may be said that the Finnish labour market is becoming internationalised through its service sector.

The overrepresentation of immigrants in the service industry's manual jobs is not a particularly Finnish characteristic, but is repeated in all of the countries that have received immigrants, whether labour or other immigrants, such as refugees, family members of previously arrived immigrants, undocumented or illegal immigrants. In most countries, however, the labour market contains a remarkable share of immigrants also at the other end of the labour market hierarchy, in various occupations of expertise or management.

Both Ireland and Finland had few immigrants prior to the 1990s – instead of trying to attract foreign labour both countries have historically bled labour force to other countries. From both countries, emigrants headed mostly to America or Canada to meet the demand for labour in the early 20th century. However, the number of Irish emigrants was substantially higher than the number from Finland. Later, during the 1960s and 1970s, 400,000 Finns moved to Sweden after jobs and a higher standard of living. A similar flow of labour took place from Ireland to the United Kingdom. Denmark has not experienced such a flight of labour during the post-war era, but it has a longer history as a receiving country, as it began to attract labour already during the 1950s.

The experiences of the three countries show how globalisation connects the flow of people and money. They show that attracting foreign investment also produces social consequences that are difficult to anticipate or fully control. Just recently, at the end of the 1980s and the early 1990s, the Finnish and Irish economies opened up to globalisation, largely on the wings of information technology. For example, foreign ownership was freed remarkably in the early 1990s in Finland, making it much easier for foreign firms and financiers to invest. Simultaneously, the number of immigrants rose rapidly in each country. In 1989, Ireland was still experiencing net emigration of more than 40,000 persons, whereas by 2005, the country was gaining about the same number in net immigration. In Finland, the foreign population was five times larger in 2005 than in the beginning of the 1980s. However, in 2005, only 3.4 percent of the population living in Finland were foreign born and 2.2 percent were foreign citizens (foreigners). One-third of them were from the region of the former Soviet Union (Alanen 2007, 17). While the proportion of the foreign population is highest in Denmark and growing fastest in Ireland, it is smallest in Finland, and the amount of net inflow is the lowest, regardless of accelerating speed in the growth of the foreign population. The structure of immigrant populations is quite different in each country. In Finland, 40 percent of the immigrant population comes originally from the former Soviet territory, in Denmark, the majority hails from Turkey and Iran, while in Ireland immigrants from the U.S. and Nigeria form the largest nationality groups (Table 1).

Improvements in the economy and employment, and liberal immigration policies have attracted remarkable numbers of immigrants to Ireland. Immigration grew steadily throughout the 1990s at the same time as emigration declined. In the space of ten years, approximately 200,000 people moved to Ireland. In the first decade of the 21st century, the annual rate of immigration has hovered around 45–50,000 annually, about half of them Irish returnees (SOPEMI 2006).

Table 1. Comparing the populations of Finland, Ireland and Denmark (SOPEMI 2006)

	Finland 2004	*Denmark 2004*	*Ireland 2004*
Population (2005), thousands	5 217	5 411	4 109
Foreign citizens, thousands	108.3 (2.1 %)	267.6 (4.9 %)	223.1 (5.5 %)
Foreign born	166.4 (3.2 %)	343 (6.3 %)	443 (11%)
Inflows per 1000 inhabitants	2.2	3.5	8.2
Outflows per 1000 inhabitants	0.8	1.7	-
Net migration, thousands	1.4	1.8	-
Nationals living abroad, thousands	1 300	-	3 000
Main groups of foreign citizens	Russia, Estonia, Sweden	Turkey, Iraq, Bosnia and Herzegovina	UK, USA, Nigeria

In Ireland the number of work permits granted in response to the labour demand created by the good economic situation has multiplied in recent years: in 1999, new work permits were granted to 6,000 people, in 2000 to 18,000, and in 2001, to a total of 36,000 people. Most of these workers originate in the eastern parts of Central Europe, such as Poland and the Czech Republic. After the EU membership of those countries in May 2004, immigration to Ireland reached its highest levels ever at 70,000 for the year ending in April 2005. About three-fourths of the inflow consisted of foreign nationals and about 26,000 were from the new EU countries. There was also some ICT expert migration, but mostly immigrant workers are employed by the service sector – the rapidly developing ICT industry uses a number of high-employment support services, including restaurants, transportation and hotel services (SOPEMI 2006).

Although Ireland has been proactive in attracting foreign labour, there have been some difficulties integrating the immigrants to Irish society. This is a consequence of the high share of so-called circular migrants, as well as the assumption that labour migration is a temporary phase. Thus, there has not been strong interest in improving the education and integration of immigrants. Recently this question has gained attention, while simultaneously, the annual volume of immigrants has grown by more than 50 percent from 2000 to 2006 (from 52,000 to 87,000), and the share of the Irish within that flow has decreased from 25 percent to less than 20 percent (Irish labour market review 2006, 16). However, when measuring the unemployment rate of foreign citizens, there is a striking difference between levels in Finland and Ireland. In Ireland, the rate is just slightly higher (about one percentage point) than among natives, whereas in Finland the proportion of unemployed among foreigners is almost threefold compared to the native population. The labour market integration of immigrants has been problematic also in Denmark, although the level of unemployment is not as high as in Finland. The large differences between unemployment rates in these three countries are a consequence of the fact that Irish immigration policy has favoured labour-based immigration, whereas in Denmark and Finland immigration mostly consists of other than labour migrants[5] (SOPEMI 2006).Finland and Denmark have tackled the challenge of immigrants' integration by introducing a wide array of welfare state measures, like language instruction, integration courses, and professional training. In Denmark, immigrant integration policy is highly employment oriented: a special "integration package for immigrants" was introduced in Denmark in 2002. The idea of the package was integration through the workplace, since the work environment was seen as the best place to learn the language and create networks (see Roseveare & Jorgensen 2004; Liebig 2007).

Irish immigrants can be found in nearly all corners of the world, and urban legends about the poor treatment of the Irish are well known ("No dogs, no Irish"). This has not, however, freed the Irish themselves from racist attitudes, and recent years have brought numerous skinhead attacks on asylum seekers in particular. Irish police, or Gardaí, have also been accused of fostering anti-foreign sentiment and of protecting skinheads (Akande 2001, 10-11). It seems, indeed, that a nation's own experience with poverty, massive emigration and other miseries is not enough to deter racist acts. A different type of change in attitudes is needed. Abandonment of the idea of the nation-state, promoting a pluralism of values, and awareness of diversity can change culture and the social atmosphere in a direction that condemns displays of racism and intolerance. Intolerance seems to be the common problem for all, Finland, Ireland and Denmark, but the most visible instances and heated international debate have concerned the Danish cartoon case[6].

---

5 Although in this book we focus on labour migration, its by-products should not be omitted. Economic growth and the increase of documented immigration have also introduced undocumented immigration and asylum seekers. Ireland is a new target country for human smuggling, and the number of asylum seekers has multiplied in recent years. In 2000, there were nearly 11,000 asylum seekers, particularly from Romania and Nigeria. Approximately a quarter of the applicants obtained asylum in 2000 (SOPEMI 2001, 187). The number of asylum seekers in Ireland has grown so fast in recent years that the parliament is demanding measures to limit their number. For example, there have been strong demands to speed up the asylum process.

6 The Danish *Jyllands-Posten* newspaper published comics of the Prophet Muhammad, which, together with tightening immigration laws and somewhat arrogant comment on the part of government representatives, resulted in an international debate about racist attitudes in Denmark.

However, as indicated, these three small European countries differ in terms of their migration policies, form of migration flows and migration histories. In addition, they differ in their roles within the global knowledge economy. Finland does not only represent a different approach in its rather passive migration policy and low labour migration rate, but it is also clearly distinctive from Denmark and Ireland as a player in the global knowledge economy, mainly due to its industrial structure, which is a crucial determinant in labour migration.

2.2 Need for foreign talent and labour

The different approaches to foreign labour may also be connected to different industrial structures and policies in the three countries. Denmark's economy is based on small enterprises and less knowledge-intensive industries than that of Finland or Ireland. This suggests that the role of multinational corporations as channels for foreign labour is more modest and the need for talent less acute. Also economic growth has been more moderate in Denmark. Growth in Ireland and Finland has been fast, but is based on foreign investment and subsidiaries in Ireland and endogenous, Nokia-led development in Finland. It seems that the countries do not apply the same logic in their immigrant labour policies, i.e. Ireland aggressively recruits people from aboard, whereas Finland aims to educate more highly-skilled professionals from among its natives and Denmark focuses on more general integration issues. This is a highly simplified picture, but illustrates the three different situations.

In Finland, business operations became internationalised very rapidly through mergers, foreign investments and other business transactions during the 1990s, although international operations have long traditions in Finnish business (Joronen et al. 2000). This kind of process is referred to in globalisation debate as "globalisation from above". However, Finnish business has not globalised from below to the same extent. Finnish businesses have recruited little foreign labour, not even the foreigners who are already living in Finland.

The Finnish economy has recovered remarkably well from the slump of the early 1990s and is one of the most competitive economies in the world. However, Ireland's economy has grown even faster, keeping up a dizzying pace: until 2000, Ireland's GDP grew at a rate of 8 percent annually, but slowed down to approximately 4 percent annually by 2002. Within a decade (1991–2001), employment rose faster than in any other European country, by more than 50 percent (OECD 2001). This is a remarkable improvement from the mass unemployment that prevailed before economic growth in both countries.

However, rapid fluctuations in employment underline the vulnerability of Ireland's economy in relation to the highs and lows of the world economy. In part, this is a result of the rapid growth strategy that works to attract foreign capital with a tolerable cost structure and thus differs from the Finnish economy, where growth is more endogenous. Both policies concerning the immigration of labour and direct foreign investment have been much more aggressive and open in Ireland than in Finland. Denmark differs from each, since the main focus in Danish debate has been the problems that immigration has introduced.

Ireland has, since the 1980s, attracted international investments, particularly in the ICT field, while this sector grew much more endogenously in Finland, due to the success of the Nokia Group, the telecommunications giant with its roots in a state-owned company. Whereas ICT grew around Nokia and its local subcontractors in Finland, many international software houses set up in Ireland to gain access to the European Union market, and to enjoy substantial tax relief and other support mechanisms that were provided by Ireland's government. Being an English-speaking country has helped Ireland's situation, as have low production costs and subsidies to entrepreneurs. Corporate taxation, for instance, has been kept at a low level – it was only 12.5 percent in 2003, compared to 29 percent in Finland. In terms of economic globalisation, Ireland is clearly the most "globalised" and liberal market economy, while Denmark is the least so. For example, according to the KOF Index measuring economic globalisation (foreign direct investments, payment compensation for non-resident workers, trade, foreign ownership, tariff barriers), Ireland is placed third, Finland 12th and Denmark 30th (KOF Index of Globalization 2007). Denmark has two specific features that have impact on its relation with the international labour market: its industrial structure is dominated by small- and medium-sized companies and the share of large companies is lower than in most European economies, and its labour market is amongst the most flexible in Europe (high professional and geographical mobility). These features may dampen employers' interest in bringing up the debate about foreign labour, because the labour market is already flexible and there is a lack of visible "global employers".

The need for foreign talent is different in each country – the patterns in the economies and educational systems that define the supply and demand of talent are different. Finland has a high share of research and development (R&D) personnel, high level of education, but its gross national product (GNP) per person is lower than in Ireland or Denmark. It seems that the stock of the unemployed and the highly educated is higher in Finland than in Denmark or Ireland, and the same is true of research and development (R&D) personnel (Table 2). These figures indicate that demand for foreign labour and talent is not as acute in Finland as it is in those countries. Although the volume of foreign and foreign-born labour has been increasing in Finland lately, its share of the total labour force is still only half (1.7 %) of what it is in Denmark (3.5 %) and slightly more than one-third compared with Ireland (4.7 %) (SOPEMI 2006).

Of course, the need for foreign talent depends in part on the supply and demand of knowledge workers. In Ireland, there are plans to increase investment into research and development from 1.4 percent to 2.5 percent of the gross national product (Building Ireland's Knowledge Economy 2004). In Finland, the share of research and development expenditures was about 3.5 percent already in 2003, among the highest in the world. In Denmark, R&D investments were 2.4 percent of the GNP. Even more importantly, parallel developments may be found when looking at the share of researchers in the total labour force. The highest share within the EU can be found in Finland (1.7 %), while Ireland is among the lowest (0.5 %) (OECD 2007).

Table 2.Comparing Finland, Denmark and Ireland (Statistics Finland 2005)

	Finland	*Denmark*	*Ireland*
GNP per person* 2003 USD	27 460	31 050	30 910
Unemployed % 2004	8.8	4.5	4.4
Higher education % (25–64 years) 1999	31.3	26,5	21.1
R&D per inhabitant (USD)	995	760	365
R&D personnel	57 196	42 206	13 996
Share of foreign labour	1.7 %	3.5 %	4.7 %**
Investments to R&D of NGP	3.5 %	2.4 %(2004)	1.4 % (2004)***

*Purchase parity adjusted
** OECD 2006
*** Building Ireland's Knowledge Economy, 2004, 13

The knowledge economy's human resources are, then, more advanced in Finland than in Ireland, and the need to acquire foreign talent is stronger in Ireland than in Finland. Not surprisingly, there is a plan in Ireland to increase the share of researchers in the total labour force. Attracting more foreign talent is part of this plan. The number of researchers should grow by 8,000 in Ireland by 2010, and about 3,600 of them should come from aboard. The proportion of foreign talent is high, since Ireland's educational institutions cannot respond to the demand (Building Ireland's Knowledge Economy 2004, 21).

The low share of highly skilled foreign labour force in Finland was revealed also in the present study. Educational organisations, universities and institutions of higher learning in particular are more international than corporations in terms of personnel structure. In Finnish society, institutions of higher education, particularly universities, have been accustomed to international cooperation longer than businesses. Higher education has a long history with globalisation both from above and below. Theoretical ideas, research trends and findings have spread internationally for as long as universities have existed. The same mobility is also true of scientists. Still, the internationalisation of higher learning in Finland is at the lowest level in Europe not only in terms of personnel but also students. Even though new technology makes the speedy transfer of people and ideas more possible than before, it has not been able to compensate for the lack of a historical process of internationalisation, which has permeated the academic field from the beginning of civilisation.

In spite of growing numbers of foreigners, as it stands, Finland's situation is not especially promising in terms of the internationalisation of innovation environments (= globalisation below). This study asked organisations that require a high level of expertise – corporations and universities – to report the number of foreigners and immigrants working in each, as well as their backgrounds and positions. Corporate representatives knew surprisingly little about the nationality distribution of their personnel. Only 22 of 40 organisations interviewed were able to provide an accurate figure *or even an estimate* of the number of foreign employees among their staff in 2004. This reveals several things. First of all, there are so few employees with an immigrant or foreign background working in Finnish organisations that management is largely ignorant of the few who have been hired. On the other hand, the privacy protections in force in Finland and other Nordic countries prohibit registering information about ethnic background in the personal register, making it impossible for organisations to gather systematic data about the ethnic structure of its personnel. Third, the "invisibility" of employees with immigrant backgrounds to managers in charge of personnel matters indicates that Finnish organisations – at least those included in the study – do not practice diversity management that takes into account different ethnic backgrounds. Exception to the rule is global ICT firm with substantial amount of foreign experts and diversity management practices.

A closer look at the share of foreign labour in Finland, Denmark and Ireland reveals interesting details. The exact number of highly skilled foreign professionals is hard to obtain, but some general trends are rather clear. According to the European Commission (2003), in 2000, the number of non-natives engaged in science and technology (Table 3) only represented 1.3 percent of all employees in the field in Finland, compared with an EU average of 4.1 percent. In Denmark, a traditionally more open society, but a less knowledge-intensive economy, the figures are reversed. In the case of Ireland, where the science and technology (S&T) sector is less developed, the share of non-native S&T labour is more than double when compared with the total foreign working population. Although somewhat simplified, this illustrates the different roles that foreign workers assume depending on prevailing economic and political conditions (Auriol & Sexton 2001, 33; European Commission 2003, 236).

Table 3. People occupied in S&T occupations, highly qualified workers and total working population; proportion of non-natives in EU nations in 2000 (%). (European Commission 2003, 236)

Country	*Total working population*	*Highly qualified people*	*People occupied in Science & Technology*
Luxemburg	41.3	45.1	33.5
Ireland	3.6	-	7.6
Belgium	7.6	5.9	6.6
Austria	9.4	8.7	6.1
Germany	8.2	4.7	5.7
Great Britain	4.0	4.2	5.4
Sweden	4.3	4.7	4.4
EU average	4.6	3.7	4.1
Netherlands	3.9	3.4	4.0
France	5.3	3.4	3.4
Denmark	2.6	2.0	2.3
Portugal	2.0	2.5	1.7
Finland	1.0	0.8	1.3
Greece	3.7	3.3	1.1
Spain	1.3	1.3	0.7
Italy	1.0	1.0	0.6

Further, it should be noted, that Ireland is even more dependent on high-tech in its exports than Finland. The share of high-tech products was almost 30 percent of all exports in Ireland in 2003, whereas in Finland it was slightly over 20 percent. In the case of industrial exports, the share of high-tech products was even higher in Ireland, peaking at over 50 percent, whereas in Finland it remained close to 20 percent. In Denmark, the share of high-tech among total exports was less than 15 percent and clearly under the EU average (25%) (NIFU 2006). This bias between nationally produced talent and dependence on high-tech exports may partially explain the prompter actions taken in Ireland as compared to Finland or Denmark, in trying to attract global talent.

Also, the general need for foreign labour is estimated to be highest in Ireland, which again motivates to prompt actions. Irish officials have estimated that there is a need for 50,000 labour migrants per annum to fill the gap between supply and demand in Ireland (Irish Labour Market Review 2005, 4-6). The goal has been achieved in terms of quantity, but not quality. It has been difficult to find suitable applicants to high-skill jobs. There are both short-term needs and a demand for more permanent solutions. The question of high-skill immigration is one that is seen as a long-term question. There has been demand especially for engineers, health-care professionals and experts in IT and financing (Noki & Kovanen 2007). Also in Finland there has been discussion about accepting 20,000 labour immigrants per year to fulfil the gap that emerges when generations born in the late 1940s retire. Again, the highest demand for foreign labour is found in Ireland. As indicated above, demand for foreign labour depends (in addition to demographic factors and economic growth) on education and economic policies at the national level.

Different demand partly explains the variation in the size of the labour flows, but the differences are so striking that demand alone cannot explain the situation In 2000–2001, according to OECD statistics, more than 50,000 foreign workers moved to Ireland, about 25,000 to Finland and less than 10,000 to Denmark. Ireland is also one of the main destinations for migrants from the new EU countries. Finland has not acquired many immigrants from Latvia and Lithuania, even though more than 150,000 emigrants have left those countries during the first years of third millennium (Economist 2006). In fact, according to statistics from 2002, it seems that the two largest single categories of migrant workers in Ireland are from Latvia and Lithuania, accounting for over ten percent each of employment permits for non-EEA permit holders. They are closely followed by Phillippinos and Poles (9 percent each), both of which are easier to explain. Estonians account for only two percent in this category (ICI 2003, 10-12).

Geography would suggest that flows from Latvia and Lithuania would head to Finland, but the attractiveness of Ireland is high in these countries. Unlike Ireland, most foreign workers in Finland are coming from neighbouring countries, including the Russian Federation, Estonia and Sweden. After Estonia joined the EU, the flow of labour has increased even more, although during 2004–2006, most were so-called posted workers, because of migration restrictions amended by the Finnish government for the movement of labour from new EU countries.

One factor that cannot be omitted when explaining this situation is the level of income taxation that is among the highest in Denmark and Finland, but among the lowest in the world in Ireland. A single worker earning up to 34,000 euros/year in Ireland pays 20 percent in taxes and may reduce this through "tax credits", so that the actual tax rate may be about 10 percent. This is substantially less than taxes paid in Finland or Denmark. However, also in Ireland, the tax rate is 41 percent for amounts exceeding 34,000 euros. These comparisons are extremely difficult to make because of the different tax systems, but the general view is that Denmark and Finland offer a rather modest after-taxes income level. For most foreign workers, the 34,000-euro threshold is high enough, but in the case of experts, whose higher incomes exceed the threshold, the benefit is less evident (Roseveare & Jorgensen 2004).

To put it simply, the key issue here is that Ireland is able to attract a substantially greater volume of labour and from more distant locations than Finland. Ireland is also to some extent more efficient in acquiring immigrant labour than

Denmark. However, there are substantial differences on the demand side, since Finland has the greatest resources in terms of "native talent" and labour force in general. Investment in research and development is also highest in Finland, whereas Ireland is most dependent on high-tech exports in this area. To summarise, Finland is clearly a more self-sufficient economy in tems of educated labours than Ireland.

2.3 Labour immigration policy

The Immigrant Council of Ireland states that "The ethical, policy and societal issues raised by these changes are very new to Ireland, simply because we were a sending society and not a receiving society for so long. We lack the experience, policy, legislation, support organisation and structures which are found in other more diverse societies" (ICI 2006, 19). This is very true in the case of Finland as well. Although the starting point for dealing with immigrant labour has been quite similar here, the approaches to seeking immigrants as well as the number of immigrants differ significantly between Finland and Ireland. Simply put, the formation of immigration policies seems to be less active in Finland than in Ireland, and the same is true for developing the content and implementation of immigration laws. Denmark, too, has launched programmes to attract foreign labour, but with rather a low profile. Danish policy has focused more on closing the country's doors, since there is fear of misuse of what have been traditionally open and generous immigration regulations. Finland has recently discussed and amended laws that favour labour immigration. However, the actual implementation and active policies are still a work in progress. The changing policies are a reflection of the demand for foreign labour and the attitudes of the nation-states to this question.

In Ireland, immigration and foreign affairs are handled by the Department of Enterprise, Trade and Employment (DETE), Department of Foreign Affairs (DFA) and Department of Justice, Equality and Law Reform (DJELR). DETE defines policies in labour migration and implements both the programme for Irish Work Permits and Intra-Company Transfer. Ministry of Justice (DJELR) controls immigration, and under its authority works the Immigration and Citizenship Policy Unit that is responsible for the development of both immigration and citizenship policies and proposals to change legislation (Noki & Kovanen 2007). In Finland, the Ministry of Labour is responsible for integration policy, and the Ministry of the Interior has controlled entry policies, including residence and citizenship matters. DETE's role in the Irish political field seems to be stronger than the role of the Ministry of Labour in the Finnish political field, and thus their policies are more actively implemented. From 2007 on, the labour migration issues are being transferred to the Ministry of the Interior, since the Ministry of Labour has been dissolved and its responsibilities assigned to other ministries. The Ministry of Trade and Industry has a minor – if any – role in Finnish work migration policy. This may be one reason why the economic and labour dimensions have been so absent from Finnish immigration policy. In Ireland, a clearly different administrative structure also produces policies that are quite different. We may wonder whether the Ministry of the Interior will produce more economic and labour oriented policies than did the Ministry of Labour.

Ireland's strategy has been to specifically attract labour, whereas Finland has been clearly less active in promoting migration policies. In 2006, the first government immigration policy programme that clearly took a side in this issue was published, but implementation has been slow, especially when it comes to labour immigration. The speed and proactive attitude in the implementation of migration policies in Ireland has also caused difficulties on a practical level. For example, the Intra-Company Transfer Permits programme was temporarily ceased because of misuse, and a work permit or visa was required also of highly-educated experts who moved to the country to work within the same company. So it may be said that Ireland has put more weight on importing labour than ensuring that each phase of administration will function. To exaggerate slightly, Ireland has managed rather than administered labour migration.

In Denmark, labour migration has increased (by almost 25 % between 2003 and 2004) and humanitarian and family-related migration decreased from 2001. However, it seems that the main focus in Danish immigration policy has been on integration issues rather than on work-related migration issues. The main policy changes have focused on tightening the laws that make family reunification, long-term residency and the acquisition of Danish citizenship more difficult (SOPEMI 2006; 176). The Act on Integration of Foreigners in Denmark entered into force already on 1 January 1999. According to the law, municipalities must arrange a three-year initiation programme for immigrants and refugees to familiarise them with Danish society and language. Although the Act was amended in 2002, aiming to ease the municipalities' qualifications for implementing accelerated integration programmes for highly skilled foreigners, simultaneously the assistance granted to newly arrived immigrants was reduced to encourage them to look for work more quickly. The focus has, then, been mostly on the problems associated with immigrants and their employment – their integration – than on attracting foreign talent.

In Ireland again, even significant growth in immigration has not solved the skills shortage, although about one-third of immigrants have been in the skilled workers category (SOPEMI 2004, 121, Noki & Kovanen 2007). Thus, improvements are continuously implemented in immigration policy in order to find a better match between supply and demand and to make the recruitment of educated foreigners easier for business sectors that are experiencing shortages (The Irish Labour Market Review 2005, 30). The Irish government introduced a so-called fast-track programme already in 2000. The aim was to ease and accelerate the recruitment of highly skilled workers. The fast-track permits did not replace the work permit system per se, but it offers a faster alternative for those whose skills are in high demand. The fast-track programme was initiated by the Department of Foreign Affairs (DFA). The DFA is responsible for gathering the statistics regarding how many and what categories of fast-track permits are granted. DETE is responsible for work visas and their authorisation. The fast-track programme made it possible for those who are eligible to apply work and immigration permits from their home countries after receiving a job offer from Ireland. Earlier, applications were processed only in Dublin. If an applicant needs a visa to Ireland, he or she has to apply for a Working Visa, but if not, a Work Authorisation is enough. Most permits under this programme are effective for two years.

The enlargement of the EU has solved Ireland's labour needs only partially. There is also demand for labour in the "old" EU countries, and competition for skilled labour is stiffening. The focus of both labour and immigration policies is therefore clearly on labour from outside of the EU. However, Ireland's Training and Employment Authority (FÀS) emphasises that immigration should be a temporary/interim solution and that it is simultaneously important to take care of updating the skills of both employers and Irish employees (The Irish Labour Market Review 2005).

The "Expert Group on Future Skills Needs" (EGFSN), representing business, labour, education and government, works as a think-tank that provides information about labour and skills needs for the Ministry of Enterprise, Trade and Employment and the Ministry of Education and Science, and suggested in the beginning of 2000 that the government should pay attention to the immigration of researchers. In 2002, a sub-committee on Research Mobility was established to work on attracting and retaining researchers (www.skillsireland.ie; Downey 2003, 2). In 2005, Ireland introduced new immigration legislation. The new Employment Permit Act, places the immigration of skilled and highly skilled workers at the forefront. This legislation was partially a result of a fear that the EU would establish a common immigration policy and compromise the flexibility of Ireland's labour market. In Ireland, a national immigration policy is seen as more suitable for small, open economies such as Ireland, that have to quickly adjust to changes and uncertainties in the international market, as well as skills shortages (Noki & Kovanen 2007). The Act also contains a list of occupations, for which permit practices have not been amended.

A significant difference between Finnish, Danish and Irish immigration policies is in the administrative role of different ministries. In Ireland, the Ministry of Enterprise, Trade and Employment (DETE) has a strong role in administration, legislation and policies concerning especially labour-based migration. This may in part explain the highly visible role of employers in Irish labour immigration policies. Until 2003, employers were virtually free to hire employees outside of the ETA-area regardless of the employee's country of origin, educational level or occupation. This substantially increased the number of immigrants arriving in Ireland – from 5,750 permits in 1999 to 47,707 in 2003. This practise did not, however, have a strong, positive impact on the migration of highly skilled workers, since most of those coming in have been less-skilled workers (Noki & Kovanen 2007, Ruhs 2006, EGFSN 2005). Still, only recently, the proactive attitude of DETE was confirmed in a speech given by its current minister.

> "Ireland will have an employment permit system, which will ensure that the economy's skills and labour needs can be addressed in a pragmatic and speedy manner, while ensuring the rights of all workers are protected"
>
> Micheál Martin, Minister for Enterprise, Trade and Employment

The differences in immigration policy between Ireland and Finland may derive partly from this division of labour. In Ireland, policies are economy-led, by virtue of being handled by DETE, whereas in Finland it has been the Ministry of Labor (since 2008, both immigration and integration matters have been concentrated in the Ministry of the Interior). In other words, economy and business have not determined the policies. The active labour migration policies are more evident, when migration is dealt with as a an economic issue along with trade and employment policies.

In Ireland, since 2007, working visas aimed to ease the recruitment of qualified workers were replaced by a Green Card programme that renews the fast-track practices. According to DETE, the new legislation[7] "puts in place a statutory framework to allow the implementation of an active, *managed economic migration policy*. The focus in terms of meeting the need for skilled labour is firstly on improving the skills of our existing resident workforce; secondly, on maximising the potential of EEA nationals to fill skills deficits; and thirdly, with a new Green Card programme and a revised work permit system, to meet the skills needs that cannot otherwise be addressed. This prioritisation is without doubt applicable also to Finland and Denmark (and most other advanced economies). However, the focus, implementation and weighting of actual policies may alter significantly between the three countries, as indicated.

---

7 The new Irish Emloyment Permits policy system have three pillars: 1) The establishment for the first time in Ireland of a Green Card for occupations where there are skills shortages, which will be for a restricted list of occupations in the annual salary range from €30,000 to €60,000 and for a more extensive list of occupations in the annual salary range above €60,000. 2) Re-established Intra-Company transfer scheme for temporary trans-national management transfers, and 3) work Permit scheme for a very restricted list of occupations uo to €30,000. (DETE 2007.)

In other words, the immigration policies of all three countries are in transition, but there were significant differences in implementation during the first years of the 21st century. While Ireland focused strongly on the economy, enhancing labour migration and actively shaping legislation to serve that purpose, in Finland, the intention was the same, but the implementation less active, and concrete administrative reforms may even have a counter-effect by enforcing a security agenda instead of promoting the economy and labour issues. Denmark, again, had greater focus on internal security and integration questions than on obtaining a supply of labour from abroad.

3 From an international to a global economy

This chapter illustrates the changing roles of corporations, nation-states and regions in transnational and global economy. The new roles are not fundamentally new, but they contain new parts that change the constitution of the whole. Regions are not just sub-sectors of national administration, but significant and independent actors; corporations are not just money-making machines, but also distribute seeds of social order and change, and foreign labour is not just the means to fulfilling local shortages, but a natural and often essential part of how employers manage in global business. These viewpoints provide the framework that outlines our approach to the globalisation of labour markets.

When corporations or organisations become global, their daily operations change. Economic globalisation is connected to migration movements, cultural diversification, and economic wellbeing. Global economic activity fundamentally transcends the boundaries of nation-states. The operators are not always national, and as the relationships among operators, both individuals and organisations, transcend national boundaries, they are not always merely limited to several national operators, as is meant in the usual definition of 'international'. Indeed, globalisation can be said to be more than mere internationalism. It represents a dimension that cannot be defined by the relationships between different nations. Such globalisation refers to activities that are characteristically less dependent on the role of nations, as opposed to international activity that occurs under conditions that are set by individual nations. These phenomena provide the backdrop for any discussion about the globalisation of the labour market and the global mobility of foreign scientists or ICT experts. When activities are clearly bound between two or more places and nations, they may be called transnational spaces. It is when they cross several national boundaries, but are independent of specific nation-states, that they may be called global. To exaggerate, international relations aim to strengthen the position of a nation-state in relation to other states, whereas global relations make nation-states more interdependent on other states.

Porter's (1990) work examining the economic competitiveness of different countries is one of the seminal studies to influence the discussion of corporations' internationalisation development Porter's central thesis is that as corporations have become increasingly global and international, this has not eliminated the significance of individual nations or their policies as factors that determine the success of corporations. Corporations receive and maintain their competitive edge through local systems, such as trade policy decisions. The globalisation process of corporations actually underlines the significance of national economic structures, history and culture in their viability. In other words, globalisation does not mean that global operators, whether corporations or individuals, are free of the effects of the local, but rather that local decisions and conditions have an increased role in the expanding operating field.

Finnish regional policy, for one, has emphasised the role of individual regions in development, and state control has been minimised in favour of giving regions more responsibility. It is at the regional level that resources are acquired and operating environments created for inhabitants and corporations, whereas the state continues to be responsible for the organisation of various administrative mechanisms. For these reasons, localities and regions play a powerful role. Local decision-making can help create and maintain global processes, while such processes can only partially be anticipated and regulated through the means available to localities. It is useful to remember that national culture rests largely on the national institutions that were built to support it. When creating new institutions, it is worthwhile to recognise the new logic that operates in the global economy[8] – the structures that were created for nation-states no longer necessarily work in the new operating conditions.

3.1 Corporations as creators of a new social order

How do the structural changes of economic life connect to cultural diversity and ethnic relations? As innovation and expertise begin to occupy the hub of economic activity, as corporations play an increasingly responsible role, and as national economies morph into global economies, all of these factors strongly emphasise not only the importance of the individual, but also the new roles that individuals and corporations play in the expanding operating field. When international trade was more export-focused – as it was in Finland prior to the 1990s – the most important aspects of an individual's or corporation's expertise, when seeking international entry, were being able to communicate with other cultures and mastering foreign customs and languages. Finns delved into the appropriate length of a businessman's socks or on how to handle one's liquor in a civilised way. A slew of handbooks and training courses about different countries' business etiquette and ways to avoid negotiating pitfalls resulting from cultural difference assisted one's entry into the world. Cultural diversity and various ethnicities were not yet part of daily working life, but only something that one experienced during export negotiations abroad.

In the attempt to master a new perception of the world, difference was contrasted sharply with familiar and accustomed daily life by emphatically underlining the differences in "other cultures". "Other cultures" were seen as fixed, un-

8 Or the similar logic during "Globalisation One" before the First World War. Then, the economy was at least as global as it is now, according to several measures, including the international mobility of labour. After WWI, many economists, businessmen and governments dreamed about returning to the world economy as it was in 1913, but the transition towards state capitalism and nation-states had already progressed too far (Firedman 1999; Hobsbawm 1994).

changeable entities that began and ended according to the boundaries of nation-states. Cultures were thought to have clearly visible differences that could be learned and managed by appropriating tips from handbooks and various courses offered by consultants. Encountering these "different cultures" was approached through various techniques and operating methods – spawning an entire cultural management industry – to manoeuvre cultural differences and communication between cultures (Dahlén 2001). For instance, the exemplary goal of the – ideologically speaking – Anglo-American diversity management is to get different ethnic groups to work together in a way that benefits a company's bottom line: diversity pays. Critics say that the approach is unduly concerned with apparent cultural difference, such as differences in values and ways of communicating, and only reinforces existing stereotypes instead of dissolving them. It also runs the risk of casually bypassing problems in the workplace by dressing them up as cultural difference, when in fact they may stem from social inequality (Trux 2000).

Cultural diversity permeates everyday working life in many global and transnational organisations. Cultural differences can no longer easily be defined as something encountered when travelling abroad, as was done during the golden export era. The surrounding reality, communities and the individuals that operate within them seem to resist categorisation. One might think that in a world where "I am constantly somewhere else and others are constantly here, and moreover, some of those among us are at once 'us' and 'them' and neither", any sense of national belonging would be history. This has not occurred, and instead, feelings of national identity become more important in maintaining internal cohesion.

In other words, the status of "other cultures" has changed radically in corporate operating environments. The change was rather quick. For example in Finland, a latecomer in the international field, this change took as little as a decade to take root. The awkward "cultural differences" that used to plague export endeavours have been quickly replaced with a situation where ethnic heterogeneity is reflected in the makeup of a company's personnel, the client base of the domestic market, and, at a minimum, the operating environment that comes with the acquisition of foreign companies – including business partners, the client base and adopted business practises. In such an operating environment, flexibility, sociability and curiosity are assets that bring success and that cannot be learned from a handbook. For example, learning conflict avoidance through negotiating techniques is not as essential a skill as the ability to see conflicts as a source of creativity, development and innovation (Trux 2000, 301). An appropriately diversity-positive management style can help avoid many misunderstandings and disruptive conflicts, and utilise various ways of problem solving in areas like the production of innovation.

Trading has always shaped culture, and in the era of the global economy, that influence is greater than ever. One may ask what kind of logic and values are being created for the new social order by the transnational conglomerates that steer the economic system. The new order certainly differs from that determined by nation-states, based as it has been in mass production and regional delineations. Whether it ends up being an improvement or a decline depends on how well today's decision makers understand and manage the creation of its institutions, its operating mechanisms and its values. Together, they are creating a new culture, a platform for a new reality in the process of forming. This reality, in turn, shapes society's structures and the environments in which individuals and organisations operate.

3.2 Innovation as the engine for labour market development

In the present situation, innovation and technological and educational policies are bound up in labour and the immigration of professionals and experts. When discussing the globalising labour market and its impact in the context of the knowledge economy, the central focus is on innovation and innovation systems that support innovative activities. Innovation systems or environments are seen as a source of economic wellbeing and competitiveness and they indirectly employ a significant number of service providers and subcontractors.

"Innovation" is often understood as technological or service inventions with commercial potential produced by individuals or small groups. In this type of innovation discourse immigration and immigrants are often treated as 'innovation potential' for organisations that are competing for skilled labour. The view is based on a model of thinking that assumes that there is only a finite number of professionals with the technological, scientific and business skills that companies seek, and who are thus capable of producing the innovations that benefit the employer (for example, Science and Technology Policy Council of Finland 2003, 3-4). The global labour market competes for these professionals. The discourse centres on individuals and is connected to an understanding of human capital, i.e. the education, work experience and occupational skills of individuals, as a limited form of capital, of which there is only a certain amount to go round at any given time. In the same way that economic capital can be bought, sold and traded, individuals with the right kind of human capital are traded on the recruiting market – at the going rate.

This view of innovation where products are a result of the human capital of individuals represents a continuum from earlier industrial research and policy. In socioeconomic discourse and in assessing competitiveness, the central role of education – which is the most essential form of human capital – is connected to the following understanding: education can be used to produce more innovators. In practical politics, education is a measurable unit that can be used to produce statistical reporting systems and concrete operating plans, because who would want to oppose allocating resources to education? The politicisation of education is further reinforced by the fact that the amount of education and the number of educated individuals and educating institutions can be geographically localised to cities, communities or nations.

A definition of innovation that is rooted in the concept of human capital is problematic. With its references to level of education and number and location of individuals equipped with the appropriate kind of human capital, it narrows the understanding of what innovation can mean. The innovation and creativity that is present in all human interaction, in information-transmitting networks, and in personnel relations within organisations that operate independently of locations, is difficult to measure and quantify. The transnational networks created by globalisation and nourished by new technology help promote the production of innovation in a dimension that is separate from the traditional spatial dimension.

Apart from the technology-centred view of innovation, another view is connected to a cultural understanding of innovation that sees innovations as new ways of collating familiar things. In this interpretative framework, innovations are seen as part of a broader social and cultural context that also fuels them, and where innovations need not have any object value apart from their context. Culturally focused innovation discourse emphasises the nourishing impact of local environments on innovation. It is characterised by grassroots diversity and tolerance, which is in turn manifested in the opportunities of people with backgrounds in various subcultures – such as immigrants and ethnic, cultural and sexual minorities – to encounter one another in the urban space. According to Richard Florida's (2002) understanding of innovative activity, innovations cannot be linked to particular, discrete individuals outside of their historical or social contexts: certain urban environments have special resources to not only produce innovation but also recognise the value of new innovation.

Further, according to Florida, environments that are characterised by openness and tolerance produce innovators and attract experts to produce more innovation. Florida refers to "openness" for new ideas, and diversity, that produce opportunities for different, even controversial ideas to emerge (ibid. 2002). However, by following this line of thought, populations that are considered marginal from the majority population's perspective, such as sexual and ethnic minorities and immigrants, may play a central role in the evolution of creative urban environments also more directly than as "indicators of openness and tolerance". They have a view from the margins, and their gaze reflects the old and the new, their country of origin and the new living environment. Therefore they can offer a wider perspective than representatives of the "mainstream population" into surrounding phenomena. Crucial for innovation, creativity is born of the very ability of see more than others, a sensitivity to the essential messages relayed by the environment, which other people lose sight of amid the flood of information and knowledge (Sthåle & Grönroos 1999). A person from another culture may be expected to have this type of sensitivity and provide new interpretations and perspectives into phenomena that members of the majority culture can longer discern.

Why the buzz about innovation? Why is innovation important? Corporations operating in the marketplace are constantly compelled to renew and rethink themselves and produce innovative products to keep investors interested, compete with new challengers, and expand their market share. Innovation, not price competition alone, is what determines a corporation's viability.

From a corporation's standpoint, innovations bring added value in the marketplace. The ability to produce innovative products requires social and cultural capital, but it also requires that traditional human and economic capital support these forms of capital. Even the expectation of future innovations and the associated profits attract people to invest in a company, and this in turn increases capital stock and share value, boosting shareholder profits. Awareness that a company is involved in innovative networks, i.e. is believed to have information and expertise as well as connections, frequently has a direct impact on the company's worth. The critical link in the innovation chain is knowing how to convert innovation into a marketable commodity. There is usually no shortage of good ideas or innovations, but knowledge and resources to commodify them are in shorter supply. A good product is not necessarily a good commodity or does not automatically elicit demand – the demand must be created first.

In other words, innovations are not just about technology, but their significance comes from the collaboration of people who have various skills and expertise. When a company comes out with a new innovation and transfers the finished product to the marketplace, the result is frequently a rapid flood of profit, in contrast with the profits from the pricing competition in traditional industrial serial production. In a rapidly changing operating environment, innovations can also take the shape of social innovations, such as working methods, ways of carrying out projects, and providing added value. One such form of social innovation is attracting expertise potential from the international market's expanding talent pool, and then being able to convert the diversity advantages of culturally diverse work organisations into an economic advantage in the production of innovation.

Recent discussions concerning innovation and the knowledge-based economy have underscored the importance of social innovation – there is plenty of information and expertise, but they could be implemented and utilised more efficiently. Social innovation also encompasses things like new attitudes and viewpoints about familiar issues. To understand the importance of benefiting from diversity, and seeing experts more in terms of a global brain exchange than as local, immovable social capital represents such social innovation. In sum, the spread of the "innovation approach" according to which economic actions (in work communities, companies, regions, nations, etc.) are organised has resulted in a novel situation. Constant change, cultural and social difference and diversity among individuals and ideas, globalisation and global communities and other issues that were earlier seen as (potential) sources of instability or even as threat, have now become acceptable, if not even desirable dynamics that boost profit making in the innovation economy.

3.3 Corporations and social responsibility

As a result of the drive for innovation, corporations are developing their international staff recruitment, cultural diversity practises, and learning to account for their social involvement. The point is no longer to appease civic organisation and avoid negative publicity, but to create practises that are convincing to investors.

Corporate social responsibility is related to economic globalisation and the objectives of sustainable development. Talking about corporations' social responsibility is relatively new, even though international economic organisations have taken up the subject publicly in recent years (Central Chamber of Commerce 2003). Social responsibility in business affects the ways in which companies operate both at home and abroad. Broadly speaking, it means that operations are guided by the emergence of ethical issues in economic activities. Consumer awareness now encompasses not only price and quality, but also a new ethical awareness of the principles of production. The discourse about corporate social responsibility was prompted by environmental questions and sustainable development. As production is transferred to developing countries, the issue of corporate *personnel accountability* has also become central, including the discussion of issues such as the fair and humane working conditions in production, for example, in terms of work safety, human rights, child labour, freedom to organise, fair trade rules and gender equality.

To some extent, the social responsibility being assumed by corporations can be viewed as a natural development – the institutions that steer the economy in society are the ones to define its operating practises and values. In agrarian times, small kingdoms and city-states functioned well as marketplaces, as the church and its teachings shaped the activities and values of the labour force. For an individual, fear of God and hard work constituted praiseworthy economic activity. The industrial era's larger units and homogeneity paved the way toward more efficient production, and the state became its instrument. A universal school system, universal education, shared language and nationalism all helped to guarantee that the large units were not called into question and continued to function. The global economy, however, is fuelled by diversity and innovation, where individuality is a characteristic of both consumers and employees. Without these characteristics, the economy, based on the diversification and innovation of products, would stumble. It seems that a growing segment of social responsibility and its institutional foundation is slipping away from nation-states to global corporations. One manifestation of this is the dynamic management-focused "managerialism", where public administration has moved away from an attorney-based bureaucracy toward a leader-centric managerialism, or the way in which nation-states are aiming primarily for competitiveness instead of stable, safe and equal societies. Even though the old structures remain, the operating dynamic is adapting to a changing environment.

A corporation that disregards the ethical dimension in its business operations puts itself at risk for boycotts and protests by civic organisations and risks negative publicity that can endanger its economic objectives. Many large corporations in developing nations, including Shell, Mitsubishi Corporation, Nestlé and Nike, have damaged their international reputation through their operations. Greenpeace, Corporate Watch and Rainforest Action Network are organisations that already have a long tradition of using publicity as a tool to force large corporations to commit to the global, moral community that is now capable of putting pressure on operators, for example subcontractors, whose activities clash with the prevailing moral sensibility.

In recent years, the discourse about corporate social responsibility and the principles of ethical business practise has broadened and taken shape as a negotiation between corporations and organisations. In 1999, at the World Economic Forum in Davos, United Nations Secretary General Kofi Annan declared that business was part of the solution for solving globalisation's problems. On Annan's initiative, a project known as the *Global Compact* was launched, and within its framework, corporations and the UN work in collaboration to seek solutions for problems in adherence to internationally accepted ethical principles. Globalisation has shaken the principles of environmental protection, gender equality, and the humane treatment of labour, particularly in the developing world. In many countries, the state is totally dependent on the profits and employment power of international corporations. From the global corporations' perspective, because the state in many developing countries is fearful of losing income, it avoids getting involved in labour issues and cedes the responsibility for improving working conditions to the corporations. Corporations are therefore under growing pressure to act in a socially responsible way and to include their subcontractors and the entire production chain within this sphere of responsibility.

As equalisers of social conditions in developing countries, corporations have substantially more power than individual nations. It makes sense for global corporations to improve working conditions and thereby enhance social stability. First of all, it is in the interest of the corporation and the brands it cultivates to share in social responsibility and to apply ethical business practises. A tarnished name comes at a high cost, and clearing it up is even more expensive. In addition, a corporation needs a stable environment to operate efficiently. Stable social conditions ensure uninterrupted and high-quality production, bring added profits, and ultimately help expand the market.

Economic globalisation has brought the issues of ethical business practises and corporate social accountability to Finland as well – albeit, with a delay. The issues emerged in part following negative publicity earned by the Finnish forestry, fur breeding and nuclear energy industries. Questions of social responsibility and ethics are thus closely connected to globalisation, and corporate social responsibility is not restricted to the geographic area of individual nations, but extends to a company's entire production and market area. The fact that the discussion is becoming more current is also tied to ideas that have been made popular in management literature that focuses on interest groups in favour of traditional ideas, where the owner's advantage, i.e. shareholder value, was considered almost important. From the perspective of social responsibility, critical interest groups include personnel, clients and the media. The principle of social responsibility means committing to a working dialogue about operating conditions and organisation (Kujala & Kuvaja 2002). This interest group thinking is on its way to Finnish economic life, although for now, companies apply personnel accountability strategies only in other countries, particularly those where production takes place and many of which are developing nations. Corporations are more interested in social equality among their employees abroad rather than those back home in the West, where the state is still considered ultimately responsible for meeting challenges to social equality. The fact that the state is so powerful – particularly in terms of research and product development – gives these countries the advantage of being an attractive location for corporations. Their social stability makes it possible to maintain uninterrupted production and offers the availability of skilled labour.

Corporations' interest in the social status of their employees is connected to the problems that many countries face in this area: if the state loses control of social stability, it will probably result in production and economic losses for a corporation that depends on its employees. The key economic operators in many developing countries are transnational and global corporations that are frequently more powerful than the state in shaping the labour market. Corporations bring their own operating cultures and create new values and institutions in their wake, for example, by replacing agrarian economies with wage labour. In this way they also have an impact on family structure and gender relations. They do not passively adjust to the demands of old social structures, such as environmental regulations or laws and agreements governing the labour force; rather, they create new transnational structures that suit their needs.

One strategy for social responsibility is that corporations and other organisations take into account society's diverse population groups in their operations. In other words, an organisation's actions should reflect the various groups in society as well as their needs, including equal representation of each gender, different age groups, the disabled, and different ethnic groups. For a corporation, the usual motivation comes from being able to show that its human resources reflect the surrounding community's social structure, and that it thereby carries a social responsibility for employing the labour force. It is also true that by utilising the various resources available in society, an organisation is a better position to respond to the needs of its operating environment. As a form of social responsibility, a diverse workforce also allows a company to market itself to interest groups, such as customers, potential employees and, through the media, to broader consumer groups.

In 2003, the Swedish newspaper *Svenska Dagbladet* published a prominent "Diversity" insert, where businesses took out paid advertisements to present their diversity strategies and market that diversity from an economic standpoint. The forestry company Stora-Enso, co-owned by Finland and Sweden, described in its 2003 annual report the strategies it had undertaken in social responsibility, and specifically named diversity in its workplaces as one of them. The diversity principle is viewed as a requisite for long-term success, because in the future, companies will have to continually expand their recruiting base, ensure that the organisation's resources and innovation potential are utilised, and respond to rapid global changes. Responsiveness improves with the multiple sets of "feelers" and networks that cultural diversity offers – not only with respect to events at home but also to global trends and occurrences (Stora-Enso 2003: 34-35, 39-40).

Although some globally operating companies have acquired a "diversity" approach, which they celebrate at least among top-level managers and in their human resource strategies, it does not mean that this is converted to practice in the company's real-life recruitment and human resource policies. Few Finnish corporations have a conscious diversity strategy, although certain projects, such as one coordinated by the Service Union United (PAM) and the Ministry of Labour, have made efforts to emphasise diversity. In businesses that operate in trade, the social responsibility dimension has taken the form of personnel accountability and has in some minor ways also been extended to immigrants in internal company policies and discussions. According to a manager at a central Finnish trade organisation, personnel accountability means that the company takes responsibility for the living conditions of special social groups, such as immigrants, to the extent that it is able to affect their living conditions through employment practises. In other words, favouring diversity translates into responsibility for the wellbeing of society's special groups.

".. [O]k, we have immigrants among us, and if we can reasonably employ them, that's great – that way they aren't being paid for by the tax payers, and they won't become socially marginalised, so there is that kind of social viewpoint in it as well."

Favouring diversity also affects a company's social image, which becomes important when companies wish to present an image that underlines their global social responsibility and, when they wish to expand abroad, avoid the usual local opposition to the outside "occupier", who is hijacking national property. When entering new countries, corporations try to don a bit of local identity, for example, by making sure that local personnel and management are adequately represented in the corporation. Such expansion strategies utilise the idea of a global "local" market and the broad ethnic representation of personnel. The objective is to manipulate the brand to create associations of "local" products that represent "us". Among large corporations, ABB is an example of a corporation that works to achieve a local image globally (Kets de Vries 1994).

Although the fringe conditions of operating change as a result of globalisation, this does not mean that nations or the nationality of a corporation have lost all meaning in a company's business operations. Other factors besides a structural dimension such as globalisation also have an impact on existing practices. It makes sense for corporations to periodically emphasise national aspects, such as a product's origin. In addition, it is difficult for people and people-driven organisations, such as corporations, to divorce themselves from the life history and cultural background, which are shaped by their nationality and are central structures in perceiving the world. Cultural and historical dimensions, as well as the nationality of management and ownership, do have meaning. For example, in multinationally owned corporations, the nationality of the top management team is much more critical in how the corporation is managed than is often believed.

In sum, the situation is somewhat paradoxical, since, regardless of the common wisdom that emphasises toughening the rules in working life and the inhumanity of global corporate giants, simultaneously corporate image and human issues are becoming more important even in terms of the economic success of a company. The bigger the global giant, the more capable it has to be in creating credible relationships with individuals who are its employees and customers. They have to adopt social responsibility in relation to the environment, as rules are set by stiffening global competition. This provides a dynamic where balancing between social justice and economic profit is a constant requirement.

4 Institutionalising the global economy

The globalisation discourse encompasses the points of view of politics, culture and the economy, and occurs both as a general theoretical discourse and concrete social discourse. In terms of economy, globalisation translates to the growth of economic trade over long distances, often conducted independently of spatial or chronological barriers. It binds and merges faraway places into a common economic system of shared trade. Economic globalisation sows mutual dependence on all sides, so that events that take place in one part of the global economic system cause reverberations in many other, geographically distant parts (see Castells 1996; 1997). They key message of this chapter is, that globalisation is not something that floats above us as intangible processes and symbols, but is acquiring tangible forms and systems that strongly impact the behaviour and decision making of individuals, organisations and nation-states. Those global forms have to be recognised, when considering policies that are meant to function in a global environment.

4.1 Building global structures

In economic implementations of the globalisation concept, the starting point is in a global *system integration* of the economic system. Global system integration means that the economy is no longer divided into national economies (Sklair 2001) and 'economy' is understood as worldwide networks and flows that unite the different parts of the network. In economic life, global system integration erodes the influence of nation-states. However, we should bear in mind that all nation-states connect to the global system in somewhat different ways.

Trade has long transcended and reached across geographic distances – the world market has been developing since the 15th century (Wallerstein 1974), but the way that national economies and corporations participate in the global division of labour has changed rapidly. Before, trade meant trading, or exporting and importing, articles. Since the 1980s, the markets and the concept of ownership have changed. For example, in the case of Finland, this means that Finnish companies have offices abroad and foreign companies operate in Finland (Vartia & Ylä-Anttila 2003, 121).

Apart from the new intensity that characterises today's global operations, another new aspect is the weakening influence of nation-states in controlling business practises. This change is so powerful that some even predict the elimination of 'nationality' altogether in corporate activity. Before, "the trade went where the flag went", i.e. nations had an important role as economic operators (Cohen & Kennedy 2000, 118). Following the liberalisation of currency and capital markets, dissolution of other kinds of trade restrictions, and decentralised production, regulations defined and imposed by nations or geographic boundaries no longer determine operating conditions as before. Many of the ways of describing international activity lose meaning as the very nature of economic activity changes. When currency rates determine political latitude, it is no longer meaningful to speak of nations as free and independent operators that exist outside of the markets. Nor does it make sense, when a growing share of international trade occurs inside corporate conglomerates, to use traditional export and import statistics to describe trade (Cohen & Kennedy 2000, 123). "National" company is likewise a misnomer, when more and more companies are controlled by foreign capital. More than half of the companies listed on the Helsinki stock exchange are foreign owned (Kiljunen 1999, 192), and key operations of companies are dispersed all over the world. The conceptual basis of 'national economies' is becoming amorphous: what is "national" in this context?

Many critics observe that globalisation has been misunderstood (for example, Hirst & Thompson 1995) and indicate that many countries have in fact relinquished economic control by eliminating trade barriers, promoting the free flow of capital, and ratifying international economic agreements that standardise economic activity. In spite of such critique, the consensus is that economic networks based in a market economy that transcends nation-states' boundaries have expanded to encompass the entire globe and have accelerated the regional merging of economies. For nation-states, globalisation means that the issues and events that they used to control are changing and taking new directions, and while certain things remain in government control, others are dislodging.

Globalisation is not really the result of a rational, internationally controlled trade policy – it is corporations and other single operators that are making the decisions. International and bilateral agreements continue to have an impact on the conditions that regulate company operations and continue to influence their decisions. In Finland, for example, the liberalisation of international trade in the decades following World War II, the freeing of capital that began in the 1980s, allowing foreign capital investments since 1993, and membership in the European Union in 1995 have increasingly integrated this particular nation-state into the global economy. Table 4, below, illustrates the degree of globalisation in industrial corporations operating in Finland in terms of the multi-nationalism of their personnel during the period from 1980s to 2000.

From the micro level, globalisation can also be viewed as an interactive phenomenon and series of events that have an impact on the *real-life experiences* of individuals. In this process, the consequences of a global system change affect the experience, self-understanding and operating conditions of individual economic operators, such as entrepreneurs, wage-earners and consumers.

Table 4. Number of employees and percentage of employees working abroad in large Finnish corporations in 1983 and 2000 (Ali-Yrkkö, Joronen & Ylä-Anttila 2002, 75).

Company	*1983*		*2000*	
	Employees	Abroad (%)	Employees	Abroad (%)
Nokia	24,000	17.5	59,000	58,0
Stora-Enso	15,000	9.8	42,000	64.0
UPM-Kymmene	35,000	11.7	33,000	37.0
Metso	15,000	12.8	22,000	50.0
Kone	13,000	66.2	23,000	94.0
Metsäliitto	8,000	7.5	25,000	61.0
Fortum	7,000	21.0	15,000	37.0
Ahlström	12,000	14.4	9,000	78.0
Wärtsilä	22,000	9.5	11,000	69.0
Rautaruukki	8,000	1.6	13,000	39.0
Total	163,000	16.3	251,000	59.0

The meaning of nationality changes in interaction with others, and individuals are required to master new information and skills. In its entirety, globalisation potentially means that people can engage in global trade and consumption regardless of geographic or political boundaries. On the way to this situation, however, many practical barriers remain, and the most difficult to transcend are the everyday beliefs and unquestioned "truths" that individuals hold about nation-states. One example of such assumptions involves the food industry: in many countries, people persistently believe in the superior quality of domestic food products. Such beliefs support continued protectionism of agricultural exports and help defend high agricultural subsidies.

An organisational model that transcends national boundaries also contains weaknesses, such as time-consuming meetings, the demands of travel, difficulties among personnel in adapting to a dual management style, or imbalances between different dimensions of the matrix. In spite of drawbacks, the model is held as essential in transnational corporations with a multinational management and ownership and with geographically broad-based operations. It is noteworthy, however, that not all companies operating in the transnational market are in fact transnational – many are merely multinational or only national. Such companies may channel business operations through national subsidiaries, or national companies may have an international department that is responsible for managing international trade. A multinational corporation may own subsidiaries in several countries, but executive control remains with the parent company and the home country.

In the late 1990s, a debate about a "subsidiary economy" and its dangers began in Finland. It had to do with a concern about the impact of foreign ownership on employment and sovereignty, and resembles the worries and fears people feel about the arrival of immigrants to Finland. But in transnational companies, the subsidiary model no longer works the way it did before. Now, certain operations may be outsourced to operate as separate, global companies that are nonetheless part of the same conglomerate. Factories in different countries may operate in the traditional manner as subsidiaries, or may be controlled through the conglomerate's main office. In the former scenario, the transnational conglomerate equals its subsidiaries – there is no discernible parent company, because the conglomerate consists of a network of companies (see Daft 2001; Barthlett & Ghosal 1998). In the latter case, the company is more like a department within a factory, with its own role in the division of labour. When compared with previous decades, the difference is that now "our factory", or the physical place where operations are carried out, has dispersed all over the globe, and in this "building", different units have their own specialised tasks that are rarely connected to their geographic location.

In public discourse, international mergers are often said to lead to a subsidiary economy. This chain of thought no longer applies in global economic conditions. As a matter of fact, it could be said that all international corporations, whose ownership and operations are distributed among different countries, are subsidiaries of global capital. This globally moving capital is not organised into units, even though it is institutionally controlled. A company's address or the location of its headquarters is no longer a guarantee of its nationality.

The globalisation of the market can be divided into multiple, mutually dependent and partially overlapping dimensions, all of which reinforce the shift away from a national to a transnational operating logic. Globalisation in the markets of capital, production, labour and trading transforms economic structures. Although the different dimensions of globalisation may seem separate, together, they constitute a trend that, as the operating environment becomes increasingly global, produces a global labour market that transcends national boundaries.

4.2 Globalisation of ownership and production

There has been strong growth in direct foreign investments in the capital market in recent years. Corporations and private individuals invest in funds and stocks outside of their own nation-states, and companies purchase foreign companies and thus channel capital abroad. Since 1985, foreign investment, some of which is connected to the decentralisation of production, has grown faster than actual world trade and production (Siebert 1999, 12). The Japanese are an example –

they own a significant portion of the economy in Europe and the United States, and American pension funds also own broad swaths of European economies.

In Finland, too, foreign ownership has increased rapidly over the last decade and a half. In 1990, approximately 70 of the five-hundred largest companies were subsidiaries of multinational corporations. By 2002, the figure had doubled. During the same period, foreigners purchased in particular service corporations, including transportation, real estate maintenance and trading companies. Foreign acquisitions were motivated by Finnish expertise in particular areas, which has in turn expanded the market for expertise. Thus far, growing foreign ownership has had a positive impact on the national economy – for example, if measured through its employment impact, the largest foreign-owned company operating in Finland, ABB Finland, is one of the five largest industrial corporations (Vartia & Ylä-Anttila 2003, 99).

Table 5. Largest foreign-owned companies in Finland in 2002.

Company	*Home country*	*Employees in Finland*
ABB	Switzerland	10,500
Kvaerner	Norway	4,570
Tellabs	U.S.A.	2,350
OM Group	U.S.A.	1,670
Flextronics	U.S.A.	1,520

Source: Vartia & Ylä-Anttila 2003, 99

Corporate investing has become global. In Finland, international investing got off to a late start in the late 1970s, but in the 1980s investments grew at one of the fastest rates in Western industrialised nations. Investments by foreign companies increased during the 1990s, spurred by the liberalisation of foreign ownership in 1993 and Finland's membership in the European Union. However, Finnish companies themselves are investing abroad at a rate approximately twice the rate of foreign investment in Finnish companies (Figure 3) (Vartia & Ylä-Anttila 2003, 108-109). Following the steep growth of the 1990s, a steadier growth pattern has taken place.

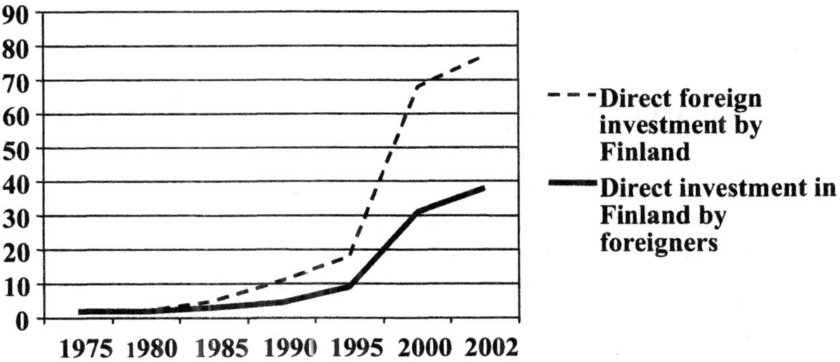

Figure 3. Development of direct investments vs. industry's domestic capital stock (gross), %. (Source: Vartia & Ylä-Anttila 2003, 108-109)

These days, the transfer of capital from one country to another occurs at warp speed and is unrelated to space or location – or even production trends. Companies with a high degree of foreign ownership are obliged to develop public relations strategies that are specifically targeted at investors. Corporate executives go on so-called road-shows to great finance capitals such as New York, Tokyo, Frankfurt, London or Milan to present their company's income development and future visions to attract more investment. One chief financial officer of a large global corporation said that investor relations take up as much time as one is able to give them. Investors often make decisions based on short-term factors that are not consistent with a corporation's long-term strategy. It is management's task to convince investors of the benefits of investing in the company. When today's investors make investment decisions, they no longer look at large corporations as representing a particular nationality, but compare them with similar corporations in the same field worldwide.

The production market engages in a global comparison of production costs: it has become important to compare production costs in all the locations where industrial production is possible. Companies make investment decisions on the basis of labour costs, tolls and tariffs, taxation, cost of raw materials, working conditions, available expertise, and various cultural factors such as the language skills, general values and consumer habits of the cooperation partners. Many production-related issues enter into the calculation that determines where production will eventually occur. In principle, companies no longer depend on geography when making decisions about location, and instead, consider the opportunities offered by various regions as part of their strategic planning. Yet investment decisions are not made solely on the basis of economic rationale – tradition, history and the management's own preferences continue to influence decision making. Anchoring in a particular cultural environment brings continuity to the operations of a global corporation.

4.3 Creating a global labour market

Over the last two decades, Finnish companies have shifted toward international production. At present, half of the employees of large industrial corporations work outside of Finland, and the majority of shareholders too are non-Finnish. What does this mean in terms of ownership, production, sales and the labour market? How does a global operating environment shape the realities of companies and the people who operate in them?

At the employee level, new operating practises concretely shape the reality of operating environments. At the organisational level, new operating rules manifest in recruitment and management practises. Such phenomena of the globalising economy as the international operating environments of corporations, intensifying global diversity on the local level, labour market expansion, and the resulting trend toward multi-ethnicity in organisations' personnel demand that management and organisational structures are sufficiently flexible to keep functioning properly in a perpetually changing environment.

An international labour market and loosening geographic ties can also be seen in organisational and management models that, in expert-driven organisations, function highly independently of geographic considerations. A demand for mobility and the ability to manage change within organisations also leads to the same dynamic in organisations at a regional level. The core operations, support functions, service networks and customers of organisations create a transnational network. The labour market is internationalising through organisations that promote mobility among employees, for example, through project-based employment, where, though connected to a particular country, a project may be managed by a multi-national project team.

"I have project groups in Finland, Hungary, China and the United States. I physically coordinate and manage operations and monitor these groups, and we are in daily electronic contact. All of the groups are working on the same project and share the same goal."

ICT manager, Tampere, Finland

Organisations expand into transnational conglomerates and create their own global labour market, which then creates its own services that become the culture of the "global nomads".

"This is a platform, a unit, that creates the company's guidelines globally, and they are then implemented everywhere the company operates. The world is looked at through global eyes, and being foreign is not a barrier – it's competence that we seek . . . and the right types of people."

Relocation manager, Helsinki, Finland

Organisations that function in a global operating environment proliferate as the logical result of an expanding capital, production and sales market. This leads to a labour market that swells beyond national borders in more and more fields. Academic research – biosciences, ICT, and management – has pioneered this development, and there is no reason to think that the labour market will not expand globally in even more fields. This widens the recruiting field, ethnically diversifies the employee base and operating practises, and promotes a management style that tends toward *diversity management*. A globally operating organisation needs employees who can negotiate a multicultural operating environment. Frequently, such people have a multicultural background and are accustomed to moving about the global labour market. The larger corporations look for tools to fit together people with diverse backgrounds and to create the right conditions for collaboration. In addition, the areas where people work are expanding: for example, Helsinki (Finland) and Tallinn (Estonia) are already often considered part of the same labour market area due to extensive commuting. The eastern parts of Finland have already embraced the concept of expanding the labour market area toward St. Petersburg, Russia as part of strategies for the future.

National expertise, innovation and competitiveness strategies promote the globalisation of capital and ownership in a way that transforms the boundaries of national economies and the global economy. As a result, the islands of global economy are growing bigger, which in turn increases worker mobility across national borders. This is where immigration enters the picture. Up to this point, immigration policies have controlled people's cross-border movement more stringently than policies that control the flow of capital or goods. When national strategies promote the expansion of the labour market across national and EU borders, is a policy that regulates people's movement in line with such strategies? How could national and international immigration strategies promote economic and labour market globalisation in a way that benefits all people, beyond national boundaries?

Because of competitive production markets and costs, the labour market becomes global as well. Simply put, every wage-earner is competing globally with employees in similar professions. On the globalising labour market, not only price matters – characteristics like flexibility, quality, reliability and above all, level of expertise, are also deciding factors. The ICT and bioscience experts addressed in the present book represent an example of global recruitment. When organisations are looking for a particular type of knowledge or expertise, the local or even national labour market is not a sufficient recruiting pool, nor are the national education systems able to respond fast or effectively enough to meet the demand. Thus, in specialised fields, the labour market expands to span the globe. Organisations recruit skilled professionals globally, regardless of nationality. There is intense competition for key personnel, and indeed, the most desirable professionals are widely mobile within global working life (Siebert 1999, 12).

The rather quick change towards global recruiting practices took place at the end of the 1990s. For example, out of the Fortune 500 companies, 88 percent use the company intranet or the internet to recruit personnel. In 1998, that percentage was only 29, but by 2000, it was up to 79 percent. Experienced managers, who have been recruited by headhunters or through personal contacts, are also increasingly seeking opportunities via the internet. In 2001, one internet portal dealing in skilled labour contained over 100,000 applications of such a calibre. The internet also speeds up recruiting and lowers costs (Deeprose 2002, 26-27; Iredale 2001, 16). Thus, national regulations and company policies are developing in a parallel direction, but this development has its side-effects.

Institutionalisation is not only about attracting experts but about the broader dynamic of transnational labour markets and the mobility of skilled labour. Germany is an example of short-term brain gain – Germany, Europe's largest economy, implemented a "green card" programme to adapt quickly to an economic boom and increased demand for skilled labour, with the objective of facilitating the hiring of Indian IT professionals to German companies. Temporary work permits, or "green cards", were allotted for 20,000 experts annually in the spirit of the well-known foreign worker phenomenon of the 1960s (Werner 2002). As early as 2004, according to a sharp statement by German employment authorities, Germany was not in fact managing to attract skilled labour, but was instead even urging professionals trained in Germany to seek work abroad to gain work experience that scarce jobs in Germany could not offer (Mattusch 2004).

The recruitment of "skilled" foreign labour has not gone as expected. One reason for this has been epitomised in the racist events that were taking place and the associated negative images thus conjured of Germany (Forsander 2002a). It may be said that the case of Germany, too, underlines the importance of immigration policies and tolerance in attracting experts, and points to the process becoming entangled with a historical context and other social processes that have formed around the phenomenon. Brain drain or brain gain represent an oversimplified picture of mobile experts, and it is therefore necessary to consider the logic according to which the dynamic of global brain circulation reacts to changes that take place in environments at a continental or national level.

The previous scenario points not only to burgeoning changes in migration trends, but also shows that politics can concretely influence the relocation of skilled labour. The international flow of experts assumes many forms and is influenced by a number of motivators and trends. The phenomenon is much more multi-faceted than simply importing or exporting "brains". The process of the transnational labour market of experts becoming an established part of the transnational social order is not yet fully complete. The ways in which the players who create supply and demand in the global economy – employers and employees – are shifted to those who regulate the global movement of labour, including employment authorities and governments, and the immigration policies that they adopt. The effects of the global economy can be seen in international agreements and in laws, regulations and practices that regulate the movement of labourl.

One can claim that the transnational labour market is becoming an institutional part of the machinery or structures that govern societies. The process is occurring alongside similar processes all over the world, thus creating an institutional foundation upon which individual knowledge holders and organisations operate within the global network. The transnational movement of labour has acquired and is in the process of developing a structure and institutions to support it.

The transnational labour market of experts is docking onto various layers of society – individual identities, organisational cultures, and institutions of the nation-state. The similarly directed operating practices of operators are bringing about and in large part have already created a foundation for the transnational constellation as a social structure, as the global networking society of experts. It must be emphasised that institutionalisation is based on the transnational activities of both individuals and organisations – in other words, the structures that are being erected already have the users and the activities to fill them.

The conditions and structures for global brain circulation are thus already being created also at the institutional level. National and international agreements and practices have long been designed to accommodate the process, albeit while focusing on particular continents. National efforts have sought to attract labour from outside of national borders, while the international agreements have been designed to transnationalise the labour market by weakening or streamlining regulatory practices. Concrete agreements regarding labour markets have been formed particularly in the scope of continents by expanding the labour market and regulation to an entire continent. The European Union, NAFTA in North America and Oceania's MRA agreement all facilitate the movement of international labour in their respective regions by eliminating restrictions that stand in the way of work and residency permits for transnational labour (Iredale 2001). The transnationalisation of such continent-sized labour markets may already be said to have become institutionalised in many work and residency permit practices.

Nation-states are trying to respond to global competition for foreign capital, investments and employees using various strategies. These can be characterised as "the race to the bottom" (Sklair 2001): various concessions, such as tax rebates, public subsidies, land use and zoning, and working life flexibility erode the safety nets of Western welfare societies and take these countries toward social standards that are dictated by the global market and by competition. For a long time now, a discussion has been waged in Finland about lowering the income tax, dismantling the social security system's incentive traps, and lowering the wages for the least productive work. These alternatives are meant to increase employment and improve Finland's competitive edge, but they contain an implicit acceptance of the resulting income disparities in the workforce.

4.4 Networking "corporate states"

In a merchant market, the trend has long been to merge different fields under the management of large trading companies that market their products widely (Nordström 1991, 43). Most large companies try to market products in areas larger than a nation-state, because, for example, in the Nordic countries, domestic markets are so small. Few of the world's top companies are European, with roots that reach to a single country of origin. A number of large American, Japanese and Korean companies operate in the world market, but European giants are usually combined companies that derive from at least two countries, along the lines of Unilever, ABB and Vivendi Environment.

Most areas of the merchant market have local and national operators, whose capacity to compete against large, global giants varies depending on the field. In many fields, product quality determines the distance between the production site and the consumers. Many services cannot be transferred too far from the consumer, whereas the immaterial products of the IT industry can withstand even long distances from production site to end-user. In fields such as dairy production, production remains local even when the original producer merges with a larger entity. But many fields, including electronics, mass media and the automotive industry, have shifted away from local and domestic markets toward international and global markets (Nordström 1991, 43).

The globalising market promotes mergers and the formation of larger economic units. Nearly all companies plan for growth or expansion, or even becoming a global operator, and see mass production as offering significant competitive advantages, among them lowered production costs and accrual of capital. Mass production is also seen as linked to the accrual of expertise capital – the investment of economic capital produces more as expertise capital grows (Siebert 1999, 41-42). Growth strategies include *mergers, acquisitions policy or organic growth.* Mergers often have as their starting point the equal merging together of different companies. The two-part names of many companies operating in today's market have this kind of history. An acquisitions policy refers to corporate acquisitions, where an active operator buys out market competitors and either merges them into a conglomerate or phases out their operations. In the third strategy – organic growth – the company works to increase its market share and size through boosting sales and investing in production.

After all possibilities of growth have been exhausted on the domestic market, whether organically or through corporate acquisitions or mergers at home, companies turn to international mergers and acquisitions. Joining the international arena introduces new risks, but also advantages that make the risks worth taking: there is less competition, a synergy effect is created through units that combine their operations, and there is the opportunity to build an organisation with the capacity to expand the market itself. For these reasons, national and international competition authorities closely watch all planned mergers and pass resolutions on them. The *risks of monopolisation and centralisation*, discussed in Marxist economic theory, that come with corporate expansion cannot always be said to lead to inadequate competition but large corporations can easily become inflexible and inefficient as administrative and management costs soar (Siebert 1999, 42).

Conglomerates can grow to become entities that employ worldwide networks of up to hundreds of thousands of employees, and that adapt various production and marketing methods depending on the region. On the one hand, while corporate networks adapt to their environments, they also mould them to suit their needs. In terms of size, the largest corporations are larger economic units than entire nations, and, as opposed to nation-states, their operational logic is characterised by a lack of regional boundaries as well as the acceptance, but also the shaping, of different national cultures.

A company's internal division of labour can be developed through solutions such as partnerships and outsourcing, where external producers take over the production of some of its operations. The result is the gradual emergence of networks of companies, where differences between the companies eventually become difficult to discern. The networks function like a single, large corporate conglomerate, or alternatively, they form a cluster of subsidiaries and affiliates. Companies working in partnership share essential expertise in the fields where they collaborate. A new area of innovation in global business is the creation of markets within corporations. This strategy can enhance the company's internal communications and product lines. It also has its weaknesses, for example, the development of a kind of parochialism at the expense of the conglomeration model. On the other hand, it can help coordinate the complex operations of large corporate organisations.

In a merchant market, companies can adopt various strategies. Global corporations can opt for a *local market strategy*, where the organisation has a presence in the local markets of several countries. This is *glocalisation*, which means that a global product is manipulated to conform to the tastes and preferences of different cultures. An example of this kind of regionally tailored approach is automatic transmissions, which are routinely installed in cars destined for the U.S. market.

In television entertainment, the same concept or format is marketed to different countries and then modified to suit different viewerships. Shows such as *Who Wants to Be a Millionaire, Have I Got News for You?*, The Dating Game, and *Idols* are primetime entertainment in a number of countries under various localised names. They are adapted into local culture and shown locally in many countries, and are reworked to suit the cultural preferences of each country's viewers. Local market strategies strive to create an illusion to make the consumer believe that the company and the product originate in his or her own country, not abroad. Consumers place a high value on the domestic origin of a product in terms of brand loyalty – in Finland, the marketing of food products, for example, is based on this. Certain brands are in fact adopted as "national property", and if the manufacturing of these products is shifted abroad, this amounts to a kind of treason. The uproar that followed a change in the manufacturing country of the true-blue Turun Sinappi mustard or the Koskenkorva liquor are examples of such loyalty.

The increased immigration brought about by globalisation shapes local markets toward broader ethnic diversity and enriches the variety of local consumer preferences. Marketing strategies respond by shaping the locally available global array of products to correspond to the divergent tastes and preferences of the various ethnicities and subcultures. Glocalisation occurs when the differing needs of immigrants and ethnic minorities show up as concrete manifestations of global diversity at the local level. One example is the Virgin music brand in Britain, which realised that young people with immigrant pasts were buying more records than anyone else. The company targeted its marketing increasingly toward this group through tactics such as recruiting young people with the same immigrant backgrounds to work in their music stores. This insight has also been utilised in Finland, where immigrants have been found to be active users of certain telephone services, and many new operators now specifically target their services to this group (Koskinen 2003).

In the United States, companies have woken up to the fact that ethnic minorities form a growing consumer group with increased buying power. The number of African Americans, Latinos and Asians is growing at faster rates than the majority population, and so is their income and buying power. In spite of the groups' internal diversity, businesses have understood the importance of segment marketing in responding to their special characteristics.

In fact, glocalisation can be said to mean *branding the local.* This concept is used in the marketing of tourist destinations, where local characteristics are bundled into a brand that is coupled with desirable, exotic or sexy images, and is then used to sell the product to target consumers. After some time of this kind of "product development", the brand image separates from the local culture and becomes its own marketing leaflet. Such examples include the Canary Islands pig roast, the Indian music from the Andes that is played on street corners of every major city, Irish pubs, and Chinese restaurants – "everyone" recognises them, but they have no counterpart in the cultural traditions of their reference countries. Minorities' different customs and practises often open up new possibilities for local people accustomed to their own customs. In many countries with high immigrant populations, immigrants have transformed consumer items like food and popular culture into brands, where new innovation is created by crossbreeding the "original" with elements of the new. The result is often a pleasantly palatable export with an ethnic flair, like the pizza of the Italian Americans or British-Indian curry restaurants. The Swedish pop music industry and the film industry in Britain and France get most of their driving force and fodder from people with immigrant backgrounds and their hybrid stars and starlets.

Instead of glocalisation, many of the world's global giants, including Coca Cola, McDonalds, Unilever and Nestlé, use the same product everywhere. They market their brands globally, even using the same packaging, thus spreading the dream of Western riches even to the poorest developing areas. The branding of global corporations often presents the imagery through advertisements, music and sports, creating the image of a trendy community along the lines of the One World Alliance tag line of *"oneworld revolves around you"* or the *"united colours"* of Benetton, with visuals of people of prominently different colours and hues, and sporting goods companies that use African American physicality and ghetto trendiness to sell products. The expansion of the market for consumer products depends on the ability to sniff out trends, and to refine, maintain and disseminate them.

The globalisation of culture is not only about the spread of reality TV formats, Britney Spears gossip, or the most recent hair styles among consumers worldwide. Cultural globalisation is supported by efficient structures that concretely globalise economic practises and the cultures of the individuals and organisations operating in the global economy. It is essential to grasp the nature of the labour market's internationalisation in this broader context. Globalisation shapes people's lives profoundly and comprehensively both in terms of their free time and work. It is reflected in what we consume and who we work with. Just as, sometimes, it is more appropriate to speak of a global instead of national economy, it is not always meaningful to speak of a national labour market as opposed to a global labour market. The conditions and requirements that determine how people operate in the field have to be interpreted from a development perspective. The whole can be seen as a global economic network, whose dynamic is determined by business, but that is controlled by numerous national and international laws, agreements, regulations and practises.

5 Reshaping national boundaries

As part of the globalisation process, the boundaries of nation-states take on new shapes. However, the process is not to straightforwardly open the gates to all flows equally, but in a highly selective manner. The process seems to follow the logic of economic globalisation and to open doors to valuable resources – investments and skills – while blocking out the flows without economic value. Further, there are supranational agreements that create common labour market areas, such as the EU and to some extent, NAFTA (North American Free Trade Agreement) in North America and AFTA (ASEAN Free Trade Area) in Southeast Asia. In addition, these agreements aim to unify certain aspects of border-crossing flows, but they rarely limit the movement of highly skilled labour from countries outside the agreement area. Thus, in terms of talent flows, several national policies and programmes aiming to attract various types of expertise globally, together with supranational agreements, create a common framework. In brief, it is important to recognise the changing, though not necessarily diminishing role of national boundaries.

Immigration is part of the economic and globalisation policy practiced by governments – whether or not this is acknowledged. The immigration policy of the United States and the country's increased anti-foreign sentiment in recent years are a good illustration of the significance of immigration policies and attitudes toward immigration in the context of global competition. America's weakened draw in attracting science and technology professionals is in part a result of the increased attractiveness of other countries – but only in part. In 2001, the United States granted 166,000 work visas to science and technology professionals, but only 74,000 in 2002 – in other words, their immigration plummeted by 55 percent. A similar but less drastic drop is seen in the number of work permits granted in certain other industries, including entertainment and finance. In part, the decline is a result of tightened immigration policies in the wake of the 2001 terrorist attack, but above all, it has to do with the country's new, aggressive and exclusive attitudes toward outsiders. A shift has taken place from a period that favoured immigration, funded research and development, invested in education, and forged international free trade agreements, toward a new time of protectionism and inwardness, which redirects the top experts in science and technology to other countries (Florida 2004). Immigration policy is not merely an administrative issue, then, but also one of ideology. It is about a country's attitudes toward foreigners and immigration, as well as the concrete manifestations of these attitudes in measures taken. This kind of information about a particular country's ideology pertaining to foreigners and changes therein travels quickly through the bush radio operated by the global economy's experts.

In the different manifestations of globalisation, it is possible to simplify and make a distinction between *economic operators* and the *administrative operators* who control the economy and society. The economy's globalisation has changed the starting points of making immigration policy – whereas before, the labour force migrated to wherever capital and production were present, it is now often the case that capital and production move to where there is available labour force. A skilled and highly educated labour force has emerged as a central production factor (Florida 2002), and Western countries are now engaged in a mutual competition for skilled labour (Mentz 2002).

Today, an administrative decision made by a single country is in many respects subject to transnational decisions. The EU has assumed a powerful role in member nations, particularly with regard to immigration issues. National-level decision making has to conform, in other words, to administrative edicts from the transnational level. The unification of the EU area's labour market and immigration policies creates a new situation, which solidifies globalisation's effects in the European labour market.

As a production factor, human capital can be compared with economic capital: accrual produces added value, but only by investing successfully. Successful investment in human capital means using the capital as effectively as possible, i.e. utilising the education and work experience of the labour force in appropriately corresponding tasks. In many fields the labour market is still clearly limited to certain regions or at most, a single nation. The human capital of a teacher, for example, is composed of the essential elements of language skills and knowledge of the local culture and operating environment. In this kind of regional labour market, the human capital of an immigrant may have little use, particularly in the early part of the immigrant's residence in the new country. Human capital is not a marketable commodity in the labour market, if it does not suit the local – or more often – national system. In ICT and biotechnology the adjustment to functioning on a global level may occur most easily, but even experts in these fields cannot ignore the impact of national and local environments.

5.1 EU as shaper of national immigration policies

The barriers that prevent the full use of immigrants' human capital are often structural, or related to the national labour market, or they are barriers imposed by protectionism in certain industries. In EU policy, expanding the labour market beyond national borders has significance also from the point of view of improving immigrants' situation in the labour market. The promotion of immigration growth, expansion of immigrants' skill sets, and lowering existing national structural barriers are ways to boost the EU's ability to compete globally – the objective is the same as in member countries' policies for immigration, labour market and integration.

In previous EU cooperation, policies on foreigners were part of the so-called third pillar – an internal issue that member nations could decide upon independently. In spite of this, the Amsterdam Agreement (1999) began the *streamlining of immigration policy*, meaning that increasing portions of member nations' policies regarding foreigners, refugees and immigrants are transferred to the sphere of the union's authority and decision-making. Streamlining has occurred very slowly over time. In reality, agreement has been reached only in terms of the minimum requirements to which all member nations must adhere to laws, regulations and the services guaranteed therein. In most countries, EU-level unified immigration policy has had little impact.

Certain specific features can help illustrate our particular case study. Finland occupies a special place in the debate about unified immigration policy: it has the fewest immigrants of all EU-15 nations, and it does not have the colonial ties that have brought many immigrants to some other European countries. During the first wave of European immigration, Finland experienced outward migration. The country has far less experience with receiving immigrants than most other nations in the union. When comparing and grouping countries in terms of their globalisation aspects, it is remarkable how old divisions and groupings disappear. For example, Nordic welfare states have several features in common in terms of their national systems (health care, social security, role of trade unions etc.), but readiness and ability to join the global labour market differ. Some are much more deeply involved with the international community through social, organisational and political relations than others. For example, Finland has only really opened up recently, after joining the EU.

International agreements ratified by Finland, however, require adherence to common principles in the nation's attitude toward foreigners and, by the same token, its policies regarding foreigners. Attitudes toward foreign nationals are manifested in the different policies toward them, such as asylum and refugee policy, immigration policy, and immigrant policy. International obligations mean that the country's policy on foreigners is no longer under the sole, independent control of the government, but that decision-making concerning policies on foreigners is influenced and bound by international agreements and other international cooperation, foremost being the cooperation within the EU (for example, Lepola 2000). Traditionally, Finnish policy on immigration and foreigners has been bound by various international agreements, such as the Geneva Convention on Refugees or ILO's Declaration on Fundamental Principles and Rights at Work, which addresses work discrimination.

Immigration policy occupies a particularly important rank on EU's agenda because of the changing age structure of every EU nation. The ageing workforce must be replaced, if the EU is to retain its ability to compete globally. According to the 2000 Lisbon Strategy, the EU's goal in 2000–2010 is to "become the most competitive and dynamic knowledge-based economy in the world capable of sustainable economic growth with more and better jobs and greater social cohesion" (European Commission 2003a).

The European Commission's statement in 2000 regarding the union's immigration policy opened up new perspectives for European immigration policy. The released statement outlined ways to promote the four separate areas of EU's immigration and asylum policy The basic points are: cooperation with the immigrants' countries of origin, a common European asylum policy, fair treatment of third-country nationals, and management of migration flows. At a later point, the EU also published a policy outline on immigration, integration and employment (European Commission 2003a). The objective is to craft a unified, combined immigration and integration policy, whose application varies from one member country to another. Thus, guidelines for immigration policies acquire common features, but what happens within the nation-states depends strongly on its particular history and actual readiness and capability of its institutions and individuals to deal with the issues.

The third wave of European immigration will be managed differently from the first wave in 1950–70s. The goals are to:

- Renounce the policy of using migrant labour, which was based on the faulty assumption that such immigration is temporary in nature;
- Clearly distinguish between humanitarian and labour-related immigration;
- Practise a selective policy in labour-related immigration;
- Achieve equality in the labour market between immigrants and the original population; and
- Support comprehensive and long-term social integration of immigrants.

The goals of a common immigration policy can be reached through a number of methods. The starting point for a common EU immigration, asylum and integration policy is rooted in a comprehensive migration management system: economic, social, cultural, and religious factors, as well as those connected to nationality, and participation and political rights are taken into account in all administration and decision making. Apart from this broad-based approach, it is also considered important that comprehensive administration be conducted with a view of the long term, which should be incorporated into both politics and decisions concerning the allocation of resources. The comprehensive approach also aims for interagency coordination. Because the implementation of decisions often gets stuck in-between administrative entities, there will be an effort to streamline the implementation of decisions through networking and new types of structuring solutions. In addition, it is essential for administrative practises to be adapted to local conditions and for services to adapt to the needs of the clientele, that is, immigrants.

From the point of view of the EU's economic policy objectives, it is important that immigrants residing in member countries are in steady employment that matches their skills. According to the Commission, the "maximal integration" of immigrants into the labour market would help the EU's economy to utilise all of its potential in terms of competitiveness, growth and employment (European Commission 2003, 19). An integration policy for immigrants is sorely needed in Finland, where their position in the labour market is weaker than in many EU nations.

Box 2. Immigration policy through the community method and the open coordination method

In practise, the comprehensive and community-wide coordination of immigration policy should occur using a community-wide method (directives) and open coordination method. The community-wide method is used to influence legislation in member nations, for example, by setting minimum standards for immigrants' rights. The open coordination method, on the other hand, is a so-called soft mechanism used to create a common framework for the policy practiced in member nations, but in a way that adapts policy to local conditions and administrative structures. Instead of rewriting legislation and structures, networking and communication between member nations and different administrative entities are emphasised.

The use of the open coordination method in social policy is connected to the fact that different countries use different socio-political models. Because of special national characteristics, the open coordination method does not aim to adapt policy – instead, member countries can themselves select the methods they will use to reach the common goals. Open coordination also seeks to produce political innovations, i.e. so-called good practises (see Ahonen 2002, Ekholm 2003, 133-152).

The common EU immigration policy as well as the union's labour market policy applies the open coordination method. Employment policy, too, intersects with immigrants' issues and adheres to the objectives of the afore-mentioned Lisbon Strategy. The Commission's public statements and proposals for directives have defined the ways in which the community and open coordination methods are used in immigration policy. Launching a community-wide immigration, asylum and integration policy is dependent on the processing timetables of the directives. Because the need for coordinating immigration policy has been defined as a central element of the Lisbon Strategy, the Commission hastens the passage of its initiatives within EU's different branches.

The EU's motivation to promote the extraction of various areas of immigration policy from a nationally administered to an EU-coordinated policy is not only connected to future goals, but also to the view that previous policies are seen as failures. According to this view, the short-term immigration policies practiced by member nations during the first wave (1950s to early 1970s) of European immigration resulted in the wasteful use and social marginalisation of immigrant labour. The second wave has ended in a crisis of the asylum system, which is fundamentally a consequence of a lack of other immigration channels (Sassen 1999, van Steenbergen 1994, Pierson 1998, Geddes 2003). In addition, the common EU policy on immigration that is emerging during the third wave also constitutes a justified criticism of the immigration policies that member states practiced in the past out of a short-term and nationally oriented starting point.

5.2 Expanding labour markets, the EU and immigration policy

The internationalisation of the labour market does not only affect the lives of experts. Immigration policies and the internationalisation of the labour market are linked, and the migration of labour in low-skill industries is also connected to this. The dynamic of the whole must be recognised in social discourse, so that political and administrative responses to the different forms of the labour market's internationalisation are as adequate and appropriate as possible.

A central cause for concern has been the enlargement of the European Union. Eastward enlargement is always associated with fears of significant numbers of labour flowing from new member countries to the old ones, disrupting their labour markets. The worry is that labour from new member countries will move to the old countries in hopes of better employment, and on the other hand, that production will increasingly shift toward the new member countries, which offer lower production costs.

The EU grants its members considerable freedom in controlling workforce mobility. Countries have the right to so-called *transition periods*, used to stem the flow of labour from new to old member nations. The first transition period is two years, then three, and finally three more years. To extend the transition period, a member country must show at the end of each period that eliminating restrictions would seriously disrupt the domestic labour market. Transition periods are used in quelling fears about the erosion of collective labour agreements and wage levels in low-skill jobs, as a greater supply of labour floods the market.

EU's earlier enlargement to include countries that were poorer than the EU average showed that, consequently, direct foreign investments into new member countries increased, technological development sped up, and the status of living improved (Kiander 2001). This will most likely be the case also with the enlargements of 2004 and 2007. Transition periods that limit workforce mobility delay the development of collective labour agreements and social security in new member countries, because governments are not compelled to fight against a declining workforce. In this situation, low production costs represent a competitive advantage: because restrictions on workforce mobility cannot be compensated for by restricting the flow of capital and investments, the most significant effect of transition periods may be the transfer of jobs from old member countries to new ones. Particularly in industries that are able to shift production or services relatively easily, employment may decline as jobs disappear to new member countries with cheaper production costs. Increasing investments into new EU member countries does, however, eventually bring wages and standards up to the EU average and weakens the new countries' relative price advantage. In the end, EU membership means conformity and uniformity in working conditions.

In countries such as France, Italy and Britain, workforce mobility is controlled through special programmes and bilateral agreements with countries that lose labour. The agreements also seek to minimise the share of the grey economy in the national economy. Agreements and cooperation with new member nations follow the same principle of comprehensive administration recommended by the EU Commission (2003), which also forms the basis for developing a common EU immigration policy with regard to third nations. Professor Michael Burda (2003) has emphasised that similar cooperation between receiving countries and countries of origin is also necessary inside the EU. This would increase the economic and socio-political benefits of expansion for the older member nations.

Policy recommendations that take comprehensive administration as their starting point undergo a complicated negotiation process in the braches of the EU, with the various viewpoints of the EU itself, its individual member nations and other interested parties come face to face during the process. Member nations may be said to be weighed down by old structures and mutually incompatible systems, and have a limited ability to adapt to the new forms of international migration. The resulting problems in controlling migration movements deter the EU's economic and socio-political objectives, put in place with the best interest of member states in mind.

The problem is that the demand for foreign labour in EU countries is constantly higher than the supply of legal immigrant labour. This has overloaded the asylum system and encouraged phenomena that are associated with the grey economy – illegal immigration and human smuggling. Member states have reacted by increasing preventive controls, in other words weakening the legal position of asylum seekers. Preventing the entry of illegal immigrants has in turn caused labour market disruptions, particularly in the south, where the labour markets depend on seasonal foreign labour.

The way that member states have responded to the increase in demand for foreign labour has exacerbated the problems, and it seems that tinkering to change current policy or creating more controls have not helped. The changing nature of the immigration phenomenon requires that administrative practises and structures adapt to the new situation, which the control structures that were originally created in the 1960s and 1970s are too outdated to handle. The global movement of capital and production as well as the flow of humanitarian immigration to Western countries have pitched the control systems that were meant to prevent immigration into a crisis, to the point that the "immigration policy problem" is more a *result* of administrative methods than something in need of administrative methods. The conflict between restricted, legal immigration channels and high demand has placed increased stress on the asylum system and led to undocumented immigration.

The situation has spawned an "immigrant industry" – criminal activity that specialises in the secret transport of people to the west. Public discourse usually busies itself by abhorring the smugglers as well as the people who choose this method of moving. The smugglers and the immigrants themselves are blamed for the repeated mass deaths that occur at EU borders. The attitude was clearly visible in 2003, when debate concerning the issue was heated.

In late 2003, almost every week, news reports described boats sunk in the Mediterranean, and the mass deaths of potential immigrants (BBC 23.10.2003, El Periódico 3.11.2003). In July 2003, fifteen people drowned on the coast of popular vacation island Fuerteventura, when the boat transporting them sank. In October 34 people drowned off the coast of Spain (El Periódico 2003). Also in October, nearly one hundred immigrants on their way to Italy drowned in several separate incidents (BBC 23.10.2003). Most governments and interest groups voiced their disapproval regarding the events, but it is difficult to identify the guilty party, and the responsibility for the mass deaths of undocumented immigrants seems to belong to no-one.

The people who drown in the Mediterranean and their counterparts elsewhere are usually workers who have no other way of travelling to the countries in southern Europe that need their labour. The factors that influence the destinies of these workers include Europe's outdated immigration policies and the indifference of authorities, as well as the workers' undemocratic countries of origin that are unable to offer their citizens future opportunities (Harris 2002, xvii, BBC 16.6.2003). The immigration policies of European countries make many people's work commutes dangerous, because with current administrative practises, the only way to prevent people from entering is to allow their boats to sink and hope that they are able to swim back to the departure port.

The first concrete proposal by the EU to control undesirable immigration to Europe was inventive but problematic. The basic idea of the model was to conduct trade with the immigrants' countries of origin and the transit countries, and have the countries agree to take back the deported illegal immigrants and the asylum seekers turned away by EU member states. The carrot was the offer of an annual immigration quota to EU countries. The stick came in the shape of economic sanctions – for example, the freezing of development cooperation.

The fact that the quotas would have been determined by the EU was opposed by many EU nations, Finland included. The model was also tricky from an employment policy perspective, because the quotas were defined primarily for political reasons, not on the conditions of the labour market. Some of the methodology of the quota model involved force and pressure imposed on immigrants as well as the countries of origin and transit, and this too caused dismay among EU members, which overturned the proposal that included the quotas in a meeting of the Council of Europe in 2003. The Council acknowledged the asylum system's crisis, which would be resolved "in accordance with the Geneva General Agreement and [the EU's humanitarian traditions]" (Council of Europe 2003). At the end of 2004, a five-year plan to improve cooperation on immigration and asylum policy was adopted in the EU. This confirmed the EU's "Fortress Europe" image, complete with strict border controls and fewer visas. Simultaneously other control policies, including raids to work sites with suspected illegal migrants, have increased.

The development of a common EU policy on immigration has been and probably will be a slow and strenuous process. The first leg of the road toward the comprehensive administration of immigration policy has been halting and many amendments seem politically impossible to implement. The situation has spurred many member countries to move beyond EU policy to respond to labour market challenges with national policies. The following is a presentation of immigration models in use in Germany, Britain and Italy that aim to manage immigration instead of restricting or controlling it more. The intent is to manage the immigration of labour through relatively light administrative methods in order to achieve the goal, which is, after all, to satisfy the demand for skilled labour (see cases 1–3).

Case No. 1: Selective Germany

A majority of the immigrants from new EU member countries go to Germany and Britain. The estimates are not exact, but even if the maximum estimated number of immigrants turns out to become a reality, immigration is not expected to change significantly from the present (Dustmann 2003, Imbusch 2001).

It has been estimated that with regard to Germany, the employment effects of the free movement of labour following EU's eastward expansion will have significance only locally and only in certain occupations. By 2030, the expected 800,000 new workers from the new countries would be enough to replace the natural loss of labour. Germany has in fact made bilateral employment immigration agreements with many ETA nations and Turkey, among others, to effectively channel the immigration potential toward industries that are suffering from a shortage of labour (Menz 2002, 736).

Germany has an annual quota of 20,000 five-year work permits to ICT professionals with an offer of work in Germany. Only a tenth of the quota has been filled. This reflects the shortage of intellectual capital at the global level, and is an omen of the fierce fighting among nations over this resource in the years ahead.

Germany's immigration policy is fraught with the problem of stubbornly holding on to the migrant worker ideal (cf. Sassen 1999; Geddes 2003). The model is rooted in the building phase of the German nation-state in the 1800s, when the country's industry relied on workforce from neighbouring countries in the east, but was unwilling to allow workers to settle in the country because of nationalist ideology. Settling was prevented through alien legislation, and foreign workers were obliged to leave the country for a certain length of time each year (Sassen 1999). Germany is now on its way to a similar migrant worker model (Menz 2002) that, when implemented in 1950–1973 in many other European countries, led to the marginalisation of immigrants and ethnic stratification of the labour market (Pierson 1998, Geddes 2003).

The migrant worker model cannot be recommended as a starting point for immigration policy, because, although it offers short-term benefits, it stands in the way of the integration of immigrants who remain in the country, and thus creates marginalisation. The model is mostly suited to seasonal work or border areas where workers cross the border regularly to go to work. Outside of that, it is based on short-term thinking to benefit one national economy that lacks understanding of the importance of integrating immigrants (Menz 2002) and causes long-term human and economic loss.

Case No. 2: Britain and new immigration channels

The difficulty that workers experience in entering Britain has overloaded the asylum system. Immigrants who work in fields that suffer from a labour shortage apply to enter the country through the asylum system, because alternative immigration channels are too restrictive.

In Britain, foreign university students are granted an automatic work permit for one year following graduation. According to the immigration department, to satisfy the country's demand for labour requires that the economic benefits of immigration are maximised. This means recruiting highly educated and young people from abroad as well as an increase in the number of work visas granted for low-skill jobs. In the latter case, the intention is to prevent the use of the asylum system for economic purposes by opening up more legal immigration channels to Britain's labour market.

The shortage in labour supply has been reflected in the transfer of jobs outside the EU. The latest trend is the transfer of top expertise and highly paid jobs to India, where there is more available labour. In addition, developments in communications technology makes it possible to move electronic support services such as telephone centres and others to areas that better suit corporations. It has been estimated that up to 200,000 jobs will leave Britain during 2004–2009, and not only low-skill jobs such as assembly or production of raw materials, but highly productive, well-paid jobs requiring top skills, including planning, business services and so forth. India is indeed challenging European production at all levels (The Times 2003).

In May 2003, Britain launched an immigration programme targeted mainly at low-skill labour that aims to recruit 20,000 foreign workers to help alleviate the shortage in two different employment areas. Britain has also launched a second recruiting programme to obtain foreign workers, this one meant to promote the availability of seasonal workers for agriculture as well as to monitor the treatment and working conditions of this workforce.

The idea of Britain's new immigration policy is to grant work visas to people who might otherwise apply for asylum. This eases the labour shortage and the pressure on the asylum system. The reason for the overloaded asylum system is that there has long been more demand for foreign labour in Britain than it has been possible to meet through legal channels. It may be said that in part, labour-induced immigration has arrived through the wrong channels, that is, via the asylum process. The problems have been excessive restrictions on labour force mobility and a lengthening of the asylum process for refugees in need of asylum.

Case No. 3: Italy and the IOM

The most evolved and well functioning labour force strategy has emerged in a cooperation project between Italy and Albania. The International Organization for Migration (IOM) participated in the project through its offices in Albania and Rome, as did the Ministry of Labour in Italy and Albania and the Italian Embassy in Tirana.

The objective was to decrease the volume of Albanian asylum seekers and illegal immigrants in Italy by offering legal immigration channels for workers. The programme aimed at the widest possible reach and publicity, and was promoted through Albanian employment offices and newspapers. Albanians wishing to immigrate to Italy were able to apply through the programme to certain occupational fields. Most applicants have been young men with intermediate education, applying for low-skill jobs in construction, health care, and the hotel and restaurant industries. During the project's initial phase, the IOM created a 50,000-person database for authorities and Italian employers of Albanians who were willing to emigrate.

The project's 45 employees interviewed approximately 20,000 workers in the course of a three-year project. Five thousand of them have cleared occupational and language tests and have been entered into the database. Of them, 1,500 have found employment in Italy, while only 63 have withdrawn from the project – some to work in Italy illegally. The project has succeeded in channelling at least a portion of those with a desire to emigrate through legal channels, while also enabling employers to find needed labour. The project has been pronounced a success as well as cost-effective (IOM 2002).

Many countries – Italy and Albania are an example – have created mutual *bilateral agreements* for managing legal immigration channels for labour. This model could also be applied to Finland, particularly with regard to Estonia and Russia. It represents a better way to ensure enough and appropriately qualified workforce, worker mobility, and better working conditions. Recruiting programmes can be tailored to the desired target groups, be they top experts or berry pickers. The flow of information about work opportunities and potential labour is an important factor in the mobility of labour, and improving the ways in which information is disseminated is critical in the creation of foreign recruiting networks.

When workers cross national borders without the availability of legal channels of immigration, they wind up entering through the asylum system or illegally, which frequently increases the amount of unreported work in the labour market (grey economy). On the whole, this has not been a problem in Finland, where the number of asylum seekers is small and asylum and residency criteria are strict.

All of the models of administering immigration policy share one thing: they aim to manage immigration and emigration in ways that meet the needs of both the country of origin and the receiving country, of the individual immigrant and the employer. This involves trying to avoid overloading the receiving country's authorities and institutions through measures that prevent the use of the asylum system for employment reasons and minimise the seepage of labour and jobs into the illegal job market. A sustainable system of controlling immigration also helps avoid the human catastrophes and criminal activity caused by illegal immigration. It is important to understand in Finland and in the European Union that it is not possible, nor even desirable, to prevent migration between the unequal nations of the global economy. Potential immigrants and the receiving countries' labour markets need each other, and if countries try to "dam" immigration through tough control measures, immigrants will find ways around the dam. In regulating immigration, the issue is primarily this: who will open up the channels for immigrants, and who reaps the benefit – the receiving country or human smugglers?

5.3 Re-defining citizens and aliens

As a phenomenon, immigration policy does not occur independently, but is strongly tied to history, economy and other political factors. It becomes easier to understand the structure of the immigrant population and a country's immigration policy when they are placed in the historical context of international economic and political development. For example, in the case of Finland, the primary economic and political context for a historical perspective is Europe. When compared with other countries of northern and central Europe, Finland was a latecomer in terms of industrialisation, economic growth and political independence. This has had an impact on both the volume and structure of immigration to Finland, whose geopolitical situation has made immigration and immigrants seem more of a national security risk than a factor that is favourable to production. A change in political and administrative attitudes is needed, if immigration strategies are to be included in the larger expertise-based innovation and information society strategy.

Finnish economic life did not undergo structural change until the 1960s and 1970s, and when it happened, it was faster and more radical than anywhere else in Europe. The flight from rural areas to cities during industrialisation urbanised society, but in addition to creating internal migration, also prompted emigration to Sweden (for example, Korkiasaari 2000, 140). Following World War II, Europe's reconstruction and industrialisation required a large workforce, which was not available within its borders. This launched Western Europe's *first wave* of immigration (for example, Stalker 2000, 11-14). As opposed to the present time, the countries that needed immigrants during the first wave were not interested in highly educated professionals – they needed brawn, not brains. *The migrant worker strategies* were born; government-controlled immigrant recruiting systems that contained the idea of meeting what was perceived as a temporary demand for labour, and then returning to labour force self-sufficiency. Reality proved otherwise. The labour market's hierarchical structures eventually made it increasingly difficult to attract the majority population to work in the less pleasant, low-level jobs (for example, Sassen 1999; Piore 1979, 17-19).

When industrialisation and economic growth took off, Europe's periphery – Spain, Italy, Portugal and Finland – all countries that had leaked labour in previous decades, had turned into immigration receiving countries by the 1980s (Carmon 1996, 16; Massey et al. 1993, 431). By then, the countries that had already recruited immigrants had come around to the realisation that immigrants settled into the country as permanent minorities, instead of returning to their home countries, as had been anticipated when industrialisation's most immediate labour needs had been met (Cross & Waldinger 1999, 29; Joly 2000, 31; Salt et al. 2000, 5; Sassen 1999, 142-143). It was not until the 1980s that efforts began to integrate immigrants into society began, through the teaching of language and social skills, for example. More attention was focused on legal and political rights, and a discussion about the rights, naturalisation and opportunity for dual citizenship began (Faist 2000, 272-279; Hammar 1990; Lepola 2000).

Integrating immigrants into the societies that received them required services, because jobs no longer provided the linkage to society for everyone. The developed Nordic welfare societies made use of their entire arsenal of measures to promote the social integration of immigrants (Necef 2000; Knocke 1993). According to critics, society's attitudes and the discourse about immigrants took a new direction, away from an economic focus and toward a social-work approach.

Finland became an immigration receiving country only in the second wave, when quota refugees and asylum seekers began to arrive in the 1980s, and to a greater extent in the early 1990s (Korkiasaari & Söderling 1998, 14-24). For immigrants who came for other than employment-related reasons, Finland was in the process of launching socially integrative measures around the same time as the rest of Europe, and the Nordic countries in particular. Finland was unique in one sense, compared with the countries of the first wave, in that it had no major existing immigrant populations who had arrived without the benefit of the new integrative services now provided to refugees and, in other countries, to the family members of previously arrived immigrants. For these reasons, the social discourse about immigration and immigrants became the realm of government authorities and was linked to the broader field of social work: the receiving, employment and social integration of immigrants.

Finland has no prior experience of attracting immigrant labour, utilising their expertise, and integrating them into society. Why is Finland such a latecomer in realising the importance of labour immigration? Why is it that Finland, unlike the other Nordic countries, has never in its history sought foreign labour? First of all, Finland became industrialised at a slower pace that the rest of Europe, and the industrialisation that had begun before World War II was delayed by participation in the war. Post-war industrial development was unable to utilise all of the labour that was being freed up from agriculture, and some of those who lost their livelihoods became a labour reserve for Swedish industry (for example, Korkiasaari 2000, 139-141; Rahikainen 2001, 32). In addition, Finland has never had the colonies that produce returnees. The country has been in Western Europe's periphery, a kind of remote island surrounded by seas on the one side and a closed eastern border on the other.

In addition to the barriers of Finland's economic situation, the position of women in the labour market has reduced the necessity of recruiting foreign labour. Women's high employment share and role in the hierarchy of working life has excluded a need for foreign labour (cf. Paananen 1993, 11). The development of the welfare society, social services and child day-care from the 1960s onward has made it possible to remove women from the homes to perform other functions. The products of an evolved family policy, such as day care, have played an important part in the Nordic countries in preventing the kinds of developments that have occurred in central and southern Europe, where European women have entered the work force on the backs of women from developing nations. The reproduction of labour, usually a women's realm, has been outsourced to legal or illegal immigrant women, who, conversely, support the families that remain in developing countries (Knocke 1991, 474-477; Lutz 1993, 137-141; Sassen 1998, 115-116; on the relationship between ethnicity, gender and class to household labour: Rio 2000; Hondagneu-Sotelo 2001).

In Finland, immigration policy and immigrants are emotional topics that are difficult to talk about, even at the government level, without getting embroiled in a debate about what it means to be 'Finnish'. At the level of legislation and legal interpretation, immigrants to Finland have been required to have a nearly biological link to Finland, such as a Finnish parent, previous Finnish citizenship, or marriage to a Finnish citizen. The same requirement for Finnish blood ties was observed in the remigration of Ingrian Finns, which began in 1991 (Laari 1997). Foreigners and in particular refugees have been viewed as a security risk throughout the history of post-war Finland, and hence protection from immigration and refugees has been considered part of the national security policy. Acknowledging and accepting refugees also represents a political stand that Finland did not feel it could afford during the sensitive relationship with the Soviet Union (Aallas 1997, 113-116; Lepola 2000, 43-45). Finland's policy on foreigners from the post-war time until 1992, when the Soviet Union collapsed, can in fact be seen as one manifestation of Finnish-Soviet relations (Paananen 1999, 42).

The sensitive and emotional responses to discussing the immigration question are reflected in the fact that Finland's legislation on foreigners has been amended on a continual basis over recent decades, as the country has ratified international agreements. The latest Aliens Act came into force in May 2004. In the latest amendment to the law governing foreigners, the objective was to write legislation that would form a streamlined structure for more open immigration policy decision making, while at the same time ensuring immigrants' human rights. In terms of content, the law is aimed at achieving harmony with the 2000 constitutional reform and the possible changes resulting from a common EU policy and its reforms in the rights of asylum seekers and refugees and in immigration policy in general. On the other hand, the law does not directly address the simultaneously ongoing public discussion about issues such as the changing dependency ratio, a consequence of an ageing workforce, or the need for foreign labour (Report by the Aliens Act working group 2001, 2-4).

The reform of the alien legislation (Aliens Act) has been a long and thorny process, where the interests of various advocacy groups have collided time and again. Politicians have been reluctant to take responsibility for the reform, because immigration policy is not something that appeals to Finnish voters. The legal reform has been showered with criticism from civic and human rights organisations (Organisations' statement on the comprehensive reform of the Aliens Act 2001), labour organisations and from within the administration (Report by the Aliens Act working group 2001). The result seems to be anything but a streamlined law, which continues to give authorities a lot of room to interpret facts as they will and offers little support for the development of a skills-based immigration strategy.

At the same time, both national and international discourse increasingly recognises the growing need for a more active immigration policy, constituting the *third wave*, as the population structure ages and the workforce declines in all industrial countries. *The Commission's statement regarding the European Union's immigration policy* (2000) stated that the zero-sum immigration policy that Western European nations have implemented for the last 30 years has reached the end of the line, and that it is now time for a new, community-level immigration and asylum policy: countries need more skilled labour, and the asylum system is in crisis. Compared with the first wave, the policy for the third wave of immigration seeks potential immigrants with education and the right skills; in other words, brain power instead of only physical performance. European Union nations compete for skilled labour not only with the United States, but also with each other, at the expense of an all-European immigration policy.

The Finnish government (Government Programme 2003) took a clear stand in 2003 in favour of the promotion of labour immigration. The motives include an ageing population on the one hand, and the so-called dependency ratio crisis on the other: "Because of an ageing population and reduction in the flow of labour to Finland, the country's population development will already during the coming decade lead to a wholly new situation. When required by the dependency ratio, the government will promote employment-related immigration. This requires broad-based collaboration and commitment among the government, localities, economic life, employees, employers and trade unions, as well as civic organisations."

The Finnish government created a programme for an immigration policy and to integrating into society also those immigrants who arrive in the country for employment reasons, by making available language and other integrative education and instruction. The intention is to divide responsibility for the cost of educational programmes for immigrants between the state and employers. In exchange, companies will have the opportunity to recruit foreign labour more freely. In cooperation with labour market organisations, the government determined the ways in which employers who seek foreign labour can participate in the costs that result from educational programmes for immigrants. The working group's proposal for the government's immigration policy programme was published at the end of 2006. The emphasis on labour migration was clear, but implementation of the programme's proposals may take new forms, since the key author in labour migration issues, the Ministry of Labour, will cease to function as of the end of 2007, and migration issues will be transferred to the Ministry of the Interior.

It is important to understand that "pure" labour immigration, where all immigrants are workers of some sort, does not exist. Employees frequently move with their families and also settle in societies for other than work-related reasons – many permanently. The hours that remain in a day after working hours are many, and during that time, people are not "production factors", but part of greater society with their own particular needs. It is therefore not sufficient to merely address immigrants' position in the labour market – other services to link them to society are needed as well, including services that take into account the entire family's needs. The functionality of services intended to anchor immigrants in society, the policy of integration, is essential from the perspective of social cohesion regardless of what kind of immigrants are being sought. One ideological starting point that has been shown to work in the model country of immigration policy, Canada, is that each immigrant should be treated as a potential citizen. Adopting naturalisation as the ideological foundation for a policy of integration means that immigrants are taken into account in structuring society, and are permitted to feel that they are an equal part of society from the beginning.

Since the new Aliens Act of 2004, the policies being considered in Finland were fairly immigration and immigrant friendly. In this regard, Finnish immigration discourse has evolved very differently than in many other parts of the EU, where security policy issues have gained importance since the beginning of the 21st century and the "war against terror", and the management of security risks characterise political development. It may be said, in fact, that in other parts of the European Union immigration policy is undergoing "Finlandisation": economic and humanitarian arguments have been steamrolled by arguments in favour of reinforcing internal security through tighter border controls and stricter regulation of immigration. In Finland, the discussion has gradually shifted toward a re-evaluation of immigration as an economic resource – for the first time in the history of independent Finland.

Table 6. Summary of the history of immigration in Finland

TIME PERIOD	IMMIGRATION-RELATED CHARACTERISTICS
Autonomy 1800s to 1917	In 1888, everyone entering the country needed a valid passport. Foreign artisans and entrepreneurs were able to immigrate to Finland. Regulations, control of foreigners. Residing and practising a trade were controlled through a permit system, which was also extended to Russians. The estate system's class divisions were also applied to foreigners, whose treatment was inconsistent and unequal. The Roma and Jews, in particular, were controlled particularly stringently. Other countries' nationals were viewed as a threat to national security.
First decades of independence 1918 to 1950	In 1918, Tatars and Jews were granted freedom of trade. Following the Russian Revolution 33,000 Russian and Karelian refugees entered Finland. Some were granted temporary residence permits. Social instability led most of the Russians to continue on to other parts of the world, whereas most of the Karelians returned to Soviet Russia. Finnish attitudes toward "kindred refugees" were more positive than toward Russians. The 1938 Aliens Act formed the foundation for rules and statutes in the current legislation for controlling foreigners, prevention of entry and deportation. The motive was to "prevent revolutionary movements from operating" by controlling international traffic → state police monitoring of foreigners. Foreigners were viewed as a threat to national security. Immigration volume was low, and the number of foreigners declined by the 1950s.
1960s to early 1970s	Legal protection of foreigners was nonexistent. Ratification of key international human rights conventions created pressure to rewrite the Aliens Act. The legislative overhaul was not carried out until 1983. Immigration occurred on a small scale under strict controls.
End of 1970s to 1980s	In 1984, Finland passed its first comprehensive law regarding foreigners, with permit statutes for legal entry and residence, and with legal protections for foreigners that were in accordance with the obligations Finland agreed to in signing international agreements. Most immigration occurred through marriage or as the return migration of Swedish Finns. Finland began to accept refugees: from Chile as of 1973 and from Vietnam as of 1979. The Council of State ratified an annual refugee quota starting in 1985.
1990s	In 1991, new alien legislation was passed, with reforms in asylum practises and other legal protections. There is continuous pressure to amend the alien legislation. The permit system for practising a trade in Finland is eliminated. Ethnic return migration from the former Soviet Union begins in 1990.

	Number of asylum seekers grows rapidly, hastening the creation of a processing system. Number of foreign nationals increases at a fast rate. In 1999, the Act on the Integration of Immigrants is passed to help integrate immigrants. In 1995, Finland joins the EU, and the movement of labour becomes easier within the EU area. The Amsterdam Agreement launches a shift to joint decisions regarding immigration and asylum policies.
2000 to the present	The Schengen Agreement goes into effect. There is an EU-wide effort to facilitate and promote freer movement of EU nationals within the Union's borders. A debate regarding a common EU policy for immigration and asylum begins. An ageing and shrinking workforce creates increasing pressure to recruit workers from abroad and from outside the EU. In 2004, new alien legislation, the Aliens Act, was passed. It is much broad-scoped and precise than earlier laws. In 2006, a proposal for the government's immigration policy programme was published with strong emphasis on labour migration.

The table above outlines the critical junctions in the development of Finnish immigration policy. It shows that the policy has largely developed as a result of outside pressures, such as the obligations contained in international agreements, and has been propelled less by internal pressures – for example, the need for labour. Protecting the state and its citizens from outside influence, be it people, money, goods or attitudes, is justifiable in certain political and economic situations, but when conditions change, holding on to the same stance becomes resistance to change and damages broader goals. Just recently, immigration has been interpreted as an opportunity and labour migration as a source of resources. However, practical implementations to support the policy are still to come.

5.4 From gatekeeper to promoter

When considering immigration policies and their implementation, as well as the attitudes that shape them, it must be remembered that the global economy is changing the operating rules of the nation-state. Frightening but baseless images about the threats of immigration abound, and from a historical perspective, protectionist decisions made in response to unfounded fears often seem senseless in retrospect. In Finland in the 1800s and early 1900s, Tatars and Jews, and a little later, Russian refugees, were viewed as problems and their opportunities to immigrate, work or practise a trade were in many ways severely restricted. One hundred years ago Finland was a different place, but the justifications behind today's immigration and employment restrictions keep alive some of the old fears about foreigners engaging in illegal work or other activities that are thought to threaten the honest work of Finnish people. Nowadays, the expertise and innovation capital that Jews, Tatars and Russian refugees brought has become an integral and natural part of the Finnish economy. Looking at these migration flows from the vantage point of a hundred years later – how they began and ended, what the situation looks like after several generations – the fears, legal restrictions and limited rights to practise a trade now seem unreasonable and irrational.

It is problematic that discussions about immigration so often involve myopic fears regarding other countries' "surplus" populations, which, as soon as the door is opened a crack, will supposedly flow freely into Finland and work at wages well below collective bargaining agreements, or live off of the country's social welfare system. An immigration policy that insists on only focusing on preventive control weakens the possibilities of attracting the highly skilled experts who comprise the engine that moves the information society forward.

Economic and sociological migration theories generally pay little heed to the various political mechanisms that control immigration, as they concentrate on the push and pull factors of immigration and emigration. Incentives targeted at different areas of life – or push factors – are not alone sufficient to determine how many people leave from a particular area and where they end up. Many other factors, such as contacts in the target country and immigration's international regulatory systems influence the volume and direction of migration.

Each country uses several systems to regulate the volume and types of immigrants. In relation to foreigners – i.e. everyone except a country's own citizens – governments prefer a system of special and preferred status, as well as excluded status. The legislation and administrative practises that regulate the position of foreigners is one practical manifestation of such a system. To put it in different terms, governments display *legalised attitudes* toward foreigners. These attitudes vary in quality depending on the immigrant's nationality or presumed reason for immigrating (Silverman 1991).

It has been said that the importance of regulatory systems for immigration has increased after the fall of the socialist system, which regulated emigration. There are hardly any nations left that regulate citizens' emigration, and it can therefore be said that control is increasingly shifting to immigration rather than emigration (Vertovic & Cohen 1999). But acknowledging the impact of regulatory systems does not make it easy to predict them. International migration has been compared to a coursing creek: you can build dams or you can create new inlets, but you still cannot predict how the creek will flow (see Widgren & Martin 2002). All of a sudden, the creek may seemingly dry up, only to reappear at another source and find a new route, and end up somewhere different. Similarly, various regulatory systems try to control the volume, nationalities and motives of the immigrants who want to settle in new countries.

In the competition for highly skilled professionals, it is not enough to identify push and pull factors. We must also understand how the current finds the channels that carry the individuals who are propelled by push and pull factors. In this kind of process, an individual can decide whether to let go, and go with the flow, or select from a host opportunities and decide where he or she wants the current to end up. And yet the push and pull factors that make up the migration flows are created from the outside, as a result of social developments, and cannot be shaped by individual decision making. In this context, regulatory systems not only consist of immigration policies and the official practises that implement them, but also of other factors that can affect a country's attractiveness quotient.

One major force on the national labour market has been the trade union movement. Traditionally, trade unions have had a negative stance toward the immigration of foreign labour. Whenever the supply of labour increases for whatever reason, trade unions customarily react by attempting to restrict the entry of the new workforce to the labour market. Frequently, this results in internal disagreements, where the trade unions' ideological principles and requirements of solidarity are on one side, while on the other side is the effort to secure benefits for existing members (Virdee 1999, Bergholm 2003).

In the years following World War II, the British labour market recruited 180,000 workers from the Caribbean and Pakistan. These immigrants often ended up in low-skill jobs that did not correspond to their professional skills. According to sociologist Satnam Virdee (1999; Fryer 1984, Wrench 1991), this was not only a consequence of discrimination on the part of employers or of structural factors, but also resulted from trade union activists operating against immigrant labour. It was feared that immigrants would water down the labour agreements and take away the jobs of the English by agreeing to lower standards. In later decades, the growing numbers of immigrant members and a change in the general political atmosphere led to a more positive attitude toward immigrants on the part of trade unions (Virdee 1999).

In Nordic countries the trade union movement has played a crucial role in all social policy, particularly when it comes to developing the welfare state, and by that token, in shaping the greater policy regarding foreigners. The Nordic welfare state model is based on the wage-earning labour of all working-age persons and the highest possible employment percentage. The labour market is the first arena where income is distributed: the labour market not only hands out economic well-being, but also confers social status. The central role of wage labour as a foundation of the welfare state gives trade unions influence on nearly every social issue. Also in terms of shaping immigration policy, trade unions play a central role. Immigration policy, too, has been built on a three-way decision-making process (government, employers, trade unions), and advocates of a national workforce – trade unions – have adopted negative attitudes toward the immigration of labour.

Again, the attitude has a history: trade unions traditionally oppose social change that increases the supply of labour on the labour market, therefore weakening the trade unions' negotiating power. In the 1950s, the growing proportion of women among wage earners made some in trade unions oppose equal working opportunities and try to prevent women's employment particularly in occupations that required education and skills. It was feared that women's participation in the labour market would lower employment and general wage levels in many fields. According to SAK (Central Organisation of Finnish Trade Unions), the increased supply of labour has led to a decrease in trade union membership and a weakened negotiating position in terms of collective bargaining agreements (Bergholm 2003).

It is indeed partially a result of the corporate three-way decision-making model, and therefore the trade unions, that the Finnish labour market has been protected so effectively from immigrants. Immigration creates pressure to adapt the labour market to a situation where there are many types of skill sets and many kinds of labour agreements. The discussion about EU's eastern expansion is a good example of how tightly the national labour market has been protected, and how even the merest threat of having to change familiar structures and decision-making models arouses a flood of objection.

The trade union movement has expressed in public a concern that a high number of employment-seeking immigrants will begin to arrive from Estonia and other Baltic countries (SAK 1998a, 1998b, 2000a, 2000b, 2001). According to SAK, "expanding to the east will bring significant changes in the labour market" (SAK 2000a), "up to 400,000 Estonians may come to Finland to work" (SAK 2000b), "a quarter of Estonians would like to work in Finland" (SAK 1998a), and "the arrival of Estonians to work in Finland is feared" (SAK 1998b).

Trade unions consider it justified to adopt transition periods to restrict the employment of Estonians and labour from other new EU nations during the first few years of membership. The adoption of transition periods as a means to quell migration is problematic in many ways. They may cause problems in the labour market, because the supply of labour to industries experiencing labour shortages cannot be alleviated through immigration. On the other hand, transition periods may also delay improvements in the working conditions and labour agreements of the new member nations, if the labour markets of these countries do not produce a demand to compete for labour with the older member nations. In the Finnish case it seems that transition periods have created a new form of foreign labour – rented workers – that are outside of all national labour market regulations, since they are merely "services" that are bought form Estonia, not employees based in Finland. Again, there are clear national and regional differences between attractive and less attractive regions. It seems that traditional "talent magnets" like London also attract these professionals and semi-professionals from new member countries. It is estimated that there are more than 300,000 Poles alone in the U.K., though official statistics only report 175,000 workers from new member countries. Also according to official statistics, there are 95 Polish plumbers[9] in the U.K., but a tabloid newspaper managed to find that many Polish plumbers in just one day by placing a small advertisement in a Polish-populated part of London (The Economist 2005).

It has been estimated that by 2030, the number of EU nationals from new member countries residing permanently in Finland will have grown by only 13,000–90,000 people from the current level, while the volume of the domestic workforce will decline by 110,000–290,000 people over the same period (Sarvimäki 2003). Immigrants from the new EU countries are expected at an annual rate of 0.1 percent of the figure that represents the Finnish population – only one-tenth of a percent of the country's present annual birth rate (Kiander 2001).

Even if transition periods are not used, the supply of labour will not increase sufficiently in Finland following EU's eastern expansion. Instead of trying to fend off migration from the new member countries, there is instead reason to contemplate ways of attracting labour to Finland. A well-functioning labour market requires that instead of preventing immigration, an active recruiting policy is needed that helps to attract labour from the new member countries and from countries outside of the European Union.

The volume of immigration estimated to arrive from the new member countries represents approximately 0.25 percent of the current EU population, which, from a demographic and labour market standpoint, is, if anything, too low (Kiander 2001, 308). In addition to immigration estimates, the low level of migration between existing member countries and the transfer of production away from Finland indicates that as the EU expands, capital will flow to where the workforce resides and not the other way around. The discussion can be absurd at times: at the same time that concern grows about the declining workforce, there are demands to implement transition periods of up to seven years to restrict the free movement of labour inside the EU (for example, Ekholm 2003, 167).

The discussion concerning the negative impact of immigration on the labour market and the positioning of Finnish workers and immigrant workers against each other seems to be based in a fear of having to adapt familiar practises and entrenched power in a new kind of labour market. Throughout history, the strength of the trade unions has been linked to the ratio of supply and demand of labour: the greater the supply, i.e., the number of workers, the weaker the trade union, and vice versa.

---

9 "Polish plumbers" have become the official icons of Central and Eastern European workers fleeing to old EU nations.

The fear of immigration's impact on labour agreements has not been borne out in studies. They show that the growing share of immigrants in the labour market does not influence the employment or labour agreements of the majority population (Dustmann 2003; Sarvimäki 2003; Cummings & Lambert 1998, 512-515). Even without the presence of immigrants, the problem in the Finnish labour market is that the workforce is more and more clearly divided into a core workforce with strong employment protections, and into an "auxiliary" workforce working under so-called "atypical" temporary employment contracts, and whose employment is dependent on economic fluctuation. The inequality of this situation lies in the fact that women, young people and immigrants are overrepresented in the group of the serially and temporarily employed.

Trade unions play a central role in the development of the Nordic welfare states. It is to everyone's advantage that labour market parties are able to develop the labour market in a way that supports efforts to safeguard the welfare state. For trade unions, the make-it-or-break-it issue is how to respond to their weakening power, as employers and labour markets become increasingly global. For the sake of their credibility, it is important to merge the efforts to protect members' benefits and the ideals of solidarity and equality.

It would also be important to separate the labour agreements that regulate low-skill jobs from those that regulate high-skill, top jobs, and to weight the ways in which the regulations directed at these different segments of the labour market affect other segments. If the fear is that low-skill jobs will be taken up by foreigners, we should think about how the regulatory mechanisms that have been designed to address this issue affect the mobility of highly skilled labour. Weakening the mobility of experts and the attractiveness of the national labour market through the kind of protectionism that is actually targeted at the low-skill job market – and based on unfounded arguments – should be called into question, when, at the same time, we expect our innovation and technology policies to be the saviours of our national and regional economies.

6 Opening the doors to skilled workers – will anyone come?

What should the labour market do in the global operating environment to attract talent, if it has no history with immigration? Will talent from the outside flood to the market as soon as the gates are opened wide? Should more be done to attract talent, and if so, how? What follows are the stories of some of the experts who did decide to move to Finland. What does the country and the opportunities it offers look like in the global field of choices? The experts we interviewed will tell us how they "discovered" and why they opted for Finland, a newcomer to migration and the knowledge economy. These stories highlight the problems that nations and urban centres face when they first join the flow of global experts. They are not isolated notes, but include the core messages from a vast body of experiences by individuals, and are consistent with the real-life changes in global and local operating environments. Innovation environments in their early stages of "globalisation from below" should not only open doors, but should actively create networks and channels within the global pool of talent.

Certain regions in the United States and Europe that have long traditions, existing transnational social capital, and large immigrant populations have a totally different starting point than a small nation-state such as Finland, that, until recently, was relatively closed off and remote, but is now keenly engaged in building wellbeing through global business and economy. The interdependence between economy and immigration in Finland's urban areas is just emerging. Whereas in more "mature" transnational spaces, for example between the United States and Asia, the trend has turned toward supporting development in countries of origin, such as China, Finland's urban centres have not yet seen the emergence of actual immigrant communities, not to mention communities of experts that centre around a single country of origin (see Saxenian 2002; 2006). A certain degree of community formation has taken place among Russian immigrants in Helsinki, but this is more of a traditional immigrant community than a confluence of economic activity and immigration. Regions and nations that find themselves at different stages of the development scale need different measures to attract and take advantage of the global pool of experts.

The attractiveness of a potential living and working environment can be measured by evaluating its status on the studied experts' global *field of choices*. Apart from the motivators that decide for or against immigrating, or individual people's real intention to move or not, the global economy's experts operate in a global field of choices, where they are in the position to evaluate the attractiveness of various options. This is not only true for potential immigrants to Finland, but also for Finnish experts who are familiar with the international job market in their own field. Many studies (incl. Raunio 2001; Virtanen 2003a; 2003b) indicate that educated Finns view international work opportunities as a realistic alternative, even though they rarely make the actual decision to immigrate. The field of choices available to the experts through the global job market's networks consists of the opportunities that they become aware of, and of regions that they consider feasible as living and working environments. Factors such as the following feature prominently in their field of choices:

- Images – i.e. interesting opportunities that are gleaned through virtual, social and experience-based channels of information. Only opportunities that produce images that correspond to one's motives and preferences appear as visible choices.
- Motives – based on preferences. The motivation to stay or go stems from dissatisfaction with the present situation or from interesting opportunities on the outside. Factors influencing motives can be divided roughly into motivators that, when of high quality, attract someone enough to begin the evaluation process, and demotivators that, even when of a high quality, do not necessarily attract, but when poor, can provide the motivation to leave the present situation or dissuade from moving to a particular area.
- Attainability – the impact of official practices, such as immigration-related permits and visas, on converting opportunities to reality.
- Experiences – i.e. the attractiveness of one's current or potential new living environment, and the experiences of adapting and committing to it. Committing to an environment requires the absence of motives to leave, or if such do exist, it requires that the environment be attractive enough to make one decide to stay instead of leave and that it contains factors that encourage commitment and meet expectations.
  (Adapted from Kotler 1988, 194; Cartwright 2002)

Companies, urban areas, nations – they all compete to be the choice that an expert makes on his or her field of choices. Each strives to appear as an interesting alternative to the expert pondering the available choices and options. Experts consider many factors before settling on a particular living environment, but the factors' role in the field of choices varies as individuals consider immigration (Cartwright 2002). Some of the important factors are motivators that attract or "pull" people to a region, but some are demotivators that – even when qualitatively good – do not draw people to the region. But if demotivators are qualitatively weak, they may prevent choosing a particular region, or push people away from the region. Motivators that make experts consider making an international move include interesting work and career opportunities, economic factors, and social relationships, whereas the most common demotivators are related to quality of life and attainability. For example, a high-quality living environment alone is not enough to motivate someone to move to another country, but if the living environment is perceived as poor in any way, that alone can prevent someone from moving to the region, or motivate them to leave it behind.

Quality-of-life factors can also serve as motivators, as a pulling force, if they are perceived to be of an especially high quality, or someone considers them in some way unique or meaningful. Experts base their "hierarchy of needs" on various quality-of-life factors, and without them, the region has no attraction at all. However, the decision to move is generally made primarily for work or relationship reasons.

A demotivator may be the reason behind an expert moving from one country to another, if the demotivator creates a desire to leave the present country. In this case, the primary reason for moving is to get away from the current living environment, and therefore the where next of the move is secondary. The foremost motive for moving away may have to do with an atmosphere of discrimination in the present country, but the factor that motivates the selection of the next location may be a job that is perceived as interesting job or a living environment that looks inviting. Push factors, such as the present place of residence or a person's life situation, may not constitute the only motives that trigger the move – the move can also be caused by motives that originate outside the region. If the primary motive is leaving a particular region, the next location will not be chosen using the same criteria as when the move was primarily motivated by a desire to live in a particular place.

Individuals rarely make a decision to immigrate rationally or to maximise economic benefit – instead, decisions are in many ways enmeshed with their life situations and values. As a matter of fact, work career and life career should be looked at together, as a whole. A career change, for example, is usually not about advancing in the work hierarchy, and instead has more to do with looking for a stimulating change (Boyatzis & Kolb 2000, 78-79). Micro-level studies of international migration have often found that decisions that people originally made on a fairly uncertain basis and with little information are rationalised only in hindsight. This way, the explanation for the move sounds rational and acceptable to the surrounding environment (Faist 2000). When regions, countries or organisations compete to attract workers, they are at an advantage if they can offer pull factors, and attain a competitive edge if they can attract and commit human resources more effectively than competitors.

6.1 Respected corporations and star scientists connecting talent

Where for example the U.S. and Britain traditionally appear as attractive alternatives with all the right channels and social networks, the world's top professionals hardly take notice of Finland in the field of their choices. The images that have drawn foreign experts to Finland are mostly connected to companies and organisations that are movers and shakers in their own fields, and to the opportunities that they provide. A country that has only recently docked onto the global information economy is able to evoke appealing images through its global fibres, i.e. by spreading the word through its transnational organisations and companies.

Being located in a particular urban area was found to be of secondary importance in terms of evoking an attractive image. Before finding out about an available opportunity in Finland, the knowledge that respondents had about the country varied from "mostly ignorant" to "aware and familiar". It is not much of an exaggeration to state that outside of Europe, the level of knowledge about Finland approaches the level of "no information, no awareness". What little most respondents knew before immigrating came from travel guides and general stereotypes. Most people had very little information about Finland or the surrounding countries, but had enough confidence in the quality of the employer to compensate for any prejudice resulting from lack of knowledge. Respondents in the ICT field were often convinced that a company with a global brand would be able to offer an interesting and challenging job and adequate future opportunities. For a company, having a credible, known brand in the operating field and credibility as an employer – in other words, not just in terms of a product brand on the market – also lends credibility to the surrounding environment and its ability to provide a sufficiently high quality of life. For bioscience experts, the images were frequently connected to a renowned "star scientist", important research, or an environment that was seen as a key player in the future of the field. Working for such an academic institution translates into performing challenging tasks at the top of one's own area of specialty, or at least near the top. Also in terms of forging a scientific career, working on a top scientist's team is very highly valued. Some respondents had also experienced working in a Finnish company or work environment, which had allowed them to form an impression of the country's work culture and of Finns as "experts".

For nearly all respondents in this study, the pull factors that actually triggered the move had to do with professional considerations or personal, social relationships. The role of the latter is a direct consequence of increased international mobility, whereas the role of professional considerations is connected to the availability of interesting professional opportunities, the possibility of doing what one is most interested in, in combination with the possibility of career advancement. Considering the overwhelming importance of work in people's lives, particularly among academic researchers, this hardly comes as a surprise. The challenge in identifying and attracting the right researchers to the appropriate jobs is finding a way to spread information about available professional and career opportunities. This type of information is often transmitted via networks of colleagues and acquaintances. The strength of images and impressions, and the extent to which they get distributed, are therefore highly dependent on the channels through which the information is transmitted to the target group. This study's ICT experts found out about opportunities in Finland primarily through corporations that engage in global recruitment and through their own social networks (n=556):

- 34 percent of respondents read about opportunities from companies' recruitment pages on the web.
- Friends or relatives living in Finland forwarded information about available opportunities to many of the experts who eventually moved – up to 29 percent had heard about the opportunity through the global "grapevine".
- Globally mobile Finnish experts and foreign experts who had worked in Finland or with Finns spread information about the country's work culture and its national culture beyond national borders. Friends and/or relatives in respondents' home countries were the source of information for 15 percent.
- Companies that operate worldwide create a strong link between the local Finnish and the international job market. An employer in the home country or a third country is often the direct source of information about work opportunities in Finland – 26 percent of respondents received information from an employer.
- Recruiting firms and headhunters provided information to ten percent of respondents. The figure probably includes at least in part information packets that companies produce for prospective employees. Experts in highly specialised fields and certain top professionals continue to be recruited by headhunters, who only send information to a small, carefully defined target group.
- 24 percent had previous experience in Finland.
- Job advertisements and recruiting campaigns in international trade magazines and job fairs are also part of the field of choices on which experts look for opportunities.

Respondents found information regarding professional and career opportunities mainly via virtual and social channels. It may be considered positive that 24 percent of respondents had previous experiences with Finland and wanted to return, meaning that they found Finnish reality appealing. Those who had been recruited through the internet frequently had had no real prior contact with a Finn or with anyone else working in Finland, and because of the absence of contact with a Finnish collaborator, their impressions of the country were often quite shallow. The internet, apart from the global bush radio, was the most important channel of information for skilled professionals who immigrated to Finland. These professionals are part of wide-ranging international networks and are highly mobile, and the bush radio is therefore an effective medium for exchanging information, channelling knowledge to regions – provided that the surroundings are satisfactory and the images and impressions of Finland that come second-hand through Finnish companies and the like are positive. A partial explanation for the prevalence of web recruiting in attracting experts to Finland lies also in the relatively low degree of international activity among individual knowledge-based operators in Finland. In other words, the traditional network of "weak ties" is not extensive enough to reach the needed volume of skilled workers from outside the nation's borders (see

Garnovetter 1973; Findlay et al. 1996). On the other hand, the operators' global network is in the process of being linked to Finland, and as it strengthens, participation in the global brain exchange will become easier.

"A friend I went to school with and who was already in Finland told me that the technological, environment and overall situation in Finland were pretty good. So I sent an application and got the job."

Chinese scientist

Professional relationships are an important channel in creating and transmitting impressions. The active international cooperation of scientific communities brings scientists in the bioscience and ICT fields together. When one of the cooperating partners is able to offer an environment that is functional and meaningful for the career of an individual and also for a common project, the cooperation is solidified in a move. Initially, collaboration may occur in the virtual realm, but may later take place in the same country and the same research institute. In this case, too, the whole is what decides – mostly professional and career opportunities and a quality work environment. The impressions and images that people have of a country or city play a very small role in those cases. In the bioscience field, the importance of star scientists – professors or team leaders who are either Finnish or foreigners living in Finland – is central in attracting other foreign scientists. Star power and the reputation of a research team or particular university carry a lot of weight. In many ways, scientists' international networks play a key role in the recruitment of new scientists.

"When I was writing my dissertation, my advisor was part of a network in Europe, that is, a cooperation network in our part of the field, and so you meet a lot of people, and eventually I met this Finnish professor. We had an idea for collaborating on a research project, but at that point I was still working elsewhere. But when we went ahead with the project, I had to come to Finland, and so I did. It wasn't that I wanted to come, but that I wanted to do that particular project and work with that particular professor."

European scientist

Among younger researchers, which is what the respondents in biosciences mostly were, at least when they first came, Finland had usually appeared on their career path because of a supervisor, professor or advisor.

"Our lab worked very closely with this group, and the professor travelled frequently to Finland to talk about plans and projects and findings. Then one day the professor asked me if I would like to come work in Finland, and I said, sure, why not."

Russian scientist

It is clear that in an innovation economy based on skilled individuals, 'globalisation from above' has created a situation where transnational connections must be built and cultivated at the level of individuals. In the case of Finland, 'transnationalisation from below', or transnationalisation through individuals, lags far behind the 'globalisation from above' development in companies that are export oriented. Still, particularly among bioscience researchers, the significance of personal co-operation and relationships were underlined as a major force in the process of deciding to move. Even a top-quality, interesting project or organisation may have a hard time acquiring expertise without credible "salespeople" and contacts, whose attractiveness derives from collaborative work or the 'swift trust' that emerges because of perceived professional credibility.

When people are at the career stage, this affects their requirements, and what decides is the whole of the opportunity that is being offered. Very often push and pull factors merge into a whole and an individual takes advantage of an opportunity for change, provided that the whole is attractive enough. Highly specialised skills increase the chances of taking advantage of an offer, and a high-quality work and research environment in the field of specialisation is a probable trigger factor for a move, and a sufficient reason for immigrating regardless of other push and pull factors.

"Actually, my friend and colleague back then, still in fact, told me that they were creating a new, super-amazing building here, and that they would need exactly the thing that I do for a living – saying, I mean, that it could be me. So it was as if there was a huge finger in front of me, pointing straight at me. Back then I wasn't really happy in my job, the research was going nowhere, and I didn't have a functional lab. And this place seemed like a good place to work. I liked the salary they were offering and the head of the department, and it seemed like the students were pretty good, which they are in fact. So, looking back at my career, it was a really great opportunity."

North American scientist

Job opportunities and reputation in the bioscience field – again, as transmitted by researchers in the field – is a factor that makes certain regions attractive to foreign scientists. On a small scale, or at the individual level, this is something that we should try to replicate for all of Finnish science and development.

"Finland seemed to be on its way to being the hot spot in this field. So I thought, if I'm going to move, why not to the centre of where the development is happening."

Indian scientist

For a scientist, working in a global scientific "hot spot" has both direct and indirect significance. The direct significance is that a scientist can absorb new things, be part of developing something new, and forge relationships with current and perhaps potential "star scientists". The indirect impact is related to the merit earned by the scientist and the opportunities for professional advancement by virtue of being part of something that is respected. It is similar for ICT experts, for whom the "looks good on my CV" effect was also an important reason behind the decision to work in a large Finnish corporation in their field. A few years' experience in the headquarters or research unit of a company that garners respect in one's field helps advance careers and provides future opportunities.

"In other words, one reason why I work where I do, and in the job that I have, is that it looks really good on my CV."

Eastern European scientist

In cases such as those above, impressions are formed in the context of present collaboration, or because of well-known scientists, research units or companies. Images of localness or nationality mostly filter through the main factors listed above and from the way potential collaborators operate. The oft-mentioned networking is, when well implemented, an effective channel for raising Finland onto the global field of choices – not promoted as 'Finland', but as a place with organisations that offer interesting job and collaboration opportunities, and as the global hub of certain lines of business. Considering the importance of star scientists, scientific cooperation and "brand" companies – the reality that the global economy's skilled professionals occupy – really does seem to have left behind national meanings, and global operators now follow the global network's own logic and values.

Although generally, when an applicant is enticed by a particular job opportunity, he or she accepts it regardless of the conditions of the rest of the environment. Still, being unknown can be problematic: some respondents who arrived in Finland for an interview found the reality very different from what they had expected.

"Sometimes it happens that the person being recruited arrives in Finland on a November's night, and walking through the city towards the hotel in a freezing snow storm, looking at the dark, empty streets, you can see in their face that they're not going to stay."

Recruiting manager, Helsinki

Because Finland is not a traditional country of immigration or otherwise well-known worldwide and hence evokes little passion, the global economy's aforementioned creative centres stand out and offer up potentially interesting images for skilled professionals. Many European nations have crafted an all-new image of themselves in the global image bank through immigration and their history. For example, large immigrant communities with a long history show that messages about those countries are being continually transmitted out into the world via global bush radios – though not necessarily by skilled professionals – as material out of which images are formed. The image projected by Finland is surprisingly conventional and stereotypical compared with the image that Finns themselves have of their country as a highly competitive information society.

"Actually before I came here I only knew about Nokia and that Finland was a land of thousands of lakes."

Chinese scientist

Many Asian respondents had had a general impression of Europe, though Finland rarely stood out independently. Asians have traditionally immigrated to the United States and Australia, and Europe has been viewed as more of a transit point. On this image map, Finland looks like a relatively radical choice.

"I really only had a concept of Europe, and the only thing I knew about Finland was that it was near the North Pole... I also knew that the work environment in European countries was generally positive, that there is freedom and so forth."

Indian scientist

In Europe and former Soviet areas, the knowledge of Finland is situated somewhere between awareness and familiarity, and mostly only Helsinki is occasionally familiar. Even when people do have an image of Finland, it is still of a cold and sparsely populated northern country, with a quiet people.

"When I came here, I only had my warmest clothes, like sweaters, even though I came in September. My father insisted that I take along a thick fur coat and hat, because, as he said, it's far north. So then I tried to look for some information at the library."

Scientist from southern Russia

Scientists from former Soviet areas – who, by the way, comprise about half of the bioscience experts in Finland, carry images that are also shaped by Finland and Russia's common history.

"I knew a little bit about the history, about the Finnish War, and that Finland had been part of Russia and was liberated by Lenin. I mean, I knew Finland from school history lessons, but I didn't really know anything about the scientific community here, or about how society works. And of course, I had a firm impression that it was like Siberia year-round; snow, always snow."

Russian scientist

The preconception regarding Finnish society among foreign skilled professionals was that it is not very appealing. Some, mostly Europeans, had an awareness of the overall level of Finnish information society, mostly in terms of the widespread use of cell phones and the internet, and the lines of business connected to them. A 1996 report revealed that when young Europeans thought of Finland, they thought of Santa Claus, Lapland, forests and the sauna, but also of communications (Kotler, Asplund, Rein & Haider 1999, 256). Inviting images that appealed to skilled professionals and gave credibility to Finland as a worthwhile investment derived mainly from the accomplishments of companies or superstar scientists well known to the experts. The job markets of the global economy's creative centres are therefore the link between urban centres and the global economic network. The role of labour markets and work environments will grow as the global competition for skilled professionals shifts into high gear. Key questions for regions who are about to connect with global labour market of experts are: Are local employers able and willing to attract talented foreign professionals and take advantage of their expertise in a meaningful way? And assuming that the ability and the willingness exist, what must the public sector do to support this type of activity? This view extends the traditional economic development approach that focuses more on business environments than on human environments, since not just expertise but also experts have to be taken into account.

6.2 The middle class on the global field of choices?

Who are these people, for whom the new roles and operating rules are being created, and for whom the new international institutions are being built, to ensure their mobility? Who are the people for whom legislation is being rewritten, and who, in return, are expected to produce economic wellbeing through their expertise? Among the study's respondents, the average ICT expert was 34 years old, with an academic education, European, male, and had lived in at least one other country besides Finland and the country of origin. One-third lived alone, one-third was in a couple relationship, and the remaining third also had a family. About 20 percent of respondents were female, and less than half were from outside of Europe, mainly from Asia and the American continent. In the bioscience field, the age structure of respondents was relatively young – most were 25–40 years old. Less than a third of the respondents had a family and one-third was female. Half came from countries of the former Soviet Union, and the rest mainly from the EU and China. Among those originating in former Soviet areas, Russians comprised the largest group.

More interestingly, this diverse group seemed to have something more in common than just an interest in ICT and higher education. In terms of their backgrounds, respondents seemed to be middle class. Many came from big cities or had at least resided in a large city at some point. While their ethnic backgrounds varied, the uniformity of respondents' professional and class backgrounds means that they comprise a group that can be characterised as a *transnational or global class*. Based on the types of jobs they hold, their commitment, and their work-related values, they are also a creative class in the sense meant by Richard Florida (2002). Florida uses the term *"creative class"* to refer to occupations where people are generally paid to create something new. About 30 percent of the workforce in the United States and 29 percent in Finland belong in this class of mostly highly educated people (Florida 2002; Florida & Tinagli 2004). In a sense, the global economy's skilled professionals are the transnational arm of the creative class.

"Countries mean nothing to me (in choosing a job). I am a global citizen."

ICT expert, China

Although the definition of the creative class has been the subject of substantial critique, it captures well the idea that working life and private life – lifestyle – are changing in tandem. In the case of our target group, choosing to work abroad has major implications for one's private life and lifestyle in the short term and long term. However, we should note that "choosing" in the field of choices is not an equally distributed opportunity for all professionals. The opportunities that appear on the global job market look very different depending on what type of expert one is and on one's international preparedness. The job market of ICT experts is mostly global, whereas the job market of a teacher of Finnish is the national labour market, which is able to offer opportunities in nearly every municipality. Similarly, the market for an engineer at a paper mill can extend beyond national borders, but only to a few locations. Different occupational groups also pay attention to different issues, when contemplating their field of choices – the same things do not attract experts in all fields.

As mentioned when discussing the ways in which images are created, skilled experts operate in a global economic network, which, as seen by experts, consists of expertise-focused companies that recruit internationally, and their regional clusters. In this network of organisations experts travel along channels that are created by countries, urban areas or regions, and companies. When the interaction and connections between these areas intensify, the distances between the different points of the *global economic network* shrink and dwindle both in temporal and cultural terms. This is visible in the ways that global experts perceive the world and form images about surrounding reality. Experts who move across national boundaries do not see the world as just cities and nation-states, but increasingly also as a network of creative centres and job markets in their own fields.

"In the world of science, you know, our field is flexible. What I mean is that it is easy to get a job in any country. Actually, the country alone does not determine where you move, and so forth. What matters is what you work on, your area of specialty, your project, and things like that."

Eastern European biotechnology scientist

This kind of image of the world is created intentionally in an international operating environment, particularly when someone is considering immigrating to another country. Skilled professionals' field of choices on the global labour market is made up of the opportunities that come to their attention and are deemed to be potential work and living environments. In practice, this means that international recruitment and, increasingly, internationally disseminated job advertisements, give people the opportunity to seek new employment globally. The experts in this study often circled the globe for their jobs and interacted with many different kinds of work environments, employees and work cultures. Their bush radio and various communication channels spread information and impressions about different organisations and environments – for example, the internet helps create a globalised image of the world and makes it possible to apply for interesting jobs worldwide.

For individual people, the issue has less to do with immigrating to Finland than with finding a better job or operating environment. In other words, the move is more about going from one job to another, rather than from one country to another. The job is already in place before the move – global experts do not first move to a region that has potentially interesting job opportunities, and then look for work: the interesting job found by the job seeker just happens to be located in a particular region. The ICT and biotechnology job markets operate globally, and recruiting is global because the applicant pool consists of professionals in every part of the world. The skills that these fields require are often so highly specialised that the right person can only be found through global networks, and particularly in the ICT industry, wide use of the internet. The ICT and biotechnology recruiting field is much broader than in many other professions that demand specialised skill. The ICT and bioscience respondents in our study and all the people who operate in these fields can be characterised as the global economy's skilled professionals. Their commitment motivation and preparedness to immigrate divide them into five categories.

- *Global nomads* consider relocating when more interesting professional or career opportunities than their present job arise. Global nomads travel from one country to another every one to few years. Their goal is not to become integrated into local culture, but to a location's global culture.
- *Career builders* value their professional development in the most inspiring work environment that is possible above all else. They are prepared to relocate when

the present job ceases to be challenging, or if other places offer more intriguing professional opportunities. Career builders may remain in their country of residence for longer periods, provided there are enough challenges to warrant staying, and in time, their contact with the local environment will become a quality of life factor.

- *Quality-of-life seekers* consider relocating when some other region besides the current one is perceived to offer a clearly higher quality of life or a living environment that better reflects a desired lifestyle. Quality-of-life immigrants are on the lookout for a more permanent place of residence where they can become integrated into the local culture.
- *Social relationships* can serve as a reason to move, and the mover's motivation to become integrated when he or she has moved because of social relationships depends on the move's intended permanence, or ultimately, on the person or community that was the primary motivation for relocating. Such movers consider relocating when important social relationships or family ties are present or are expected to transfer away from the present living environment.
- *Adventurers* see the world as a web of interesting job opportunities, and changing jobs and countries is connected to having the opportunity to obtain new experiences and expand one's horizons. It is not essential for them to have a clear image of Finland – rather, the image's exoticism is precisely what appeals to them.

Although it is possible to group respondents according to their reasons for relocating and their level of commitment (above), and although their attitudes regarding work in many ways correspond to those described by Florida for the 'creative class', it is not possible to define the characteristics that are external to work in the way that Florida did with regard to the creative class. Recent years have seen the "discovery" of new lifestyles in the United States among certain highly educated professionals. These occupational groups are perceived to share certain consumer lifestyles, as in the case of the creative class and the 'bohemian bourgeoisie' (Florida 2002, Brooks 2000). According to this view, when skilled professionals make relocation decisions, they are largely affected by things such as the presence of an active nightlife, the availability of a wide selection of free-time activities, rich cultural offerings, and a lively urban setting.

Since the 1960s, the lifestyle of the 'rock 'n roll generation' has been actively linked to the values of the hectic business establishment of yuppie values and lifestyles. As far as the *choice of living environment*, no such linkage is possible in the case of the transnational arm of the creative class. People today come from widely varying cultural backgrounds, and respondents very rarely even mentioned the factors above, not to mention emphasised them as being important influences on their choice of living environment. Issues of lifestyle are seen more in terms of forging social relationships or, more broadly, as a preference for either rural or urban living. Although some of the respondents enjoyed the fact that they were able to combine a high-tech occupation with rural-style ranch living, or conversely, placed a value on their urban living environment, these factors had little impact when making the decision to relocate. It is true that they may affect the level of happiness with the living environment and the degree of integration, but also in this respect respondents were highly flexible and able to change their consumer habits, as long as quality of life was otherwise perceived as good.

In general, defining a certain target group solely on the basis of consumer choices must be conducted very carefully and with many caveats (Zuboff 1987). In fact, it would be more consistent to talk about a "global middle class" than a "global creative class". The middle class has always been the force that stabilises society's institutions. So it seems to be in the case of the globalising labour market as well. Well-educated and well-off mainstreamers from various cultures are creating an important resource for the economy and for societies, and consequently, the regulations of institutions and the recruitment policies of companies adapt according to their needs. However, even the "global middle-class" is something of a question mark, since its role as stabiliser of the global economy or even "global society" and supporting institutions is an emerging hypothesis rather than confirmed fact.

The respondents of our case studies were highly work-oriented, and the lines between work and free time, professional identity and private persona, were very malleable. Classified according to their motivation to relocate, most are global nomads or career builders. Among bioscience experts, career surpassed nearly all other needs and personal relationships – as one researcher commented: "Career is everything." Career building was frequently a deliberate process, and even those who did not express a systematic method in forging a career were aware of the building blocks of a "great career" and of what kind of story a good CV should tell. The importance of attractive, interesting jobs is highlighted in Finland, because people's general impressions of the country are less alluring, and especially in the case of people whose move is not connected to social relationships or previous experience of the country.

Economic wellbeing is a central factor that motivates people to become mobile – and economic factors are especially noteworthy in the dynamic of relocation as push factors that propel people away from a particular place or region. Disparities in economic wellbeing often translate into differences in the career and professional opportunities and quality of working environment that a place can offer. As an example, the economic dire straits of many former Soviet areas were identified as a push factor by scientists who originated in those areas, and were viewed as barriers to career advancement upon a possible return.

"Well, yes, I think about going back all the time, but from a scientific point of view it's fairly uncertain... Maybe if I wanted to become a professor quickly, that would be one way, but scientifically speaking it would amount to an absolute catastrophe. For that reason I'm in no hurry to go back.'

Scientist from the former Soviet Union

Some respondents who worked in the ICT industry had moved in search of better economic opportunities. When discussing economic wellbeing, it is useful to distinguish as a separate group those who come because of special contracts or on assignments, and whose salary levels and other financial benefits are markedly superior compared to local workers with local job contracts. For workers with special contracts or on assignment, the employer may, for example, pay for the tuition of the family's children at an international school. It ought to be pointed out that in purely economic terms, Finland does not even come close to being the best option among global choices. Many foreigners who have moved to Finland have had to accept a lower salary when they first arrive, decide to stay longer or continue their assignment. Finnish salary levels, i.e. the local labour agreements, usually do not correspond to amounts paid abroad or the salaries and other benefits awarded to workers who are on assignment from elsewhere.

Economic factors, particularly for people moving away from Finland's adjacent areas, can mix with a yearning for added security. Finland makes sense because of the proximity of the home country and of social networks. Finnish society and lifestyle may also evoke positive images, though these were rarely deciding factors in making the decision to immigrate. The images were primarily based on personal experience of Finland as a place to live and work. Such experience-based images highlight the importance of real characteristics in the attractiveness of an urban environment: experience has allowed the immigrant to evaluate the society's culture and deeper values, norms and lifestyle.

"I had studied and worked in Oulu before. However, we moved to Australia for work and to obtain citizenship. We did become citizens eventually, but my family in particular wanted to move back to Oulu, because they considered life here to be much more pleasant than in Australia. I found a more interesting job here, so we decided to move even though we are now Australian citizens."

ICT expert, China

The mobility of global experts occurs mainly during certain life stages. Being a wandering nomad, a quality-of-life seeker who would prefer a more permanent place to live, or someone who moves for the sake of social relationships, varies depending on family status and life situation. All global experts are nomads to some extent, and some remain nomads for their entire lives – but being one does not necessarily mean moving frequently. It can be manifested as an awareness of one's global opportunities in terms of work, in the event that it becomes necessary to change jobs and move to another country. Often, though, being a nomad occurs in life stages when there are few ties that bind to a particular place. Experts –

whether Finnish or foreign – without a spouse are more likely to move than couples; couples without children are more likely to move than couples with small children; and couples with children under school age are more willing to move than families with school-aged children.

Being mobile is encouraged by the internationalisation of the experts themselves and by the new labour market dynamic, which no longer expects the same kind of long-term commitment to one employer or task as before. Careers consist of a series of assignments that last perhaps a few years each (Bergström 2001), and the ability to be flexible in the choice of working and living environment has become an important value. It is said that in this type of operating environment individuals fare best, or are happiest, when working as consultants, not forced to commit to a single employer and instead "sell" their expertise to the employer that offers the best deal (Sennet 2002).

"What happens with a lot of people is that they've been assigned to Finland for a few years, two or three, looking for merit points, so that they can get a better job in their home country or in the same corporation or in another country. Then there are those who have been here longer, who are concerned about their career future, because typically, the people who are willing to change countries for the sake of a job are fairly career oriented, and they have high expectations for what they want."

ICT business manager, Tampere, Finland

Changing jobs is a career development and lifestyle issue, but in the individual's mind, the best job offer may also contain other factors besides purely economic or career-building benefits. Employers are increasingly forced to pay attention to their location in terms of the attractiveness of the living environment. Workers who work without a strong sense of dependence, loyalty or commitment, will go where the job offer is the most ideal. Professional development is an important consideration, but for those who move because of social relationships or quality of life, it is merely a complementary factor that is one part of the total package offered by an employer.

Bioscience researchers had fewer experiences with international relocation than ICT professionals, of whom more than half had lived in at least one other country apart from Finland and their country of origin. Only five of all of the bioscience researchers interviewed had lived in a third country, and for some Asian scientists, relocating to Finland was in fact the first trip abroad. Less than one-quarter of respondents in the biosciences could be defined as global nomads. It is noteworthy that all of the nomads were Europeans, who can easily move within the European Union, compared with people from more faraway places. In the ICT field, however, many immigrants from East Asia and Africa were nomads by virtue of their many international relocations and future plans. The fact that ICT professionals had moved more frequently than bioscience experts reflects the different nature of those fields: in the fast-paced ICT world, the workforce moves at a faster rate than in bioscience research, which requires lengthier work processes.

Growing international migration does not come without consequences. The fact that so many people in an individual's work environment take off to work abroad easily creates a "culture of immigration". Many Russian bioscience researchers and some Turkish and Hungarian ICT experts had ended up in Finland via classic chain migration, where first, one person with existing ties to Finland leaves and is then followed by others. The culture of immigration creates chain reactions in that when the scientists go, others have to go too, because the level of the science that is practiced declines with the departure of the star scientists. One respondent described a laboratory in the former Soviet Union that nearly emptied out because everyone went to Finland. It is difficult to change the culture of immigration once it begins (Stalker 1999), and the phenomenon has undoubtedly been launched already within many post-Soviet natural science communities. A similar culture of immigration was also described by two South African ICT professionals, who characterised the atmosphere at home as thwarted and obsessed with compensating for the "sins of the fathers" following the collapse of apartheid. An atmosphere of blame and oppression creates push factors, and for these young, native English-speaking men with a globally marketable skill set, the global job market offered a natural way to resolve the situation. Neither respondent came to Finland directly, and first moved to an English-speaking area. It is part of the new dynamic that the culture of immigration is linked to the global economic culture on a permanent basis.

It is often difficult to discern the primary reasons for why someone immigrates, and usually they are manifold and consist of a combination of push and pull factors. For many respondents, immigrating to Finland was the end result of many factors and even coincidence – but even coincidence must be consciously recognised and allowed to take place.

"I came to Finland – it was a coincidence. I mean – I have thought about this a lot myself, I think that many people's decisions, even about huge life changes, come from being in a certain place at a certain time, there's a certain moment in time when a person decides... I was supposed to be here for two months. Well, I've been here nine years now. So this is how it happens."

Estonian scientist

People immigrate when the formula is right; there are push factors that make a person leave an unsatisfactory job or location, and suddenly the right channel opens up – or a scientist consciously seeks opportunities – to a university that is interesting for his or her area of specialisation and that employs interesting researchers, who in turn open up possibilities for future career development. Personal reasons may also complement the formula.

> "I wanted to get away from that job. In other words, I wanted to move for personal reasons, I wanted to move for scientific reasons, and I wanted to move for political reasons, and all of these were very strong motives, and I was much happier from the first moment that I walked in through that door."
>
> European scientist

The motives to immigrate to another country arise from societal, personal and professional explanations. Societal justifications have to do with the possibilities and quality-of-life requirements offered by different regions. Personal reasons are connected to personal life situation, and professional reasons include work and career prospects. Motives and reasons can become concrete decisions to immigrate, because international job market clusters are constantly expanding and creating a spiritual distance to "local" environments. Regardless of individual immigrants' motives, the labour market increasingly offers the opportunity to realise whatever change is desired, whether the desire for change comes from social push factors in the current living environment, economic factors, or personal reasons. Immigration is frequently associated with a better and more interesting job, but it is not necessarily the actual reason for looking at another country. To view the transnational job market merely as a career development channel is to see it too narrowly to appreciate the phenomenon's diversity. Individuals who acquire globally applicable expertise are shaping their own opportunities to operate as part of the transnational or global network society, with many of its own operating rules, and its own culture and geography.

Russkij Finlandia: the global economy can be only a short distance away

Skilled professionals from the area of the former Soviet Union stand apart from other skilled immigrants in terms of the operative push and pull factors, and they should therefore be discussed separately. In the biosciences, they comprise the largest single group, making the former Soviet Union an important brain reserve for Finland. The views expressed by these experts underline the fact that even in a global operating environment, geographic and cultural proximity between the old and new place of residence facilitates many aspects of life.

Push factors are notably important for immigrants from the former Soviet areas. Many of the nations that were formed after the fall of the Soviet system are struggling economically, which is reflected in scant public resources and allocations. Equipment is spotty, and in an equipment-reliant field such as the biosciences, this is crucial. There are also problems in the payment of wages, and when they do get paid, they are hardly enough for survival. In addition, career advancement and opportunities are limited, because most of the best scientists have left to go abroad.

"Most Russian scientists think that if someone paid them even half the salary that it is possible to earn abroad, no-one would leave. Everyone wants to stay in Russia, but unfortunately the situation in our university, which has been recognised as the top of its kind, is very bad. It's really difficult to survive, because prices are so high that only the rich can afford them. So, the options are either to leave or to quit and cross over into the business sector, for example. Of course, there're a fair number of those half-crazy scientists who will just do research and ask for nothing. Unfortunately, I'm not that crazy – I value the opportunity to do research, but I also value being paid for it." (Russian scientist)

For people from former Soviet areas, particularly the Baltic countries and Russia, the proximity and a certain similarity in Finland act as pull factors. The fact that Finland is culturally and geographically close to Russia and the Baltic countries makes it an appealing choice for people from these countries. Finland is a kind of "next-door Europe" – a Western European nation that is close to home.

"I would say that out of all the European countries, Finland is most like Russia. The differences aren't that great, which makes it a little easier to tolerate the differences that there are. The nature is the same, the people are different, but they still have some of the same characteristics." (Russian scientist)

The opportunities that skilled professionals from former Soviet areas have to maintain close ties with family, relatives, and friends are important. This was highlighted in the fact that respondents emphasised Finland's proximity and the availability of good transportation channels between Finland and former Soviet areas.

"I like working here just for the work, and also because Finland is so close; I no longer have to fly to the United States, I can just hop on a train. If I were looking for a new job, I would look in Europe, maybe in Scandinavia, or Germany. But not in America or Australia, they are so far away from Europe. My family is in Russia, so it's easy when I'm this close."(Scientist from Moscow)

The Russian community's size in Helsinki in particular is so large by now that it offers cultural and other services as well as a feeling of home to newly arrived Russians. The community is nothing new, and in fact represents a return back to normal after 70 years of isolation and stalled relations. The larger cities, Helsinki and Vyborg in particular always had sizable Russian communities with their own linguistic and cultural services. The situation is also a common one in the sense that almost everywhere, a neighbouring country's immigrants make up one of the largest immigrant groups. The attractiveness of Finland for Russians is not only connected to the factors discussed here, but also to the presence of an unusually long border between the two countries and the economic situation of the areas on the other side of that border.

"In the beginning there were almost no Russians, but now you can speak Russian with many researchers. There are a lot of Russian permanent residents, and a good Russian community. You can hear Russian in the streets and in stores, too." (Russian scientist)

"I'm trying to keep in contact with Russians. It's nice sometimes to have coffee and speak Russian. And then there are the concerts... when I have the time, I buy tickets. Luckily Russian life is much better in Helsinki than in Turku; for example a lot of theatre troupes come here, and musicians, and Russian ballet. I also listen to the Russian-language radio station, Sputnik, it's my favourite, the music is great. As far as magazines, I subscribe to Spektr. I used to have a Russian TV-channel, but it got to be too expensive." (Russian scientist)

Without specifying whether the above speaker takes advantage of Russian high-culture offerings such as concerts, ballet or theatre, it nonetheless adds a feeling of security to know that they are available if a hankering for Russian culture strikes. The visibility and entrenchment of various cultures in Finnish urban centres is clearly something that improves the chances of not only attracting but binding foreign labour to Finland. Even when global workers operate partially in the sphere of a "third" culture, the presence of one's own culture acts as an adhesive at least in some measure. In this, Finland's urban centres have a long way to go, especially outside of the capital city. This can be seen in internal migration, which showed indications that foreigners' desire to leave smaller urban centres for the capital city was founded not only on better job opportunities and greater diversity, but also on the presence of representatives of one's own culture. This is in part typical of the birth and entrenchment process of global clusters that are born also out of geographic and cultural factors. When geographic or cultural distances are not too long, it is easy to come together.

For many Russian-speakers, Finland tempts because for someone starting out a career as a scientist, the country looks attractive and offers a high-quality framework within easy travel of many former Soviet areas – again, a Western European land with Russian add-ons. Since it is Russians in particular who are attracted to Finland, and since the Russian natural science curriculum is of a high quality, it would make sense to market Finland especially to Russians as a good place for professional opportunities.

Political and historical realities have traditionally made Finns view the proximity of Russia, the Baltic nations and the rest of what used to be the Soviet Union as more of a burden than anything else. However difficult, it is crucial to reverse such thinking. The saying that for Finland, Russia is both a threat and an opportunity, is a worn one but useful nonetheless. The former Soviet areas can help Finnish society remain dynamic by providing skilled workers and innovators, a market area, and opportunities for greater cooperation. Taking into account the capacities of the skilled workers who arrive from these areas is both relevant and essential, for example, when designing various student exchange and other academic programmes. The probability that students remain or eventually return to Finland is relatively high, if they know that it is possible to maintain their social relationships and cultural ties.

6.3 Permits, visas and official gatekeepers

Born of images and motives, a decision to immigrate still must become an actual, solid moving process. Several Finnish urban centres and companies are in the process of building the channels to facilitate and speed up immigration of skilled workers. This process involves a series of official practices and regulations and the statutes concerning their practical interpretation. Seppo Paananen (1999) speaks of the "small" policy on foreigners, based on the ability of companies hiring foreigners to recruit and maintain a diverse workforce, and on the practices applied by authorities to foreign workers. This "small", real-life policy occurs largely in encounters between individuals, in recruiting situations, in the workplace, in government agencies, and is manifested in attitudes regarding foreign workers and the hiring of foreigners in general. The "big" policy on foreigners is the official series of laws and statutes that the "small" policy interprets. Frequently, the significance of real-life policy becomes emphasised when immigrants enter the Finnish labour market. The gatekeepers of companies and organisations are in a key position in creating an attractive image (Wrench 1991; Paananen 1999, 127). Their attitudes, service competence, and willingness to hire foreigners decide the extent to which the big policy, i.e. government laws and statutes, affects the country's image as an attractive choice on the international labour market. The official policy on foreigners forms the framework in which people operate, but its practical functionality is determined by gatekeepers who interpret statutes and official viewpoints within the limits that the framework permits. In order to understand the connectivity of the certain place with experts' global field of choices, both "big" and "small" policies of that place should be known.

In terms of skilled workers, discussions about an active immigration policy and a total overhaul of the law on foreign nationals are at the centre of the greater immigration policy. The Finnish work permit system has characteristically had employers evaluate labour needs and the level of expertise, and it has not been considered necessary that the public sector develop special programmes – fast tracks – to maximise the efficiency of the process (Sorainen 2001). However, improvements to the immigration and work visa process do get recorded into law and incorporated into the practices of officials. The work visa system was updated in conjunction with the renewal of the legislation on foreigners so that it better serves labour market needs and is a more effective tool of employment policy. As far as the official policy on foreigners is concerned, the objective is to respond to the issues that companies recruiting foreign workers most often encounter. At least in principle, the trend in developing the greater policy on foreigners is a correct one. However, no fast-tracks or special programmes for experts have been introduced. One exception is "FiDiPro" (Finland's distinguished professor programme), that was initiated in 2007 and offers funding for universities and research institutions if they hire foreign top professors or researchers. Funding is provided by the Academy of Finland and the Finnish Funding Agency for Technology and Innovation (Tekes). The funding period is temporary and lasts two years. However, the programme focuses on funding rather than on providing broader special programmes for experts.

We should note that obtaining a work or residency permit did not present significant problems for the study's skilled bioscience or ICT experts. The real problem has to do with a lengthy process and short duration of the visas. In particular, the awkward application and granting process for continuation visas and customer service inefficiencies have been problematic. Companies' willingness to hire foreign experts is in fact tempered by the bureaucracy of the work permit process. An employer's need for specific talent is often immediate, and the time and effort that are invested into recruitment are wasted if the potential hire receives a better offer elsewhere in the course of the long waiting period. This decreases the probability of getting the needed and possibly best available worker for a given position, and even when a worker is already living in Finland, bureaucracy results in frustration and loss of working hours.

"Often there's competition. If someone is good, many people tend to think so, and we're just one of the employers trying to get this person. You call the person and say, 'So, you applied for this position' and they say, 'Yes, I've already had a couple of interviews, and I'm not interested anymore,' or if the process is long, they say they already have another job. If they have a family, we can maybe tell them to come in the beginning of the next month, and ask them to bring the family in three months. The longer the process, the greater the likelihood that the person ends up going somewhere else, but if we're able to keep the candidate revved up and can show them that the process is going somewhere, everything is alright."

Manager, Espoo, Finland

In practice, the real-life, "small" immigration policy is implemented by entities such as the police, the Social Insurance Institution of Finland (KELA[10]), and companies themselves. As a rule, the immigrants in this study viewed government agencies as places that offered equally administered services, though there was some criticism – and relatively often, poor treatment was seen as related to the client's ethnic origin. Lack of language skills on the part of agency personnel was also considered a drawback, as were seemingly illogical justifications for decisions. The last two complaints are probably connected to some extent. In addition, lack of knowledge about the agencies' operating methods and their frequently complicated practices, for example at the Social Insurance Institution offices, may provoke a sense of unequal treatment.

Two of the official agencies that every immigrant to Finland must encounter are the local police and the Directorate of Immigration (Finnish Immigration Service from 2008). Dealing with the residence permit system and the associated bureaucracy elicited many comments from respondents. Skilled immigrants who arrive to work as experts in a particular field differ in many ways from immigrants who come without a pre-arranged job, but in the face of the permit system that governs residency, all people are equal, and hence their experiences greatly resemble one another.

It is paradoxical that immigrants who have a job offer from Finland encounter more difficulties in the permit system than immigrants who, by virtue of their reason for immigrating, including family ties, refugee status or Finnish ancestry, have the right to permanent residency. In most cases, having a job lined up in Finland in most cases is not a sufficient justification for permanent residence, and therefore work and residence visas only apply for the term of the employment contract. Universities, for example, largely operate with short-term project funding, and serialised temporary and irregular job contracts are among the most common types of employment contracts. At universities, all sides suffer from this, but it is worst for immigrants for whom the duration of their residence and work permits as well as eligibility for social security are tied to the term of the employment contract. This kind of situation breeds fragmentation in lives and careers and uncertainty about the future, even in terms of country of residence. Were it as easy to renew a residence visa as it is to continue an employment contract, there would be less of a problem.

Official attitudes are also highly important. Some respondents complained of poor treatment at police departments, and many assumed that the reason was rooted in other foreign clients. In practical terms, poor treatment was mostly manifested as

10 KELA, the Social Insurance Institution of Finland, is a state institution with primary responsibility for the implementation of social security in Finland.

unwillingness to serve or provide information about the process and its duration, and as inappropriate comments directed at clients.

"When I go to the police station, they have a really negative attitude toward foreigners, and I understand why. They mostly have to work with refugees and other foreigners who cause problems, and so they have the same attitude toward all foreigners. It feels very insulting when you're treated like a second-class citizen."

ICT expert, South Africa

"[There is] discrimination and racism even in public agencies like the police and the Directorate of Immigration."

ICT expert, Liberia

"I have to say that Finland's residency system is horrible, at least in Helsinki."

Bioscience expert, Britain

Some of the horror stories told by immigrants about the residence permit bureaucracy are actually connected to strategies that are supposed to make dealing with the bureaucracy easier. Foreigners can apply for an extension for their residence permit with the local police, regardless of where they officially reside, and people who have been in Finland longer know how services in different localities differ. The most paradoxical aspect of the awkward residence permit system is that a new permit costs a lot of money. A foreigner working in Finland, compelled to renew his or her residence permit annually, particularly during the first few years in the country, not only has to relinquish his or her passport to the police for up to half of the year, but to boot, has to pay for it.

"It's very … well, in the end we got a residence permit, but the process could have been easier. What I mean is that it takes a long time. After you file an application, it takes three to five months, sometimes even longer than six months, until you receive another brief permit which you have to renew almost right away. It's very impractical. If a person is beneficial to this country and has the documentation to prove it, the permits should last longer. I can't believe that it would really take that long to process. And then there are the travel restrictions. If you don't have a residence permit, you can't travel. And without your passport, you can't apply for a visa in a third country. And one more thing. Even when they are polite, I doubt that they give us all the information that would be helpful. Maybe they only give you the information that you know to ask for. As an outsider you can't know, you don't know how to ask the right questions. And another problem is that the process is not cheap, in fact it's pretty expensive: more than 100 euros."

Chinese expert, who has resided in Finland from the early 1990s

In certain cases, police and the Social Insurance Institution, in collaboration with companies that recruit globally, have developed services aimed particularly to this new group of clients. This has involved developing new operating practices together with the businesses that recruit foreign workers, by streamlining existing practices or naming an advisor on issues pertaining to foreigners. But if the quality of the processes to apply for residence and social security rely on cooperation between isolated businesses and officials, this raises a question about the principle of equal treatment. What about the official matters of those foreigners, who work for a smaller employer with no resources to ensure better cooperation? Skilled foreign workers and the businesses that employ them do, however, create pressure to develop tolerance and quality of services at Finnish agencies. The best-case scenario is that the pressure will streamline the practices applied to foreigners and improve policy.

The role of the Directorate of Immigration was mentioned by a relatively high number of respondents, naming problems such as long application processes and, to some extent, the attitudes displayed when providing services. Long application processes and the short duration of granted permits are problematic, especially for this study's respondents, in whose job descriptions travel is an integral part.

"Dealing with the police is problematic. I mean, when your residence permit runs out and you need a new one, it's really an unpleasant situation. At least this past year I was really angry, because I had to wait too long, more than five months, and the permit is only for one year, which I think is really stupid. I think that all foreigners who have to extend their permits would agree with me, that it takes way too long. In Germany it took like 15 minutes, if you're working there. And I've been here more than three years."

Bioscience expert, Russia

It is possible to obtain, or "borrow", one's passport from the police department in the midst of the application process, but many respondents reported that this required additional bureaucracy. One manager-level scientist, for instance, with a number of foreigners in the same unit, said that it takes a significant amount of time to write all the affidavits and reports. According to the manager, it is also difficult to delegate those tasks, because Finns themselves do not know the system very well, and as a foreigner who had had to go through the same formalities, the manager was familiar with the residence permit system. As someone who had recruited numerous foreigners, the manager felt an obligation to help the employees as much as possible.

In the respondents' opinion, the primary reason for the occasionally very long application processes was the lack of resources and depth of the bureaucracy – the police being a case in point. They also felt that there were opportunities for making the system more efficient, and considered increases in resources and duration of permits to be sensible options. Business and academic managers in charge of recruitment agreed that attitudes at the Directorate of Immigration were not very positive with regard to customer service for foreigners.

It is easy to overemphasise the importance of officials and bureaucracy in the discussions and "horror stories" among foreigners. On the other hand, one important – even very important – factor in choosing a particular location worldwide was "non-racist attitudes toward foreigners among local and government officials". Even though a well-functioning and tolerant official system does not actually draw people to a country, a malfunctioning system that evokes negative imagery can be an effective inhibiting factor.

As the profile of immigrants has undergone a change, public agencies have entered a new operating field. Apart from family members, Ingrian-Finnish remigrants and refugees, Finland constantly takes in workers in every occupational field, and their numbers are on the rise. People who immigrate to work often have other options besides Finland, and hence their impatience with the bureaucracy is perhaps more emphatic than that of immigrants who have either an ethnic or social bond with Finland. For skilled workers, adapting to the bureaucracy is in fact optional.

The attitudes and practices of employers also shape the real-life, "small" immigration policy. Respondents who had received little assistance or experienced negative attitudes immediately upon arrival recalled such experiences long afterward, underlining the importance of high-quality integration services. Attitude and desire to help are crucial, because the first impressions of not only the employer's attitude toward employees, but also of Finnish people in general are formed at this point. People who received useful and friendly assistance were also very satisfied and based part of their impression of Finns as a friendly and helpful people on this early experience.

"When I first came here, the human resources department was the biggest problem, because the attitude was that 'you're coming here for two years to make money, not to work hard, because you're American'. Their attitudes were really morose, and some of my friends have had even worse experiences. One family was told to look for an apartment through the newspaper, even though they spoke no Finnish. Some families have gone back, and part of the reason was the way that they were treated by the HR department."

ICT expert, United States

"My employer picked me up at the airport, took me to my apartment, and showed me where I worked. They could have been more helpful in social matters, and I would have needed someone who spoke Finnish. In a lot of things it really makes a difference that you're a foreigner, especially this far up north. People aren't very eager to help."

ICT expert, South Africa

Attitude is crucial, regardless of who helps with the initial integration process – an outside company, the human resources department, the unit's manager, or a colleague who is chosen as a "buddy". Integration services help at least some new arrivals to initially orient to their new surroundings. Those for whom this type of service is not available receive their first impressions of Finnish society and its attitudes through public agencies.

The accessibility of services depends on how well informed the new arrival is of their availability and how effectively such information is disseminated to the intended target. Universities and research institutions do not have the services that many businesses offer, including relocation services for foreigners. Foreign employees frequently have to rely on information provided by earlier immigrants, or, in some cases, department staff step in to help with practical matters.

> "At first I did not understand how in hell I was going to get organised in the social sense, I mean getting a social security number. Or what do I need from the police department and in what order things need to be done. I was completely in the dark about what you have to do to be a resident of Finland, and there is still very little information about that. That's frustrating. I remember how I would run around Helsinki, back and forth, to get these things done, and it was really confusing. I thought back then that it had really been different in [previous country of residence]. There, the university had an office whose job it was to manage affairs for foreigners, and they gave you a packet that included the forms and instructions for what you had to do and in what order. What makes it worse here is that Finns tend to only give you the information that you know to ask for, and nothing more."
>
> British scientist

For "regular Finnish people" working in organisations, the problem is that few are familiar with Finnish society and its official structures from an immigrant's perspective. Particularly in workplaces with few foreigners, there is no support, not to mention systems to help resolve everyday issues. Taking care of the official business of registering after arriving in the country is important in the sense that, to be able to use the services of most welfare states, one must be registered as a resident of a municipality. The images that immigrants form of their new country and of its attitudes toward immigrants largely emerge during this process. In a survey of ICT professionals, asked to rank 24 statements in order of importance, the largest number selected as most important "non-racist attitude toward foreigners on the part of government officials". The significance of such impressions in creating the reputation of an open and welcoming society cannot be overstated. Bluntly stated, the gatekeepers have to be well-mannered and the service has to be prompt, if these officials, with their practices, are going to help reinforce the national expertise base.

7 Creativity, cultural competence and careers in job markets

It seems that regions with liberal market economies and emerging economies with high-incomes for highly skilled and deep job markets for talent may be the places that eventually attract the most of global talent. In order to compete with this, regions with welfare regimes should make an effort to enhance the human aspects of their innovation environments to offer an authentic competitive advantage in the race for talent. The key message of this chapter is that the genuine qualities of a welfare state's work environment may offer extremely attractive environments for creative and scientific work, if cultural competence and career opportunities are available. As labour markets become more global, the attractiveness of a country or region and its ability to utilise knowledge are dependent on how well local job markets are equipped to provide incentives at a global level for highly skilled labour, in the event that they decide to use their talent in this particular innovation environment. Knowledge and its creative use are the cornerstones of innovation economies, and to draw its full benefit, the *human* nature of the resource must be fully understood. The integration of labour markets requires two approaches: on the one hand, enough talent and knowledge must be tunnelled to the region and to organisations, and on the other hand, knowledge and expertise must be utilised in a way that produces added value for both the employer and in particular for the employee. Regional job markets (i.e local employers) should be able to adjust to global labour markets (i.e. foreign employees) also at an organisational level.

7.1. Toward global creativity

There are several dimensions to a work environment. In the context of our discussion, we will highlight the innovation environment as viewed through an individual's viewpoint – a creative *innovation environment*, which gives talented people the opportunity to actualise and develop themselves through challenging work. It is appropriate to separate innovation and creativity in this context. Innovation involves three phases: conception, which includes creativity, and development and implementation. Innovation results in a novel, repeatable product, system or process that provides a definable benefit to someone. Antecedent, however, emerges from the creativity of individuals, whether working in teams or independently (Basset-Jones 2005, 171). Thus, innovation environments that are produced to support the innovation process of companies should not be confused with environments that support the creative work of individuals.

Creative innovation environments open up new opportunities for the future, offer work opportunities in operating environments that are maximally interesting and innovative and characterised by high-quality, and a diversity-sensitive management and work culture. Management and work culture should be able to take into account the personal needs of each individual to a certain extent. A creative innovation environment also entails that there are opportunities to develop and utilise one's talents in official and informal arenas, networks, institutions and organisations (Raunio 2002).

In a global context, in such environments, central issues include the cultural competence of the working environment and the ability of the Finnish innovation environment to adapt to and function as part of the culture of the global economy and its diverse community of talented professionals. The ICT industry, for example, has rapidly become part of the global culture, whereas in academic institutions, internationalism has long been built into the very nature of scientific endeavour – although information technology has served to intensify that cooperation and accelerated the work pace in communities of scientists as well. The challenge for professional life is to combine an increasingly diverse and multidimensional workforce with structures and practices that were created for the welfare state's traditionally homogenous workforce.

We should note that diversity management, which aims to take into account individuals and cherish difference, has its roots in the multicultural soil of the United States corporate world and legislation. According to Gordon (1995), the emergence of the corporate cultures in the United States was a response to a structural crisis that large corporations faced during the 1980s. He refers to "corporate culture as a mode of governance designed to provide a new type of sense-making for the citizens of the corporation". The core component of the new corporate culture was manifested in diversity management that recognized the racial and gender identities and (potential) conflicts emerging from diversity. New corporate culture does not demand assimilationism or undifferentiated social control, but "links a vision of diversity to something that might be called multicultural corporatism". He saw that corporate multiculturalism had the potential to support the rewriting of the wider social contract of the United States (Gordon 1995, 3). In fact, diversity management was largely a result of "rewriting the social contract", since the roots of diversity management are in Affirmative Action (AA) and Equal Employment Opportunity (EEO) policies, i.e. antidiscrimination legislation of the United States. Both Affirmative Action and Equal Employment Opportunity policies were established in order to improve the situation of racial minorities and women in the labour market (Kelly & Dobbin 1998). Thus, it was not just a case of economic incentives to manage diversity in order to be more creative, but there were also legislative push factors that forced employers to change their behaviour.

In Finland, diversity management and corporate cultures have played a much more moderate role, and legislation concerning equality has not enhanced the emergence of diversity management as was the case in the United States. Employers' capabilities (and management modes) of facing difference are at a much lower level than in countries where diversity is a part of societal structure. This discussion does not delve deeply into critiques of diversity management, but merely points out that this kind of discussion has not yet even occurred in Finland. There has been no diversity to manage or any diversity management to criticise. Once again, a novice of internationalisation must find its own way of coping with the new situation, as immigrants slowly but nevertheless increasingly find the Finnish labour market.

However, viewed from outside, the Finnish system contains many positive characteristics that the local population pays no attention to because they are considered givens. To simplify slightly, one could say that, in the competition for talented professionals, the work environments of small Nordic welfare states are a strength factor in terms of quality, but a weakness in terms of quantity. Other qualitative strengths include security, family friendliness and emphasis on equality, all arising from the traditions of the Nordic welfare states. In spite of a lack of social interaction, respondents saw the Finnish working environment as pleasant and less competitive than in many other countries – Finnish working life is not characterised by cut-throat, me-first individualism, where each colleague is seen as a competitor. Many respondents placed a high value on family-friendly working life, manifested in long vacations (possible to take when agreed), working days that mostly end at five o'clock, and the possibility of staying at home when a child is ill. Compared with many other societies, Finnish working life is fairly flexible in favour of individuals and families.

"Working hours are better here, basically eight to five. That when you have a kid here, you can leave your job for a year and then return to the same job, is fantastic. I would love to bring that practice to the United States. The playgrounds also are a great part of this society, because they offer mothers the opportunity to meet other people, when they are at home with small children. I think those things are great."

Spouse, United States

"It was a positive surprise that families, not just work, are valued very highly."

ICT expert, Australia

"Working life is still pretty relaxed here, so it's possible to enjoy Finland's nature and so forth. You have time for yourself, which is pretty rare these days."

Bioscience expert, Britain

Apart from isolated cases, respondents expressed satisfaction with the quality of their jobs and the opportunities that they afforded. For a work-oriented professional, an interesting and challenging job is a strong promoter of integration and commitment even to the degree that most researchers in the bioscience field seemed to have virtually no free time or social context outside of work, and for them, the flexibility of the work culture meant being able to forge their entire lives out of the context of research. In professions requiring expertise, for many experts who are committed to their work the freedom and flexibility in working hours has meant that work has become a total lifestyle that defines human relationships, free-time activities and even consumer habits. The line between work and play gets murky, as suggested by Florida (2002) to be the case among the creative class (see ibid. 2002). Work has become the strongest identifier, overruling other parts of life, including relationships, hobbies and family. This is illustrated in one of the responses to a question regarding free time and the living environment:

"That's a difficult question, because most of our lives take place inside the lab, so there isn't really much time left over for other activities. Yes, my only social network is at work."

As a lifestyle, total devotion to working life means an acceptance, at least up to a certain point, of slower or more difficult advancement in the integration process in other life areas, because the work itself is so interesting and meaningful. On the other hand, when work itself fails to meet expectations or is unpleasant in any way, it has a major impact on a worker's willingness to remain in the country. In this study, there were virtually no respondents who were clearly dissatisfied with the content of their work. What did present problems was the relative shortage of professional and career opportunities for non-Finnish-speaking professionals and particularly their spouses (Figure 4).

Another qualitative strength is the low level of hierarchy in working life, making it easier to approach colleagues and superiors. The relatively restrained, expressionless-seeming Finnish way of conversing, however, diminishes some of the benefit of non-hierarchy, when communication is easily limited to mere exchange of information required for taking care of business (Figure 4). Developing diversity management, cultural competence and communication skills within companies offers an opportunity to boost the attractiveness of not only one company, but also cities and the country as a whole on the global job market of experts.

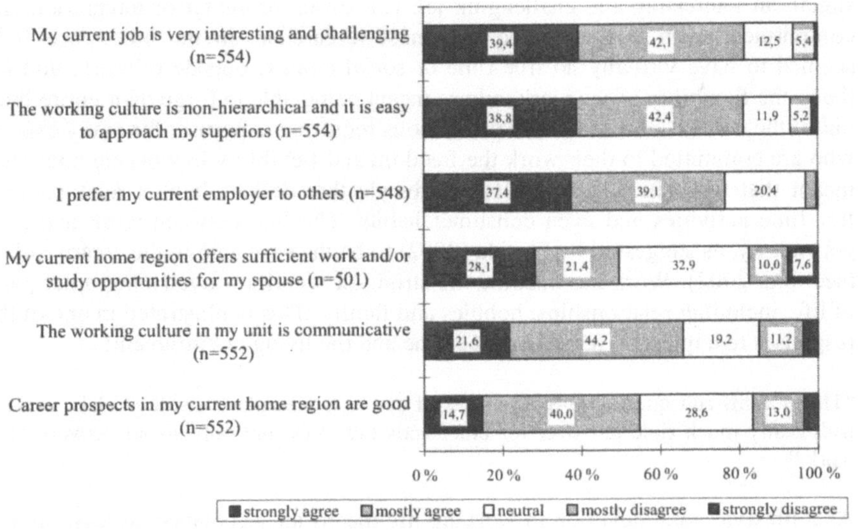

Figure 4. Satisfaction with aspects of ICT work environments in Finland. (Source: Raunio 2003)

For some respondents, multicultural work culture was an important commitment-promoting factor. Although few Finnish work environments could be characterised as multiethnic at this point, many research units in the biosciences are at the forefront of this development. Such global culture communities make it easy for foreign scientists to enter and become a part of the community. Multiethnicity is also perceived as giving a unit a competitive edge in productivity.

"It really is the case that when you look at successful teams, they are the ones that take in foreigners. And I don't understand why some teams won't do that. Maybe they just don't have the necessary contacts. But yes, it's pretty clear that the teams that succeed are the same ones that bring people in from abroad. And I think that the connection is in expanding the talent base and the perspectives."

Manager, Western Europe

There are examples of ICT units that are permeated by multiethnicity, and managers who believe that the social influence of immigrants is a strength and gives the unit a competitive advantage. Not only immigrants, but also other groups have had to learn to reconcile different cultures and viewpoints. Some managers have observed the opportunities that this talent brings in the global operating environment. In certain operations, for example in units that localise products for the global market, the very nature of the work requires the understanding of diversity and different viewpoints and their conversion to a relevant form. However, we should note that diversity as such is not the source of creativity that leads to economically feasible innovations, but has to be combined with cooperative organisational culture and leadership that facilitate effective group functioning (Kochan et al. 2003, 18).

As special case even among Nordic work cultures, Finnish work culture presents challenges particularly in terms of communication and personal interaction. The lack of a culture of conversing has an impact on business practices and the individual's ability to participate in and utilise his or her talent in the organisation and in teamwork, or become personally integrated into the work community. Knowledge-based organisations often implement individual-driven management and practices that are geared to earn the maximum benefit from employees' creativity, skills and talent. Companies such as IBM, Texas Instruments, Nokia and Microsoft emphasise *respecting the individual* in their corporate cultures. Individuals are *empowered* to bring their own viewpoints, ideas and operating practices to the company, and the managers' role is to forge good relationships with staff and support their opportunities to utilise their skills autonomously. In operating environments like these, power is delegated down the command chain and the importance of individuals in the company's success becomes emphasised. For employees, this entails freedom on the one hand and independence on the other, in managing their work flow (Brown 1999; Castells & Himanen 2000). These characteristics emerged clearly also among respondents' work environments. The impact of Finnish culture also came through, frequently in ways that indicated that it may at times impede the realisation of operational goals. Empowerment and individual-focused operating practices got stuck in the Finnish way of communicating and interacting and in views regarding independent work.

Finnish organisations presume an inherent equality among employees regardless of position or status, and this affects the ways in which power and influence are manifested and used. In many societies, managers are managers even outside of the workplace. In Finland, 'supervisor' is usually seen as just one among many social roles that people may have (Trombenaars 1993, 74 adapted from Törmälä 1998, 23). Even internationally speaking, a non-hierarchical, shallow organisation is a typical way of organising a knowledge-based organisation, but the low level of hierarchy becomes highlighted in Finnish working life. Similar structures create similar operating frameworks, but it is the way people operate inside the framework that forms the process that individuals experience as surrounding reality. The fact that organisational models appear similar does not therefore entail similar operating practices. Easily approachable managers and the absence of hierarchy are regarded as very positive and enhancing for the work environment, and ultimately create a good foundation for open communication.

"Relations between directors and staff are completely different here compared to England. It's much less formal, and the organisation is shallow; it's shallow in England as well, but there you have more of an "us and them" mentality between employees and senior staff. If someone gets promoted, that person's relationships with previous colleagues changes, but that is not the case here. Here, my boss can freely get drunk in my company, whereas in England there would be a built-in resistance to something like that."

ICT expert, Britain

"Once, fairly early on, I asked the professor if I could go home. The professor started smiling and laughing. It was like 'hey, wow, you don't have to ask that!' But I come from a country where there is more of a distance, or hierarchy, at least in my previous lab."

Scientist, former Soviet Union

Finns respect, even cherish the rights of the underdog, so woe betide the Finnish boss who tries to bully or unduly coerce subordinates. This informality in the corporate climate of Finnish companies facilitates the interchange of ideas and builds mutual respect (Lewis 2002, 272). The informal relationship between superiors and staff can nonetheless create confusion among foreign employees in terms of job descriptions and roles. Many employees crave more direction and clearer guidelines in their work (see Törmälä 1998, 51-59).

"You're pretty much left to your own devices whenever you start a new job or task, and there is very little direction; you are expected to come up with your own way of handling the task and problem solving. This is in complete contrast to what I'm used to."

ICT expert, Germany

In a multicultural environment, it has become extremely important to understand one's own cultural characteristics and peculiarities, in order to recognise the role of international management fads and organisational innovations in a particular local cultural context and with a particular set of multicultural staff. The role of managers clearly has less to do with oversight, and individuals have far greater leeway to fulfil their work functions than in more hierarchical work cultures. Once a task is assigned, the expectation is that employees will know what to do, and if they have problems, they are expected to proactively bring them up with the manager. Finnish working life emphasises personal initiative, and employees are expected to express whatever requests or needs they may have (Törmälä 1998, 49-51; Trux 2000b, 280-300; Hämäläinen 2001, 75 and 81). When the lack of informal conversation is coupled with the expectation of autonomy, and the individual is left to negotiate a broad and loosely defined task alone, the following problems may arise:

- Difficulty in being able to place one's work in the context of the whole
- Lack of clear objectives in the task itself
- Even when an employee has adopted the independent working method, the two problems above may make it difficult to ask the right questions, if too little information about the task is provided
- An employee from another cultural background may not have adapted to the independent, "ask when necessary" culture, as the manager supposes
- Viewpoints among team members regarding their role in the project and the extent of input required may differ.

Lack of oversight and active critiquing can also seem like a manager's lack of interest or appreciation toward an employee's work. A "valueless"-seeming task or one not clearly connected to the whole robs employees of motivation to make the best possible effort in terms of performance in the task. When employees encounter operating practices without understanding the whole, misunderstandings will probably occur. Respondents from faraway countries, Asians in particular, felt that independently working employees and a lack of oversight led to selfishness and to some employees leaning on the work of others and "coasting" in project work. The Finnish sense of individualism is often concerned with independence and autonomy, whereas in many other societies such characteristics are more connected to attempts to stand out and be competitive, while at the same time working in closer collaboration with others than is common in Finland. Seeing one's work as part of a greater whole and understanding the operating practices of the workplace may turn what is perceived as a negative phenomenon into a positive one. Lack of oversight and independent work can be reinterpreted as trust in the employee's own skill and ability, and respect for his or her independence, as opposed to indifference. However, to recognise this everyone must understand the different ways of interacting in different cultures. If employees understand the operating rules and receive enough direction, they will more easily appreciate their freedom and independence.

"To me, the atmosphere is relaxed, and it is easy to approach your managers, compared to Germany, where they are fairly distant. I like this kind of system – you are free to express your opinion, whereas in Germany it's hard to even get access to a supervisor. The informal system here is good."

ICT expert, Brazil

The culture of conversing and social interaction affects the workplace broadly, not only in terms of team work or management. Conversations about non-work issues are an essential part of creating social networks, which enable people to learn to interpret one another's values and ways of interacting and thinking, but also help people feel part of a community. In practice, the process is often compromised – for example, the wide use of e-mail as a communication channel in place of personal contact is often seen as a way of avoiding personal interaction. Writing informal e-mails in Finnish on mail lists, and merely attaching a brief English-language summary can be positive, but also indicates to a foreigner that he or she is not a full part of the conversation. The foreigner is a bystander and only informed of the main points of a given issue. The fact that many e-mail messages are written in proficient English also underlines the unwillingness to interact on a personal level – the e-mails show that the reason for the minimal interaction has nothing to do with lack of language skills.

The so-called coffee break syndrome can make it difficult to integrate in the workplace. Foreigners already feel that there is hardly any conversation culture, and so conducting coffee-break small talk in Finnish makes those who do not understand the language, or only do so in a limited way, feel like total outsiders. Over a long period, this may come to feel quite awkward and even oppressive, and when foreigners find themselves treated as unequal participants in the informal social context, it delays their integration. Respondents were understanding of this problem and viewed it realistically. They reported that they understood the prevalence of Finnish and emphasised that they themselves had opportunities to learn Finnish if only they had enough time and motivation. Most respondents also had experiences with other cultures, and compared with many other non-English-speaking countries, English is used rather widely in Finland, even in informal conversation (Bayer 2002).

The total commitment of bioscience experts to their work may pose problems with regard to the production expectations imposed on them in exchange for today's investments – but under what conditions will bioscience inventors become the cornerstone of a new "Nokia" The substance of the work – research – is what is most important to a scientist, and the object value of the work – financial wealth or social status – is secondary to this central consideration, the content of the work itself. Most scientists in the biosciences are motivated by a strong ethical dimension in their work, for example helping to cure illness. Because academic freedom and individualism, or the freedom to fairly independently choose the subject of research and decide one's work schedule, are important values for scientists, working for a corporation is considered diametrically opposed to academic freedom.

"In the academic world you have a lot of freedom to do what you want, when you want. But working for a business, you're in a commercial situation, and you have to work nine to five and do what your supervisor tells you to do. It may even happen that you've achieved something really interesting, but the company doesn't view it as interesting or profitable, and you have to just leave it and start doing something completely different."

European scientist

For most scientists, working as a scientist is the only real aspiration, a total lifestyle, and only possible in an academic institution that places a high value on individualism. The bioscience job market is highly international, and it is common to have worked in several countries. The scientists interviewed for this study also expressed appreciation for how the field cultivates its own community through conference travel and scientist visits.

"There is really no other occupation where you can travel around and meet people with similar interests, who get their kicks from the same things. I mean that it's not like you can walk down the street in Finland and say to someone, hey, you know what, I discovered a really cool structure just recently."

European scientist

Scientists fear economic risk taking and loss of academic freedom. Their firm attachment to the academic community is problematic for the future expectations of the bioscience field, which is expected to collaborate with the business sector to produce commercially viable innovations and form new "Nokias" to make the profits to offset the investments into the field. It is, however, unlikely that many scientists, with their academic ideals, are willing to go the entrepreneurial route or even work for a business enterprise.

In sum, welfare states and their national labour markets have certain strengths that, instead of eliminated or dismantled, should be taken advantage of in the global competition for expertise. However, nationally and regionally designed applications of diversity management would enhance the emergence of creative innovation environments that are appealing to global talent. It would also be useful to understand the differences between target groups: where a career-oriented university researcher mostly appreciates professional contacts and career opportunities, a more established engineer with a family may value family life and lifestyle in general very highly. Here, 'lifestyle' refers to general opportunities to realise oneself outside of working life, regardless of what that lifestyle consists of. Linking lifestyle to certain consumer habits distorts the image, when we discuss broad, diverse population groups – including the one comprised of transnationally mobile experts. More detailed insight is needed, as interpretations to back up policy recommendations are constructed.

7.2 Equality in professional and career opportunities

When considering how to attract global talent, the reality behind the fancy words concerning diversity management, equal opportunities or business's need for the "best brains" should be acknowledged. What does an individual expert confront in his or her rendezvous with the local work environment? How available are the rewards of career advancement and social status to foreign talent? The reasoning behind the legislative elements of Affirmative Action and Equal Employment Opportunity should be taken seriously: an attitude that assumes difference and diversity as desired resources rather than as a burden to be avoided does not necessarily automatically arise from a multicultural, global reality.

It may be said that the greatest obstacle in working life is the inability to communicate with difference. Difference not only separates individuals from the work environment, but the inability to negotiate difference results in people's innovation potential getting lost in the process. While avoiding naïve interpretations of the possibilities of diversity management, we do claim that employers should at least be able to connect foreign employees to the innovation process, even if absolute fairness is a Utopian goal. Diversity management also engulfs gender differences, and in spite of the long tradition of working to equalise the opportunities of both genders in working life, hardly anyone would say that the situation is perfect. Similarly, even a long tradition of dealing with diversity probably will not guarantee absolute fairness between different ethnic groups in working life. It might, however, when competing for talented professionals, provide a significant advantage, especially in fields where individuals place a high value on professional opportunities and career development.

Relatively often, foreign respondents saw their opportunities for advancement in companies as weaker than those of their Finnish colleagues. In some cases they even felt that if the choice in a promotion was between a Finn and a foreigner, the Finnish person was promoted almost without fail. The reason identified by respondents was usually the social networks, where those who are already acquainted hire one another. The bias was more evident in cases where a manager needed some local knowledge and cultural skills, than in the case of more technical projects.

If an organisation's top management was exclusively Finnish, respondents saw this as reinforcing the idea that valuing "Finnishness" was part of organisational culture in choosing managers or giving promotions. This emphasises the importance of integration and encouragement of commitment. Unless employees are able to participate in social networks and have a real understanding of a company's operating methods in the context of local culture, their opportunities for advancement are probably weaker, at least in certain managerial positions.

The "coffee break syndrome" and other cultural traits of Finnish homogeneity and inwardness, various 'big brother' networks, and other forms of informal social interaction can affect the advancement opportunities of outsiders. Particularly respondents who had been in Finland longer were able to offer sophisticated analyses of the impact of being non-Finnish on career and professional opportunities.

"There is so much nepotism in the Finnish scientific world, and who you know is more important than what you know... The way I see it is that many job descriptions are tailored to particular persons, even though there is a whole host of others who could be really good in a particular job. And as far as recruiting the best people to Finland, that is not the way to operate... And there are also a lot of strong individuals in various departments that everybody bows down to, and these people make sure that the little researcher that the strong one happens to like gets a position either in that department or another one. This kind of thing is kind of exclusionary, like you have to be part of the sauna culture, smile and be pleasant and so on, so that you'd be popular. All of that is difficult for someone who's new."

Scientist, Europe

This phenomenon is probably not limited to universities and their organisational culture; respondents in the ICT field mentioned similar experiences. It is indeed likely that, for outsiders, the difficulty of entering the "Finnish sphere" is a broader reflection of a close-knit, homogenous and homogenising community and way of thinking. Such conclusions are supported by studies on the status of first- and second-generation immigrants in Finnish and Swedish labour markets (for example, Forsander 2002; Knocke & Herzberg 2001).

We should note that similar "glass ceilings" were met by Asian professionals in Silicon Valley in the United States. In a 1991 survey, two-thirds of Asian immigrant professionals working in the private sector believed that their advancement to managerial positions was limited by race in Silicon Valley. The exclusion from "old-boy networks" and lack of "role models" were considered more important than "racial prejudice" as factors that prevented the career advancement of Asians. As the number of entrepreneurs from ethnic minorities and connections with professional networks increased, also the glass ceiling seemed to become much more permeable (Saxenian 2006, 55). However, in a global operating environment, having strong social capital that is built on trust based on sameness and exclusive social relationships can turn into a weakness, when what the environment really requires is innovation and the ability to change rapidly. This suggests that despite the fact that the phenomenon is quite natural and universal, the steps from a regional social capital towards a "global social capital" should be taken intentionally.

Close communities and trust may be considered a strength of Finnish society. The "strength" is a problem, however, when we are trying to create the kind of global talent-reliant work environments that support and promote innovation. An open and interested attitude toward technological, social or organisational ideas presented by employees supports the creation of a rich problem-solving environment. The innovativeness of a diverse community is probably manifested not only in new types of problem solving, but also as social innovations – for example, as the emergence of a new kind of conversation culture among members of a workplace. For a community to be innovative, it is essential that it be able to accept, receive, discuss and embrace suggestions that are different and even surprising.

Many of the study's foreigners had advanced in their careers and felt that their chances of moving forward within the company were good. However, even some of them assumed that they would have advanced slightly faster if they had been Finnish. Still, respondents thought that this was probably fairly natural and something that existed in organisations in many other countries as well.

As a whole, career advancement was considered easier for Finnish than foreign candidates. The study cannot confirm the veracity of this, but what is essential is how widespread this interpretation was, as it evokes at least some negative attitudes toward managers and working in Finland in general. If the organisation is thought to treat representatives of the host culture differently from other cultures, this can weaken the bond and trust that an employee feels toward the employer, whose credibility as a truly international company suffers. In most cases, though, respondents viewed their development in realistic terms and did not expect rapid career leaps. The fact of being foreign and lacking social networks were nonetheless considered only a partial aspect – or in some cases even a non-issue – among all the impediments to career advancement. Other impeding factors included shallow organisational structure and respondents' specific areas of specialisation, which frequently entailed a shortage of available jobs. (see Raunio 2007)

Many respondents considered their broader career opportunities in regional terms (Figure 4) or in Finland as a whole (Figure5) somewhat more negatively than they viewed their possibilities of advancing with the present employer. Figure 6 indicates that Finland's success in many international studies measuring competitiveness does not necessarily extend to one key area of competitiveness: attractiveness on the global labour market available to talented professionals. Up to 27 percent of respondents mostly or completely disagreed with the statement that "Finland offers a globally competitive job market and good career opportunities". As a rule, career development is one of the goals in moving to another country and also part of the dynamic that prevails in the working lives of global experts, emphasising the phenomenon's significance and increasing the probability of immigrating, particularly among people who place a particularly high value on career development.

Figure 5. "Finland offers a globally competitive job market and good career opportunities" (N=553), ICT field (source: Raunio 2003)

When respondents considered changing jobs, they did not consider finding a new one in Finland as likely as moving to another country – the Finnish job market was not usually the place where foreign experts looked to find new work. Exceptions were usually people, who had a Finnish spouse whose job was tied to Finland specifically. On the other hand, the Finnish job market does not offer endless opportunities for someone who does not speak Finnish. Apart from language problems, respondents also felt that their options were to some extent limited by the inability of Finnish companies to integrate non-Finnish-speaking and culturally different experts into the work community.

Whereas Finnish working life welcomes the global economy's talented professionals with open arms, their spouses, if they work in less global fields, encounter a completely different reality. Out of the 33 spouses interviewed for this study, only one was completely satisfied with current employment and in a permanent job. Four others were employed, but only temporarily, and were not very satisfied with their work. Twenty-six of the spouses had not worked at all in Finland, though they had applied for work. All unemployed spouses were certain that if unemployment were to continue, the family would leave regardless of the other spouse's permanent position. Finland's limited professional and career opportunities available to spouses were an obvious bottle-neck, particularly outside of Helsinki.

A spouse need not find employment immediately, but in the longer term a lack of engagement probably results in a decision to move on, because the spouse who is already working and has globally applicable skills can usually find another job in many other countries as well. But many spouses were satisfied with their current situation, which allowed them to be at home with small children, provided that the move was relatively recent and the adapting process was still ongoing for both children and the family as a whole.

"I thought of working here, but the prerequisite is speaking fluent Finnish, which is completely understandable, so now I'm learning Finnish. On the other hand, it's quite alright to be spending more time with my family right now, when the kids are getting used to a Finnish school and Finland in general."

MD, spouse, United States

This situation was, however, seen as temporary almost without exception. At the end of the day, people wanted to start working as soon as their children had adapted and/or were old enough, in the parents' view, to be in day care. For people who were planning a long-term stay, a spouse's employment was a precondition for staying. When people do stay in spite of a spouse's unemployment, it significantly lowers the level of economic wellbeing and complicates the spouse's integration into Finnish society and its social networks. Törmälä's (1998) study also found that a central problem among foreign experts with families was the spouse's unemployment. In long-term unemployment, the situation led to difficulties in making friends and learning Finnish. Social networks and Finnish language skills would probably make it easier to find work, and so the situation becomes a vicious circle (Törmälä 1998, 67-70).

The biggest problem in finding work came from a lack of language skills, but employers' attitudes toward foreign applicants were another factor. Many job-seeking spouses had encountered prejudice toward foreigner employees. They had experienced unmitigated discrimination, where the employer did not want to give the job to a foreigner, or the foreigner was offered a significantly worse employment contract. Such interpretations indicate that Finnish job applicants are at an advantage at both employment agencies and with employers. Foreign degrees and work experience are also not valued as highly as Finnish ones. There is a vast difference in the situation of a foreign expert who arrives to an already existing job – their spouses understandably had a much more negative view of their own employment possibilities.

Adapting the labour market to cater to a more heterogeneous pool of job applicants will make it possible to take advantage of global talent resources. One of the most noteworthy projects at the moment is EU's revamping of the education system, intended to produce a much more clear-cut and uniform education system. These are institutional changes that transform "others" to "us" in official practices. Although informal recruiting practices and attitudes will remain, they are not supported or nourished by institutional structures. Steps towards a "global community" are and should be taken cautiously. These are the steps that employers should take.

8 The dilemma of the welfare state

As global and transnational migrants become an increasingly central resource for the global knowledge economy, nations must weigh the economic and social policies they practice from a standpoint that is entirely different from what was intended by their founders. This chapter examines the dilemma of the welfare state in a global world. To simplify, the dilemma emerges from the clash of the nation-state, which was designed to serve people who spend their whole life as members of this imagined community, with mobile individuals who share their productive and less productive life-phases between several nation-states. Welfare policies provide equality at a national level, through taxation and public services, but simultaneously weaken the development opportunities for private services and lower the income level of experts. Individuals who interpret the dilemma through their regional or local environments – where they live and work – instead of by gazing at national averages, may view this environment as a lower-quality environment, compared with a local environment in a nation-state, which provides higher-quality services and a higher income, although at the expense of national equality. This is one of the key questions to balance when considering strategies for maintaining the welfare state as a competitive social model in the global economy.

The relationship of non-citizens to European welfare systems is perhaps one of the most complex yet under-researched areas in contemporary policy. According to Baldwin-Edwards (2004), what little comparative literature exists spans the gamut of possible analyses: from Freeman (1986), who suggests that European welfare states are almost uniformly exclusive owing to their citizen-based provisions; through Baldwin-Edwards (1991), who argues that different states interact in very different ways with their immigrant populations; and more recently, Soysal (1994) and Jacobson (1996), both of whom claim that European countries are almost uniformly inclusive of their resident aliens owing to the important impact of international human rights law (Baldwin-Edwards 2004, 318). It would therefore be impossible to conduct any European or global analysis at a more detailed level – hence, here we concentrate on just Finland, while broadly defining its position among welfare states (Table 7).

In order to provide some answers to the complex question of the relationship between non-citizens and the welfare system, we have defined the target group and the relationship quite narrowly here, and yet clearly one source of complexity emerges immediately. The target group consists of highly educated professionals working in Finland – a somewhat manageable approach. However, in order to say anything meaningful from an individual's point of view, we cannot omit the individuals' primary social relationships. This introduces the spouses, children and other social relations that indirectly connect individuals to the welfare system.

Much has been made of the importance of highly evolved information societies for educated citizens and of the knowledge economy for innovative companies in ensuring international competitiveness. As information society develops, it is nevertheless crucial to keep in mind that the Nordic welfare state and information society need not be mutually exclusive, and that in fact, a successful information society and knowledge economy are preconditions for a welfare state that can operate generously. Information societies cannot create welfare states, which are founded on society's prevailing values and the broad-based support of the citizenry. The concept that information society and knowledge economy are necessary for the welfare state can be interpreted another way: to counter anti-globalisation sentiment. One can argue that without a strong, global welfare state, globally oriented information societies and knowledge economies will encounter powerful opposition that will impede or even halt their development.

Finland is a case in point – even in the depth of recession, the country was able to continue developing its information society, because the welfare state made it socially acceptable to follow the trend. One would think that because information society's revenues were slower to accrue than the expenditures of the welfare state, as occurred in Finland in the late 1990s, this would have angered the country's population and resulted in an economic crisis. But in the end, the very services that the welfare state is able to offer so effectively buffered the exacerbation of the problems that did arise, so that there was no need to radically change the course of development (Castells & Himanen 2001, 86-67).

As nations' economies become increasingly linked to the global economy, welfare states can no longer ignore this development and continue as if the national dimension were the only consideration. There is no fundamental conflict in realising the ideals of both a developed information society and an equality-seeking welfare state – as long as no conflict is built into those structures. Creating living and working environments to attract foreign experts is part of this broader development and also serves to highlight its problem areas – it is a central challenge for a society that bases its welfare on expertise.

The aim of welfare state ideology is to ensure the wellbeing of all *citizens*. Various entities that can be called basic welfare state models have been established to support this objective (Table 7). This translates into the creation of national "boundaries" within society, because many national measures to promote equality in fact increase inequality at a transnational level. In some ways, however, from an individual's perspective, society's institutions and its high-quality, equality-securing structures may not seem all that high-quality or represent a notable improvement in terms of the quality of life.

8.1 The welfare state in shaping the standard of living

It is often pointed out that as a Nordic welfare state, Finland is more competitive. But is it true that the welfare state, with its comprehensive services, really attracts foreign innovators? The present study suggests that a comprehensive welfare state and its societal effects, such as security, do have an impact on the contentment of particularly immigrants with families. As mentioned previously, however, in themselves, excellent social services do not constitute a reason to move to a particular country, but they can play a role in the willingness of foreign experts to remain in the country.

Immigrants who come for work reasons mostly use employer-provided health services, and unless they have a family, hardly use any other public services. This does not mean that a comprehensive welfare state does not have an indirect effect – its services help make publicly funded jobs in particular attractive to experts. After all, it is society's very investment of its resources that makes it possible to develop the organisations and train the people who work in them.

A highly evolved welfare state also encourages foreign experts to commit to a new society. A safe and child-friendly environment and a comfortable, orderly social realm can anchor individuals to their living environment, even when economic incentives fall short of expectations. Built upon the comprehensive welfare state, a global competitive advantage in attracting innovators and investments is not a permanent one, and must be re-earned over and over again. Many of the factors that explain the success of Nordic welfare states in global competition are connected to the welfare state and to an education system that makes people equal. In fact, both have changed, and Nordic countries are now reaping what they sowed previously. How do we stretch the welfare state to create a foundation also for future competitiveness?

Welfare state models are divided into three categories, or regimes, depending on the principles that formed them. The monikers of the regimes vary in different classification systems, but the basis for how they are classified is approximately the same in each case. A typical classification speaks of residual, corporatist and universal models (Esping-Andersen 1990). The table, below, summarises the key characteristics of the different welfare state models.

The universal welfare state's central socio-political tenets are more than half a century old, but basically they have not changed. The two cornerstones, considered useful for society as a whole, were established to reduce social disparity. First, there are income transfers "from the rich to the poor," which were seen as supporting consumer demand and therefore employment – the cash of the poor reenters the consumption cycle more readily than that of the rich. Second, the education system was built with the central objective of eliminating poverty, putting a stop to the class differences that each generation inherited from the previous one, and freeing up all available talent reserves for use by the labour market and by society.

Table7. Three social policy models, as adapted from Karisto et al. (1998, 284; Mishra 1981, Kangas 1986) (cf. Esping-Andersen 1990, Kangas 1986).

	Residual model	*Attainment-based corporatist model*	*Universal Nordic model*
Role of state	Minor	Varies	Central
Social expenditure in GDP (gross domestic product)	Low	Relatively low	Substantial
Population segment that social policy targets	The poor	Active participants	Citizens
Level of social benefits	Low	Good	Reasonable
Typical form of assistance	Selective assistance based on careful need assessment	Selective assistance based on work income	Universal assistance to all
Clients served by social policy	Stigmatised as freeloaders	Have earned their benefits	Regular citizens
Assistance oversight	Widely and openly monitored	Widely used but cloaked monitoring	Little monitoring, cloaked
Role of private organisations	Important	Fairly important	Unimportant (Finland is an exception in the case of employment pensions)
Examples of countries	United States, Britain, New Zealand	Germany, Austria, France	Nordic countries, The Netherlands

The Finnish version of the universal welfare state sought to create a nation-wide, class-less uniformity and efficiency in the socio-political arena and in the national economy. Its achievements are in fact a success story: in just over a century, the country has emerged from a poor agrarian society to an internationally competitive leader. The welfare state made it through post-war structural changes with honour, and continued its expansion, though this development was halted during the 1990s recession. The current debate centres on the fate of the welfare state's services, as structural unemployment, a declining workforce and shrinking income tax base shake its foundations.

The discourse of the meaning and future of the welfare state boils down to this: what can we do to keep Finland competitive and to continue to guarantee that Finnish trade and commerce can operate in favourable operating conditions? In political debates, a strong welfare state is often viewed as awkward, useless or inhibiting competition. The reasons for demands to reduce and overhaul the public sector can be weighed from various points of view, but whatever the reasons, dismantling the welfare state, resulting in a rise in social disparity, will have an impact on Finland's attractiveness in the eyes of foreign experts – a positive as well as a negative one.

8.2 What the welfare state takes: taxation and wages

To attract innovators, one needs money. Studies about immigrants' values and choices show that already when they consider relocation, many immigrants create an equation out of the factors of immigration and working and living in the new target country, and weigh the result. The amount of money left over after taxes and living expenses is therefore significant. In this sense, too, our target group deviates from other groups of immigrants in several ways – from the less educated who migrate for work reasons, as well as from those who are educated, but for whose expertise there is little demand or for whom the transnational job market is more limited for one reason or another, than it is for experts in the ICT and bioscience fields. In the presence of global options, objects of comparison also adapt to the global and asymmetric operating environment. Comparisons are less concerned with averages or the average income distribution of a particular country, but instead focus on the position of the highly educated in a given job market and in different geographic locations. This is reflected onto the evaluation of income level, which is nearly always compared to the major job concentrations in various industries in the United States and Great Britain. Finland does not shine in such comparisons.

In the research and development field, Finland is almost a country of cheap labour: although the average wages of industrial workers fare favourably in international comparisons, wages for experts and for management positions that require a high level of education are lower than in many other countries. Not only that, prices and taxes are high. Figure 7, below, gives the net earnings for married and single engineers and mid-level managers in Finland, Germany and the United Kingdom. In Finland, taxation does not depend on family structure, so differences among married experts or managers are even higher when compared with countries with policies that support families (such as Germany). This of course reflects national culture and values. In Finland, women participate in working life more often than in Germany and households are expected to be two-income households even if there are children, and, consequently, tax breaks for the "breadwinner" are not considered necessary. In the case of the United Kingdom, the difference is simpler, since the United Kingdom is more of a liberal market economy than is Finland, and progressive income taxation that aim to diminish income disparities does not fit into its political agenda as well as it does in the coordinated market economy of Finland.

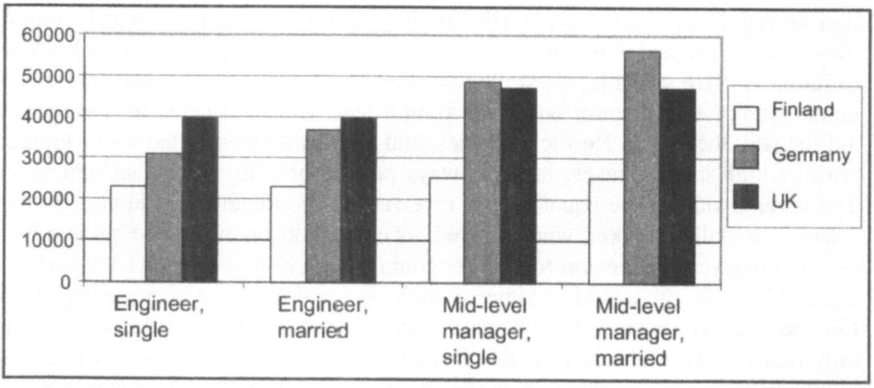

Figure 7. Net earnings in Finland, Germany and the U.K. among single and married engineers and corporate mid-level managers. Figures are based on earnings and tax data for 2000–2003. Child and family benefits are excluded (Coddan 2003; Kurjenoja 2003a; 2003b, Survey of German Tax Laws 2004; TT 2002, 3).

Among economic incentives, taxation is one point of comparison. It may act as a pull factor in attracting workers and investments, leading to tax competition. Low corporate or income taxes can invite foreign investments – a strategy upon which Ireland, for instance, has built its IT clusters, creating a rapid economic boom, higher employment and a fast-growing volume of immigrants. Income taxes are low in Ireland, only 20 percent on incomes of up to 34,000 euros per year, and substantial tax reductions are available. In fact, an internet site for potential immigrants to Ireland[11] claims that one of four Irish employees does not pay income taxes because of thresholds and reductions. However, for high-income (exceeding

11 (www.movetoireland.com)

34,000 euros/year) professionals the rate is 41 % (www.revenue.ie). EU membership determines the latitude that member countries have in terms of national taxation systems, and within this framework, Ireland's strategy has been controversial. It is clear that, compelled to finance its sizable public sector welfare system, Finland will never become a tax haven. Something can, however, be done to make working in Finland more appealing to foreign experts. A total system overhaul is not needed, but some of the parts can be modified to better work in the new environment. Simply put, the principle of national equality must be adapted toward the principle of transnational justice. The collisions of these two ideologies that strive for equality in different arenas can be seen in the encounters between foreign experts and Finnish society, to follow.

The global economy and greater mobility make it possible to reap the benefits of a number of systems. This has intensified the international income tax competition for highly educated experts, who are in a position to choose in which country they want to live and work, and who can therefore fall through the cracks between different welfare systems. An skilled worker who financed his or her pricey academic studies in a country with high tuition fees, where students do not receive aid the way they do in Nordic countries, and who subsequently moves to Finland with its high income taxes, in some ways pays double for his or her education. The reverse side of the equation has received more attention in Finland. In that scenario, a skilled worker, who received his or her education for free but at a high cost to taxpayers, moves on to another country with high wages and low income taxes. Thus far, the actual volume of such "brain drain" has been negligible in Finland – approximately 10,000 people leave the country annually, but usually only temporarily. For many, a stint abroad only represents a temporary phase of career development. Any loss of the brain reserve has thus mostly occurred in the form of brain circulation. The issue here is a broader societal one, and the reason that one aspect of it is now brought to the forefront is a result of the different interpretations of society among foreign experts.

Finland's response to the international income tax competition has been to create a special tax category for foreign "key employees". Taxing foreign workers differently can breed resentment because it places people who live in Finland in an unequal position in front of the state and therefore goes against the principle of equality that characterises the Nordic welfare model. An argument in defence of special taxation is that foreigners are not permanent residents and that immigrating to Finland comes with special costs to immigrants. The Nordic welfare state and the relatively high taxes that pay for it are based on the concept of the so-called life course: at different times in their lives, people who live in the country are either a payer or a beneficiary. Roughly speaking, the universalism of the Nordic welfare state relies on the fact that paid taxes go into a common account and, in principle at least, individuals need not seek additional security through private funds or insurance plans to finance pensions, health care or their children's education.

At the heart of the issue is finding a method of combining the different social models during the life of an individual in a way that is fair. If the desire to eliminate institutional barriers is real, we need to figure out how to combine the different operating models of, on the one hand, a society that is founded on a private insurance system and individual responsibility, and on the other hand, a universal welfare society, in the lives of individuals in a way that is meaningful and fair. As Baldwin-Edwards (2004) suggests, it is both costly and complex to adapt welfare systems to immigrants, but it is also possible that excluding immigrants from welfare services has as much of a cost as including them. Since welfare regimes are now undergoing a radical restructuring, non-citizens could be incorporated in a rational and orderly manner. In its reports, the OECD suggests that current labour market trends should form the basis for social policy (Baldwin-Edwards 2004, 330). This structural change is also underway in Finland, making it the right moment to re-examine not only social policy but the associated taxation – both play a role in the commitment of skilled workers, as described in this chapter. Even beyond humanitarian reasons or questions of global justice, from an economic point of view it is more important to make the effort to attract and commit (skilled) workers than to restrict the access of non-citizens to the services of the welfare state.

From national equality toward global justice

The findings of the present study underline the significance of the low earnings potential, high taxation, other taxes, and the employment pension system as a confluence of factors that lowers the appeal of Finland for skilled foreigners. The question is not one of specific salary amounts or tax percentages, but also of the impressions and stories that circulate among foreign innovators. Only six percent of respondents were completely satisfied with their wages and three percent considered the rate of taxation reasonable (Figure 8).

The negative perception of high taxation and low wages is not only an economic issue, but, because of worldviews that are founded in different value systems, it also takes the form of a moral conflict for which we must find new solutions in the changing environment.

Although foreign workers are generally aware of wages and tax rates before immigrating, their significance often emerges only after settling in the job and the country. On the other hand, many come assigned to Finland under the security of an economically superior expatriate contract, but upon the renegotiation of the contract, the economic benefits are brought down to local levels, which can be problematic. Often, too, Finnish wage levels are compared with wages in high-tech regions of countries like the United Kingdom or United States, and the differences are quite significant. It is true, however, that it is difficult to make such comparisons and that they should be viewed with caution and as fairly unsophisticated and simplified representations of reality. Whatever the case, Finland has been mentioned as a "country of cheap labour" for research and development (Castells & Himanen 2001).

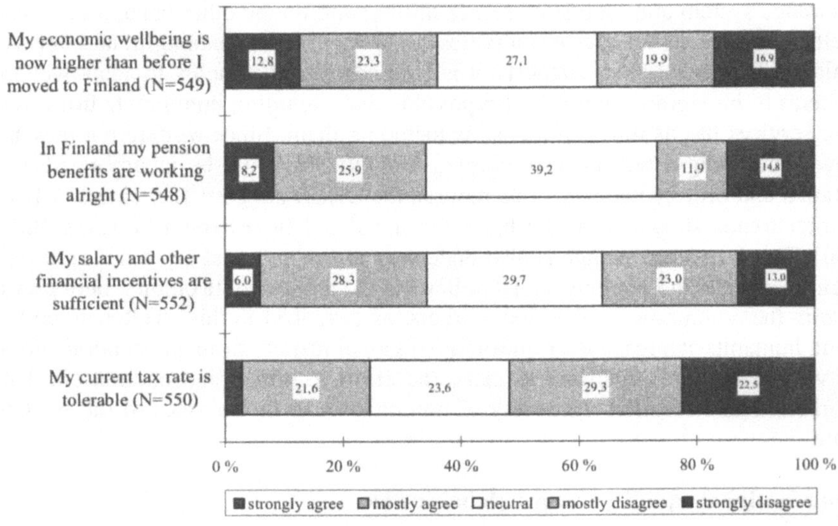

Figure 8. Satisfaction with economic environmental factors – ICT field. (source: Raunio 2003)

It should be realised, that although absolute figures or percentages are, indicative as they are, often misleading when interpreting comparisons such the one above from an individual point of view. Not every immigrant respondent's wage level declined dramatically after moving to Finland, although many made concessions in terms of their economic wellbeing or at least their net earnings. Only less than 13 percent of respondents had experienced a clear increase in economic wellbeing following relocation to Finland. On the other hand, this is also an indication of the high value that global experts place on career opportunities over economic considerations, but it can form a barrier to competitiveness in attracting and committing global experts.

"Well, the kind of people we get is pretty dependent on money. Money decides. Wages and... I think it does decide. Foreigners – maybe not people from Estonia, but other countries – always ask how much we pay, and ask about the high taxes... It's been a deal breaker for many people. Or the taxes could be lower, so that you'd have more left in your hand. That could be one way, a way to seal the deal. People who have worked elsewhere – they ask questions like "oh, why so little".

Manager-level Estonian scientist

Temporary and permanent residents view taxes differently. For example, a staggered taxation system for foreigners is often seen as a fair practice. In such a system, the tax percentage increases from one year to the next and reaches the local level, for example, by year six of residency. Immigrants feel that staggered taxation is justified because someone who is only working in Finland for a few years has not benefited from the free education and will not be around to benefit from retirement benefits or services for the aged. Also, high taxes do not necessarily translate into high-quality services among those that this target group encounters. In addition, single people and couples with no children use very few services. Staggering taxation would diminish the amount of taxes paid for "nothing in return" in the case of short stays, and after a sufficiently long period of residence in the country, the realisation of society's benefits in the life of an individual would "justify" bringing the tax rate up to the local level. On the other hand, the issue is not income taxes alone but taxation in general.

"The taxes would be OK if you had been born here, studied here, and were planning to retire here. Why should I pay them when I only work here and am in no way a burden to society? I pay 47 percent in income taxes, 20 percent on everything that I purchase, a 75-percent tax on gasoline.... my overall tax rate is 75 percent, and that can't be right – why do I have to pay the state that much?"

ICT expert, South Africa

The importance of economic wellbeing becomes topical particularly during certain life stages, and at such junctions people give serious consideration to factors like taxes, wages, or the opportunity to improve their economic standard of living in another place. It is also difficult to take an economic step down and accept a lower income, even though global experts are not primarily propelled by financial success.

"I think that wages are the biggest reason why people leave. In Italy the wages are almost the same, but taxes are lower and my family has a place to live there, so our living expenses would be lower."

ICT expert, Italy

"I wish my husband were earning more and that we could get a bigger home. It wouldn't matter if we were younger, but we're 35 and we have a family, and both of us are highly educated. In the U.S. our standard of living was clearly higher, and it's hard to take a step down."

Spouse, United States

Finnish taxation is high and research and development salaries are relatively low. That's not all – overall Finland is seen as a "tax state" that also caters to "freeloaders" at the expense of tax-paying workers. In many cultures, the appreciation of work also comes with opportunities for significant financial benefits and for securing the future and wellbeing of one's family by working hard. In Finland, without option programmes, there is little possibility to accrue any substantial wealth, even among the highly educated, and the public sector, for its part, has assumed the role of "safety net", ensuring elder care, education and basic security for families. (Raunio 2007.) While not eliminating the ability of individuals to attain a desired standard of living for themselves and for their families, an extensive universal safety net does limit such opportunities.

Because the salary levels "force" both partners to work – if they have a family – lifestyle itself is shaped in some ways to be dependent on the public sector and its child-care systems. The welfare society finances public services that, elsewhere, are funded through private foundations or insurance. For someone from another culture, it may seem unfair to be forced to pay for a public sector that offers health care, child care and pensions, when the individual could just as well decide to give some or all of the money to the private sector, or even choose higher net earnings instead and save money for his or her old age.

Taxation and the expectation of two-income, nuclear family households

Many countries grant different kinds of tax breaks to foreign workers, mostly to skilled workers. The government's proposal to the Finnish Parliament for a law on taxing foreign workers considered the 'key person' tax system in use in several European countries, including Denmark, Norway, Sweden, Netherlands and Belgium. Neither Sweden nor Belgium, for example, has a particular system in use, but people can apply for special status. The Danish system seems the most generous from a foreigner's perspective, which is possibly perceived as a counterbalance to Denmark's steep income taxes. The highest progressive bracket is 63 percent, whereas foreigners whose income exceeds 43,500 Danish crowns can be taxed only 25 percent in total income tax. Special status may be granted for up to three years instead of the maximum two years in Finland and Sweden. Denmark also allows even scientists with smaller incomes to be eligible for the special tax bracket.

Finland adopted 'key employee' taxation in 1996, and accordingly, foreign workers whose income exceeds € 5,800 per month pay 35 percent in income tax. The defence of the government scheme that proposed a special tax break for foreigners alluded to Finland's ability to compete internationally. The proposal examines tax programmes in use in other countries and concludes that international comparisons show that the taxation of foreign wage earners is regulated through special provisions in countries where income taxation is at a level that resembles

Finnish levels. At the outset, the tax programme was to remain in effect for only two years, 1996 and 1997. A two-year extension was ordered thereafter. In 2000, the application of the law was interrupted, because the commission was asked to determine whether the tax break amounted to government assistance that could be construed as contrary to European Community legislation. It was found not to do so, and was renewed for three more years (2001–2003), and has subsequently been extended until 2007. The law was changed at the beginning of 2007, and "specialists" or "key employees" who have arrived in Finland after 2006 have been eligible for the special flat rate (35 %) for 48 months instead of 24, the limit for those who arrived before 2007. According to the temporary Act, "it is required that the key employee has not been a resident of Finland at any time during the five years preceding the year when he/she accepted employment in Finland" (Finnish Tax Administration 2007).

It is hardly a wonder that each time the law's continuation is debated it arouses passionate support as well as opposition. The 'key person' tax law contains many points that tug on people's emotions about taxes, the money-making elite as well as foreigners. The idea that the foreign elite should be granted an exception in taxation, which is meant to apply strictly and equally to each and every person, so that more of this elite could be tempted to work in Finland is controversial. The law has been discussed rather widely considering the small number of people it actually affects. During 1996, the year when the law was adopted, only 40 individuals were affected. Thereafter the number of those within its sphere of application has increased, and by 1999, the special tax bracket applied to 150 foreigners who were temporarily working in Finland. The € 5,800 monthly wages, however, are high even for highly educated workers, which restricts access to the tax programme, even though in principle, the law allows an opportunity for inclusion. No studies exist as to what role special taxation plays in foreign experts' decisions to work or not to work in Finland.

Finland and other Nordic countries tax spouses separately, and the same rules apply to spouses as to single people. In countries with corporatist social security, such as Germany, Belgium and Holland, a married couple is taxed as one unit with the result that the tax burden is less when only one spouse earns the income. The idea behind this is that supporting the spouse who manages the home – usually the mother – is a financial burden on the working partner. This model of taxation supports women who stay at home instead of working. The model with two heads of household, where society supports child care outside the home is a characteristic of the Nordic welfare model, which aims to employ as many women as possible.

For immigrant families this becomes problematic, however, because most spouses, even highly educated ones, again mostly women, stay at home because of the difficulty of finding work. In foreign families, typically only one partner is employed (this is atypical among Finns). In this way the fairness of taxation is connected to prevailing attitudes and the ability of employers to employ people who speak only some Finnish or none at all. The new Aliens Act eases the conditions for employment of the spouses of skilled foreigners who migrated to Finland to work, and now automatically grants work permits to spouses. The issue is therefore increasingly one of how successfully employers can utilise the international labour market, rather than one of legal limitations. In most families of foreign experts, the single head of household model is a reality stipulated by circumstance.

The Taxpayers Association of Finland compared Finland to eleven other nations in terms of families' net earnings after taxes and child subsidies. The Nordic equality ideal does not use taxation to support stay-at-home spouses (Figure 9.). As an ironic result, the stay-at-home spouses of foreign experts come up against a different set of invisible, built-in borders set up by society.

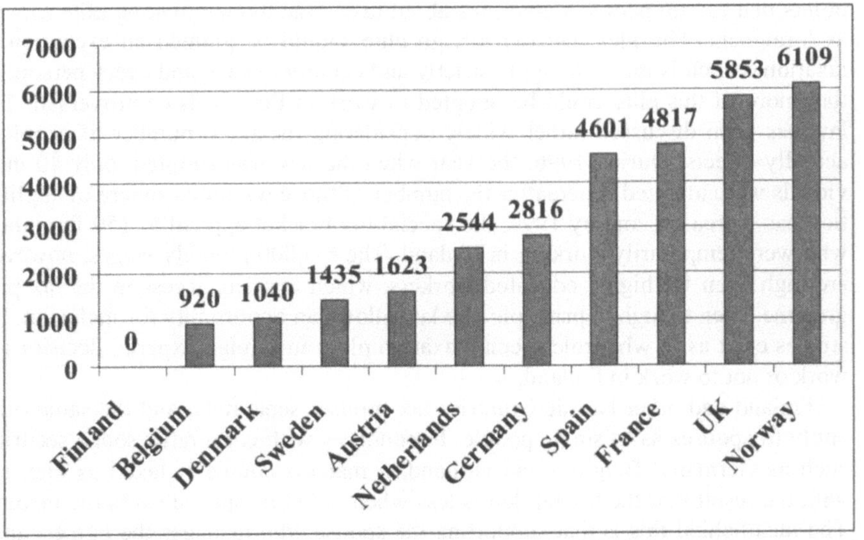

Figure 9. Differences in family net income compared with Finland, after taxes and child subsidies. Annual wages of employed spouse € 43,470, two guardians, one wage earner (Kurjenoja 2003a).

Taxing spouses individually is justified when there are two employed adults in the family, but this is usually not the case in families of skilled immigrants. The achievements of Nordic welfare states end up going against the principle of equality and against immigrant spouses – usually women.

Box 3. The story of the Campanis

The Campanis, originally from southern Europe, are facing a gruelling financial situation. The family's father, Nico, was recruited to work in a Finnish ICT company, concluding a long search on the part of the company. The Campanis carefully calculated if it made sense to relocate to Finland for this young family, which includes Nico, a four-year-old son and the mother, Monica, who is a trained pharmacist. The proffered salary exceeded Nico's current earnings by a slight margin, but on the other hand, they would have to pay more taxes in Finland and they had also heard that living expenses were higher. Child care would be another expense, because Monica's mother would no longer be caring for the boy. The couple thought it probable that a pharmacist would find employment in Finland. Even though the equation promised nothing spectacular, the family decided to leave, because the new job would help Nico's career path and the move would give them all new experiences.

Once in Finland, they easily found a place to live with the help of Nico's employer. The family felt that the apartment was in the middle of the forest, but it was very comfortable and within easy access of where Nico worked. The neighbours, too, seemed pleasant. Their son was accepted into a nearby day-care centre, where, after initial difficulties, he has been happy, and even the language has not been a problem. The real problem is that Monica has not been able to find work, no matter what she has tried. She went through all the area pharmacies, pharmaceutical companies and academic institutions, used every possible contact, and made phone calls and personal visits. Like any wage earner, Nico pays taxes, because his salary level does not reach the minimum required for key person tax status. Yet, because of Nico's high wages, Monica is not eligible for any kind of unemployment benefits. She understands that she has been unable to find work because she lacks Finnish-language skills, and has therefore enrolled at an employment agency-organised language course, even though, as the spouse of a temporary foreign worker, she is not technically eligible for this benefit. The expenses from the move, daily travel expenses, rent, and day-care fees that are tied to a higher income category, and other living expenses all mean that Nico's salary gets used to the last drop. Most unfortunate is that they cannot afford to travel home for Christmas, even though they all miss it terribly. On the positive side, their son enjoys his day care and Nico enjoys his job, which has great career opportunities, as his duties grow increasingly demanding and bring more responsibility. Monica wants to work, but a job that matches her qualifications seems to elude her more and more each day.

For immigrants who come because of a job, the equation of low wages combined with high income taxes that do not recognise the cost of caring for dependents with no income of their own is a heavy burden. Most immigrants come accompanied by a family, and while the experts have pre-arranged employment, their spouses do not. The spouses of educated professionals are usually themselves educated professionals, but finding employment is commonly thwarted by the same difficulties that most immigrants who arrive in Finland without a job waiting for them face. In real life, the employed spouse must support the unemployed spouse and the children. Spouses are also outside of the sphere of KELA's (Social Insurance Institution of Finland) unemployment benefits, because the employed spouse's earnings exceed the minimum limit for eligibility for basic unemployment assistance. In the absence of sufficient professional experience in Finland or trade union membership, the unemployed spouses do not meet the employment conditions and are therefore blocked from eligibility for the unemployment allowance.

Previously, when skilled workers migrated between different countries, it was more common for their employment contracts to be so-called expatriate contracts, which more generously took into account a family's moving expenses and loss of income. Expatriate contracts are still used when employees remain within the same employer but are transferred to another country. These days, skilled workers' employment contracts usually adhere to local employment agreements, including their wages. For foreign workers, the shift to local agreements means that their standard of living is affected more by local regulatory mechanisms such as taxation, wages and social security than by any benefits offered by the employer.

Should you pluck a hen that's laying an egg . . .

Because divergent tax systems cause tax competition and various complicated key person tax systems, it would be useful to create regulations that span at least the area of the European Union, to prevent competition in taxation schemes. In addition, a common regulatory base could facilitate mobility within the EU.

As it stands, taxes, including income taxes, have been lowered over recent years in nearly all OECD nations, including Finland. It is difficult for the systems that typify vastly different social models that are engaged in global competition to coexist side by side – including taxation. Singapore, for instance, where the tax rate is 20 percent, intends to further cut taxes in order to trump fast-developing China in the race for innovators (Kaseva & Vartia 2002, 84). In light of solutions like these, it is clear that the EU does not employ the same competitive means as countries with developing economies. On the one hand, this points to the importance of creating an internal EU system, and on the other hand, to the impossibility of tax competition being a viable competitive advantage. The question is more about ensuring sense and fairness in the tax system than about achieving global competitive advantages. It is also true that promoting such characteristics that are emblematic of a democratic welfare state, probably represents a competitive advantage for Europe – so that they and Finland – can distinguish themselves from other parts of the world.

Because it seems that particularly single professionals without a family prefer private over public services, they often lack the motivation to pay taxes. The relationship between what you pay and what you get in return may seem remote. As we have described above, a connection does exist, but not in the form of services and benefits that can be commodified.

In one sense, by paying taxes, foreign skilled workers contribute to maintaining the environmental characteristics that they value. On the other hand, from a national-economy perspective, there is no justification for taxing foreign workers highly. First of all, the demand for services is concentrated in the private sector, which means that at least part of the income after taxes is rerouted back into the economy through direct consumer demand. Second, the contribution that foreign skilled workers give to the national economy through their work may be viewed as more valuable than their potential tax contributions: they produce added value for their employers. The Finnish income tax model is founded on the life course idea in which each person moves from the role of payer to the role of beneficiary. The employed work force pays for those who are outside of the workforce so that children, students, homemakers, the unemployed and the retired can receive services and financial assistance. Third, immigrants bring with them a substantial amount of education capital – free of cost – that someone else already paid for. Higher tax rates may be justified among Finns by arguing that in most cases, Finnish society paid for their education, and in exchange, they pay their taxes. It is not unfair that someone who was educated in another country pays less in taxes than a comparable Finnish employee who, at a minimum, received his or her basic education in Finland.

In addition to taxes and the added value of their labour, work migrants make the same social security payments as everyone else. Finns know that all the money they pay will eventually come back to them when they need it, as pensions and unemployment benefits. For immigrants, social security payments merely look like another tax-like burden, because frequently, restrictions in residency permits make it impossible for immigrants to be eligible for unemployed status or to receive a pension.

In view of the national economy and all of the considerations described above, expanding the special taxation system for foreign workers may well be justified. It would certainly make it easier to attract and hold on to skilled workers, and moreover, it would increase consumption and promote employment within the private service sector. Still, the limitation of this approach should be understood. We should note that increasingly sophisticated and illustrative rankings from an individual's point of view are continuously produced to compare the economic well-being of different occupational groups around the world. These detailed analyses often include novel views that may be more interesting for an individual decision maker looking for a job on the global market, as opposed to the traditional national averages or other macro-economic comparisons that are typical in scientific analysis. For example, Mercer's Human Resource Consulting ranked countries according to total pay (including bonuses) for information technology (IT) managers. The highest paying countries for IT managers were found in Western

Europe, with Switzerland, Germany and Denmark holding the top three positions (Table 6). The traditional talent magnet, the United States, was placed 14th.

A totally different picture emerged in Hay Group's "World Pay Reports", where the average *disposable* incomes of senior managers (head of function/department) were compared. When costs of living were included, Western European countries were at the bottom of the list and emerging economies in the Gulf States occupying the top ten. The report compared true purchasing power in the region and thus not only was Finland placed at 46th out of 47 countries (just below other Nordic welfare states), but also traditional high-income countries, including Switzerland (13th), United States (24th) and United Kingdom (40th) were excluded from the new top ten (Table 8). (McMullen. 2007.)

These comparisons provide novel insights into the economic wellbeing of very narrowly defined occupational groups on a global scale. This suggests that the economic environment of Nordic welfare states and advanced economies in general have to be readjusted to the global age at least to some extent. It is evident that tax competition with emerging economies will not be the solution. It does become even more important to understand the viewpoint of individuals along with macro-economic views, when considering the "attractiveness" of a region. Benefits from trade-offs between quality-of-life-factors and monetary incentives should be more carefully considered in this context from different target groups' points of view. Evidently, Nordic welfare states are not the best place for money making phases of life, but they may have other advantages that experts value extremely highly.

Table 8. Comparing salaries globally for IT managers and senior managers (McMullen 2007; Mercer 2005)

	Highest paying countries for IT-managers (total pay)	*Average disposable income for senior managers (real purchasing power)*
1st	Switzerland $ 161,900	Saudi Arabia $ 229,325
2nd	Germany $ 126,700	United Arab Emirates $ 223,939
3rd	Denmark $116,000	Hong-Kong $ 203,947
4th	Belgium $ 112,300	Russia $ 157,348
5th	Japan $ 109,600	Turkey $ 154,762

It is worth remembering that economic factors alone are rarely the number one reason for why top experts decide to relocate or remain. Among bioscience experts the central motivator is the content of the work, its humanitarian impact and vocational nature. Similarly, ICT experts did not include economic wellbeing among their primary criteria – instead, the content of the work and the future opportunities that it opened up by allowing strategic career planning were their primary motivators, nearly without exception. From this perspective, it almost smacks of utilitarianism to emphasise the role of salary as a motivating factor.

"Well, I don't think anyone is happy with their pay. My salary is at the same level as other people who are in the same position in Finland. Sure, salaries are better in the U.S., but the U.S. is known for using money to try to attract people. My colleagues in Germany pretty much make what I make, but their living expenses are lower. Still, I wouldn't switch countries just because of money. That's not what this is all about."

Russian scientist

It would be to underestimate our target group if we did not emphasise that they do have an understanding of – and frequently value – the relationship between high taxes and small income differences, and a system that produces equality and social stability. For non-citizens, though, the life course model makes less sense than for citizens who remain in the same country all their lives. Finnish citizens appear to find high taxes acceptable as long as they receive concrete benefits in exchange. In a 2004 study, Finnish Business and Policy Forum (EVA) found that almost two-thirds of citizens agreed that taxes should not be lowered, if it would impair social protection and public services. On the other hand, when more or less the same argument was put in a more abstract way, arguing that high taxes are part of the Nordic welfare model, and should thus be accepted, only slightly over a quarter agreed, and close to half disagreed. Other formulations of the same basic argument give results in-between these two extremes (Torvinen & Kiljunen 2005; Haikonen & Kiljunen 2003). From the perspective of foreign workers and skilled experts, the actual services do not necessarily offer the best justification for the welfare state's high taxes. Many respondents do, however, consider the positive effects of income distribution to be the foundation of social equality, stable operating environments and security, even if they use few of the services that welfare states offer in return for the payment of taxes.

"Well, basically this is worth paying for, it's pretty well produced. But it should be possible to produce it even better. It pays to pay taxes because then you don't have the nuisance of lots of crime. You don't have to see people starving all around you, and things like that. You know that it just doesn't happen. When I go to Manhattan, I feel really uncomfortable, I feel – I think that a wealthy society should not allow people to live like that. But is just happens anyway. And Finland is a wealthy society too, but it doesn't [allow it to happen], and I find that a good thing."

American scientist

The welfare state helps hold on to scientists, not through direct services but indirectly, by virtue of the impact that they have on the living environment and thereby to the creative problem solving environment as a whole. The working environment, too, reflects welfare society in the sense that bioscience respondents in particular viewed their employers as very well organised and as providing the necessary high-quality, reliable support services that are essential for productivity, as they free up employees to focus on their core expertise.

Society's services, which make everyone equal and are produced through high tax rates, create social stability and an infrastructure that supports equality and productivity. It is nevertheless timely to reconsider the reorganisation of taxation and social security, including pension payments, as people's careers are increasingly divided between different societies and their different systems – and not least because this plays a role in being viewed as an internationally attractive choice (see Hjerppe, Kari & Lönnqvist 2001). As a whole, as pull factors, economic considerations are usually a weakness for a country, rather than an advantage, and they frequently prevent long-term commitment.

8.3 What the welfare state gives: social harmony

It is the welfare state's structure that determines the relationship between society and its various demographic groups. The welfare state's *quality* is directly connected to how Finland's foreign experts experience that society. Typically, Nordic welfare societies have a strong state role in doling out wellbeing founded on the principle of equality. Each person in each municipality, including immigrants, regardless of nationality, receives welfare services. Benefits are not limited to people with a low income or those who have earned benefits through various insurance mechanisms – day care, child subsidies and free basic education all are examples of universal benefits. The fact that welfare services are intended for everyone maintains broad-based support for the welfare state even among the well-to-do, who view themselves as the net funders of such services (Blomberg-Kroll 1999).

The international integration of social security systems follows the general distribution system of ILO's general convention. The systems are divided into three columns that complement each other vertically, and into five horizontal areas of social security. Also EU legislation and internal legislation are based on this division, familiar in EU15 countries. The first column consists of actual social security, meaning all mandatory systems required by law, which defines all such benefits and the right to them. They are nearly always part of public administration, usually mandatory and funded through tax funds, tax-like fees or social security payments. The system in the second column complements the security of the first column through collective or employer- or business area-specific arrangements. Some systems in the second column may be mandatory and regulated by legal statutes, but they are not required by law in the same sense as the systems in the first column, because the law only applies to the ways in and conditions by which the funds or foundations operate, not to the benefits they grant or the right to such benefits. The system itself determines such conditions and rights. The third column represents private insurance provided by insurance companies. The line between columns 1 and 2 may be unclear at times, but the difference between columns 1 and 3 is always clear-cut. The first provides basic security, and there are differences between countries in terms of how much complementary insurance is needed and whether it mostly comes from column 2 or 3 (Kari et al. 2001, 7-9).

In Finland, social security traditionally comes from the first column, and the roles of 2 and 3 are lesser, though the importance of column 3's private insurance in particular is growing. The present study is concerned with the different ways in which people, who come from various types of systems, interpret the Finnish system. Commentary regarding a state that first taxes, then distributes the achievements of people who work for their income to "freeloaders" does not just reflect cultural difference, but also the tangibly different practices and laws of income distribution in systems that are basically similar. It is not always about profound cultural difference, but of laws and institutions that operate differently and that it is possible to change.

According to this study, in and of themselves public services do not constitute a pull factor to attract foreign experts, since they hardly use them. If all it took to entice immigrants was a strong welfare state, labour migrants would be better advised to opt for corporatist welfare states, where there are fewer entitlements and services, but whose quality – for those who are employed – is superior.

It would seem that the way in which the universalist, Nordic welfare society bolsters social stability, the feeling of security and prevents social isolation would be a more powerful pull factor for experts than whatever public services they are able to use. Instead of targeted public services, these characteristics can anchor skilled workers to their living environment. The first column's social security cannot be replaced by simply producing similar services within columns 2 or 3, because the gist is not the services and their quality, but the social harmony and stability that are a consequence of reduced social inequality. The issue is to achieve equality in income distribution without unreasonably obstructing the financial attainment opportunities of the highly educated.

Public health care as a competitive advantage?

Nordic welfare states are often marketed to foreign experts as a society that can offer high-quality public services equally to all citizens – a fact that is frequently used as a justification for high taxes. The quality of services should meet expectations – and as a result of all the marketing and the reputation that welfare societies have, they can be quite high. The data in this study revealed much the same, with respondents generally assigning a very high value on Finnish public services (Figure 10).

On the other hand, those who had actually used the services reported many problem areas or shortcomings in both quality and accessibility. The areas that received the most mentions (apart from immigration-related processes) were health care and children's schools. Not all issues are directly connected to the respondents being foreign and the problems that ensue from that, but had to do more generally with the quality of services in Finnish public organisations. If the welfare society and its services are supposed to justify the high taxes and are meant to entice more foreign workers, we should cast a critical eye on the services we produce as well as how they fit in with foreign experts, whose demographic is financially relatively well off.

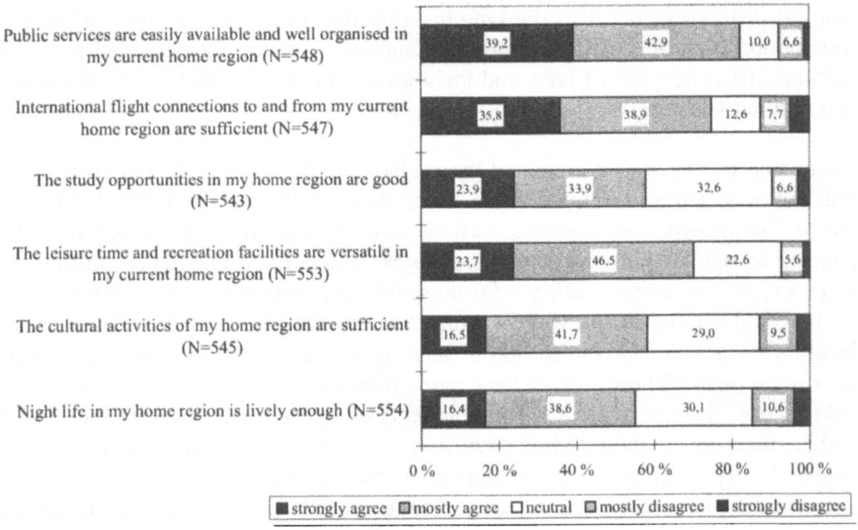

Figure 10. Satisfaction with functional environmental factors – ICT field. (source: Raunio 2003)

Baldwin-Edwards (2004) notes that even when there is universal health care, as in Belgium, the United Kingdom and Sweden, immigrants encounter serious difficulties in using it. For countries that have insurance-based systems, there are clearly greater problems, even including access to services (Baldwin-Edwards 2004, 329). To varying degrees, the same issues plague all systems regardless of how different they are in principle. In the case of skilled workers, the problems were minimised by their low level of participation in the services, possible assistance received from the human resources department of an employer, or agreements that were in place with local KELA branches. Nevertheless, those who did use the services encountered obvious problems, including eligibility of spouses and families for social security, and quality of services.

People had encountered problems in gaining eligibility to health-care services in the first place, as Baldwin-Edwards has described to be the case in many other European countries as well. Spouses in particular, but even some professionals who came to Finland for a job had problems obtaining the 'KELA card', which entitles the carrier to health care. Many respondents were never told that foreigners have the right to the same coverage for illness-related expenses as Finns. Several respondents reported that it took a relatively long time until they even became aware that there was such a thing as public health insurance.

Respondents found practices related to health care coverage, which were dependent on the length of residence in Finland or on the status of the residency permit, to be confusing. Many people were asked to re-file their applications, and the process was often slow moving. Major stumbling blocks in the process were lack of English-language skills among officials and letters addressed to foreigners that were written in Finnish. Companies themselves have made efforts to resolve problems by collaborating with local 'KELA' offices, and in some cases have been able to come up with new practices that work. It is fair to say that the public health-care system does not welcome foreigners with open arms, and if it takes a long time to gain access to services, this further erodes the motivation to pay the taxes that go toward maintaining the public sector's services. Even if, for individuals, there is value in the system in preserving social stability, the very fact that services are available to everyone can mean not only that those without means are served but also that there is a lack of high-quality services directed at highly paid individuals.

Often expectations that are placed on the quality of the system are too high, and the result is disappointment. Many respondents had negative experiences with the quality of health care, and those with a longer-term perspective on the services had noted a deterioration of health care.

> "Services have become worse over the last ten years. They were better when we first came here. But they're still acceptable."
>
> Estonian scientist

According to respondents, the right kind of treatment was not always available or the quality of service was poor, either when compared to their home country, or in general. Waiting periods were often thought to be unreasonably long. In part, these complaints are directed at the culture of the Finnish health-care system as an institution that is geared toward caring for a proactive client base, but in part they had to do with the actual quality of services. Many experts in the bioscience field have themselves received basic physician training, or reported turning to a colleague who was a physician. The opportunity that particularly people from former

Soviet areas or Eastern European countries had to obtain treatment at more affordable prices and in their own language won over turning to the Finnish health-care system.

"I myself am a doctor, so I take care of myself, and of course no-one can do it as well as I can. And the things that you can wait with, like the dentist, I take care of when I go home. It's better in the end when you can explain what you want in your own language. Even though I speak good English, they sometimes don't. For these reasons I have never used the health-care services here."

Russian scientist, in Finland for nine years

Many countries have a tradition of family physicians, where the same, familiar doctor cares for an entire family or all the relatives, in some cases from the beginning of the doctor's career all the way until retirement. A family doctor is almost like a member of the family and helps arrange health care for issues that are outside the sphere of his or her specialisation. Home visits are a normal way to consult with the sick patient. If used to the provision of such intimate services, it is perhaps difficult for a person from such a culture to appreciate the benefits of the Finnish service culture. The frequently long waiting periods, and bouncing patients from one place to another, take away from the personal, people-friendly nature of the service. In many cultures it is possible to see the doctor without any delay, or at the very least, to have a nurse assess the situation's acuteness as soon as the patient arrives at the doctor's office. Some respondents, whenever they had noted this, also expressed surprise at the use of student doctors as doctors – students who had either not yet graduated or were only in the process of becoming specialised. A student in the shoes of a physician – a position with very high prestige in many cultures – can erode the credibility of the system's quality.

Some respondents were, however, quite satisfied with the quality of the services they had received, for example, child-birth or other health-care services that required specialised treatment. Cultural or language problems were rarely mentioned, and most had been able to receive service in English. As clients and consumers, global experts probably demand greater service and quality, but are also culturally adaptable. Even though the quality and resources of Finland's health care are being debated even at a national level, the issue is exacerbated in the case of foreigners, who often expect concrete proof of the high quality of Nordic welfare services particularly in health care. The fact that the services are "free" does not necessarily represent a major advantage for skilled workers, because in countries with less comprehensive health care systems employers often pay for employees' private health insurance.

In the United States, for example, most full-time employees and their dependents are entitled to employer-sponsored health insurance. Improvements have also been made in recent years to employees' ability to retain health insurance when they change jobs, and to the coverage of family members (Kari, Laitinen-Kuikka & Markwort 2001, 214). Skilled workers are thus able to use the services of private doctors as part of their employer's benefits package, as through taxation in Finland. It is nevertheless true that private insurance does not extend to spouses or families as automatically as in the Finnish system – another sign of the family-orientedness of welfare societies.

Is a nationally successful education system attractive in the international context?

Another often-mentioned system of public service is comprehensive school. By a slight margin, the majority of ICT respondents wanted to place their children in a Finnish school with teaching conducted in Finnish (Table 9). But over half of families with two foreign parents favoured an international school or a Finnish curriculum taught in English. The popularity of official international schools is probably tempered by relatively high tuition fees. However, 37 percent of respondents with a Finnish spouse wanted their children either in an English-language Finnish school or an official international school. Sometimes, the availability of an English-language school is a precondition for a family remaining in the country.

"If we don't get the kids into an English-language school in Tampere, we'll go – otherwise, we'll stay."

ICT expert, India

"Salo does not offer enough English-language schooling opportunities for when my child reaches the normal school age in Britain."

ICT expert, united Kingdom

People often time their relocation to accommodate children's schooling, so that they can enrol in the home country or possibly in a third, frequently English-speaking country. It seems that, families with school-age children are most likely to remain in place, at least for the duration of the children's education. The issue has therefore less to do with finding Finnish schools deficient, and more to do with valuing the preparation that a different growth environment and English-language or home culture is perceived to offer to a child's development. While a high ranking in international school system comparisons, such as PISA, is important, individuals also place a key value on factors such as learning a particular culture or social conventions. This points not only to the need to invest in the quality of education but also in its diversity and applicability in the transnational job and education markets. The challenge to a school system that many view as the longest-standing pillar of the nation-state and a builder of national culture is notable (Castells 1997; Allardt 1988). How is it possible to convert a bastion of national culture into something that produces citizens of the world, who are able to succeed in the global operating environment? For many, the possibility of learning Finnish as a native language gives pause.

Table 9. What type of school would you prefer your children attend – according to spouse's nationality (%) – ICT field

What type of school do you prefer? (%)	*Nationality of spouse*		
	Finnish	*Non-Finnish*	*Total*
Finnish, taught in Finnish	61	44	52
Finnish, taught in English	17	22	20
Official international school	20	33	27
Special pedagogy (Steiner, etc.)	2	2	2
Total	100	100	100
N	176	192	368

Apart from substance, if the school system does not convince with its cultural and social expertise, it is fairly unlikely that foreigners will choose to send their children to a Finnish school in favour of a school in the home country or another school system that garners international respect. The quality of teaching at official international schools, as well as English-language schools or classes frequently gets evaluated on the basis of language alone. Moreover, typical Finnish customs, such as the relative freedom of students in school-related routines and other school activities should be better explained to parents of foreign students – to someone on the outside, such freedom may look more like indifference. The independent work ethic that adults encounter in the Finnish workplace already manifests in schools, but to a person from another culture, it may be interpreted as something else altogether.

"Over here, an hour before school starts, the children are already playing and fighting in the school yard, and also afterwards. In the U.S. children are taken to school and the school takes responsibility for them, and they get picked up when school is over. The structure is much clearer. Schools here also perhaps have less structure in terms of teaching and in providing guidance to students. There's more of a do-it-yourself mentality, and that's something of a problem for my son. In the U.S. the discipline was almost military and the kids were given clear limits as to what was allowed and what was not. That was good for the kids. If there was a fight or some other problem, it became a big deal at the school and at home, and that was that. Here they don't seem to care what kids do in the playground. Sometimes my son comes home from school crying, after someone has beaten him up. In the States we're not used to this kind of thing."

Spouse, United States

"Well, if you compare schools in Estonia --- I do think it's a bit lax here, in primary and later on in secondary school. There could be better order... The reins are a bit tighter in Estonia, they require a little more, and here, it feels like they often require nothing at all."

Estonian scientist

Schools play a critical role, and in the process of creating new generations of multicultural experts, it is essential that parents have faith in schools' ability to offer the best possible education for their children. Teachers' multicultural preparedness is becoming increasingly important when classrooms no longer consist exclusively of the children of the majority culture. In a broader sense, multiculturally oriented schools also help children adapt to a new culture, which – at least when a family moves repeatedly – can be very stressful. Various mechanisms geared to facilitate the adapting process can significantly enhance a region's draw in the eyes of people who come from different cultures and language areas.

A number of foreign spouses underlined the critical role of the culture of child-rearing and role models in a high-quality school system. The perception of Finland's "free" views on child-rearing may seem to complicate the formation of good manners and a well-developed social identity. In the long term, schools in particular bear responsibility for adapting the second generation of immigrants to Finnish society and for shaping the impressions that those who leave the country form about Finland.

In our study, Chinese bioscience researchers differed from other professionals in their views regarding children's education. Most planned to return to China at least when it was time for their children to begin school. According to these respondents, it would be difficult to enter the Chinese school system midway through, and remaining "in the West" with the children would mean that they would miss out on the opportunity to achieve success in the Chinese system. Chinese respondents also made quite far-reaching career plans, and in those plans, children's schooling was a key consideration.

"... We have to plan now, because in China, if our child has been in school here and we want to return to China, it will be impossible to gain a grasp of the Chinese school system, because it's more demanding than here. So we have to plan carefully whether we should put our son in school here, go back to China, or go somewhere else – it's important. We have to decide what kind of culture we want to attach him to, and he can then decide himself if he wants to have a career in China or somewhere else. But the problem is that if you don't take your child back to China in time, he'll lose his chance to become successful there."

Chinese scientist, father of a one-year-old child

Foreigners encounter the same difficulties as Finnish citizens in enrolling their children in a particular day-care centre or school, or obtaining fast, efficient service whenever they require health care. The particular problems with health care affecting our target group were in the system in general, rather than being connected to multicultural issues. The lack of discipline and shortage of structured activities was viewed as a lack of overall structure, which is related to the view of the country's perhaps excessively free-form philosophy of child rearing. The same phenomenon probably occurs in the workplace: the emphasis on individuality and independent initiative is a natural aspect of Finnish culture, and moreover, is also reflected in health services, schools and day-care centres, all designed for self-organising individuals, and extends to many other public services as well.

According to the study's findings, highly educated immigrants have less appreciation for welfare society's services as such, although they do value the way that they are reflected more generally in society in the form of security, social stability and a well-oiled infrastructure. These characteristics have evolved in Finland specifically because the welfare society targets all services, including education, to the entire population, reduces inequality and prevents the segregation of a society whose two extremes are, on the one hand, the wealthy who invest in their own security mechanisms, and on the other, the underprivileged who have ended up in society's grey zones. Equality-oriented public services and entitlements can have meaning for foreign experts in that they determine the degree to which such welfare society mechanisms guarantee a safe and peaceful environment and quality infrastructure. Hiding behind cultural difference is not useful in this instance – in the end, it is the system and how well it functions that are at issue.

9 New elements of competitiveness – living environment

The individual's point of view brings in a new element to be given consideration in the global competition for talent: the living environment. Although the living environment as such is not enough to attract global talent, it is an important part of the competitiveness of a region and should not be omitted when policies are being created for succeeding in the global knowledge economy. This chapter illustrates the role of living environment and local culture as elements of competitiveness.

We get one step closer to the heart of local culture when we examine the everyday living environment of individuals. Instead of focusing just on the social system and its institutions, we will consider the physical, functional and social dimensions of the living environment. For a long time now, the quality of the living environment has been an important focus of urban development and initiatives to attract skilled workers. A good living environment has also traditionally been one of the basic components of regional development strategies based in technology and expertise, as well as a basic requirement for attracting skilled labour. Particularly in regional development that is founded on knowledge and high-technology, the role of the living environment is seen as a factor that influences the ability to attract commerce, investment and skilled workers (Willoughby 1995; Saxenian 1989; 2 Castells & Himanen 2001). Studies examining such overall policy recommendations have found, however, that a region's professional and career opportunities are an especially strong determinant of where skilled workers go (Green 1997; Malecki & Bradbury 1992).

Nevertheless, living environments do play a role in how competitive urban centres can be, although it does not make sense to look at their environments apart from the professional and career opportunities, discussed in previous chapters. A high-quality living environment can also bring direct, economic benefits to companies. Numerous studies show that they are able to save on wages in regions that offer high-quality living environments, because employers are often forced to compensate for less attractive environments by offering higher wages (Granger 1993; Granger & Blomquist 1999).

There is proof that a high quality of life is attractive, and many urban centres have tried to shape this into a pull factor to attract global capital. It is no coincidence that in recent years, quality-of-life rankings and listings for cities have been so visible in the media (Rogerson 1999, 982). Simply put, regions that can offer a high quality of life will also attract human resources. Some claim that the wonderful living environments and their high quality of life in certain areas came about precisely as a result of developments in high-tech commerce, rather than being the instigator for them (Rogerson 2000). The multiple interpretations and definitions of 'quality of life' and 'living environment' are often the concepts used to explain an area's attractiveness. For a better grasp, we will divide the characteristics that make a region inviting into five main elements, of which career and economic considerations were already discussed. The other three components are the physical, operational and social dimensions in an environment (Raunio 2001: Linnamaa 1999). The most visible recent discussion of this issue has been the creative class's location preferences as described by Richard Florida (2002). He too divides the environment – or the quality of place, as he expresses it – into the three areas used here. Quality of place describes the unique combination of characteristics that can make a region inviting and ideal also in the eyes of the transnational creative class. In other words, quality of place contains three ideal dimensions, which, adapting Florida, can be defined as follows:

- What's there: combination of natural and developed environments, or the physical environment that provides the backdrop for creative lifestyles.
- Who's there: diversity of the population and the relationships among its groups, which may make the inclusion of new arrivals to the community possible – the social environment.
- What happens there: urban forms of life, such as culture and street life – the operational environment (Florida 2002).

For individuals, these ideal dimensions describe the physical, social and operational environment that shapes life outside of work. Studies not only in the United States but also in the U.K. and Sweden have pointed to the increased significance of the living environment also in internal migration between different regions (Laakso & Loikkanen 2000; Breheny 1999). In an international assessment, it is useful to emphasise the characteristics of Finland's urban centres, including a small population and the environment's small-town ambiance.

In evaluating the attractiveness of Finland's urban centres, their size and characteristics are important. International urban research has found that the declining quality of life in cities is especially connected to the flight of wealthy and middle-class populations from urban areas. There is talk of so-called de-urbanisation, as social conditions, physical environment and availability of services decline. In international discourse, the problem cities are usually the world's great metropolitan areas, and the migration away from them is toward small towns and semi-rural surrounding areas of metropolitan areas. In terms of their size, with the exception of Helsinki, Finnish city regions are more comparable to the definition of a small town or semi-rural environment.

In the United States, for example, Malecki and Bradbury, in their study on the importance of living environment in selecting a location, define an urban centre as a place with over one million inhabitants, while medium-sized and small cities are defined as those with fewer than one million inhabitants (ibid. 1992). In Britain, Breheny (et al. 1999) have defined as a small town or semi-rural area a place with fewer than 250,000 inhabitants and as an urban area a concentration of over

750,000 inhabitants. In Finland, the only urban centre with more than one million people is the Helsinki metropolitan region, other city regions having between 150,000 and 300,000 inhabitants.

In numerous international studies that have found semi-rural physical or social environments to attract businesses and skilled workers (Green 1997; Breheny 1999; Rogerson 1999), such areas have mostly been of a comparable size to Finnish city regions, located a reasonable distance away from major cities. According to Wiklund (1995), the particular nature of Finnish urban areas also differs from the dense, urban life of Central European cities quite markedly. "Northern cities" are by nature spacious and adjacent to nature. Even Finland's sole urban metropolis, Helsinki, is very close to natural areas and is a typical Nordic urban area, where even the most problem-ridden section of town is a far cry from the slums of the big cities. Even Finns who do live in cities have a very close relationship with nature, and in this sense live a "non-urban" way of life even in the Helsinki metropolitan area, at least outside its immediate downtown centre (Wiklund 1995; Helsinki by district 2004).

Finnish people generally find their living environments satisfactory, which probably has a lot to do specifically with being a "northern city" and the fact that even Finland's city regions look more like small towns when measured by international standards (see Strandell 1998). The typical problems of big cities (rush hour, lack of safety, expensive real estate etc.) are often associated with all cities without taking into account their vastly divergent appearance, particularly of city regions. The Helsinki metropolitan area is in fact a large city that is only in the process of becoming congested, and all of the other city regions have exactly that attractive small town ambiance that was so often mentioned in the technology-driven regional development plans of the 1980s (see Saxenian 1989; Tattari 1989). Very similar patterns and environmental qualities – a dominating but still quite small-town-like capital city-region – may be found in all of the Nordic countries.

9.1 Living environment

Most of the study's foreign respondents had adapted well to their Finnish living environment and considered it functional and satisfactory, in spite of the relative scarcity of architectural brilliance or historic towns. For the most part, factors like cleanness, functionality, small-town character and proximity of nature are the qualities that Finnish urban environments can offer to those from elsewhere. Among ICT professionals, 66 percent of respondents agreed completely with the statement "My living environment is clean and unpolluted", and 28 percent agreed with it for the most part (n=548). Many bioscience researchers took engaged in outdoor activities, and for them, nature was especially meaningful.

"I like Helsinki a lot. I like the planning. You can access nearby woods no matter where you live. You can find nature whenever and wherever. We like to cycle and this place offers great opportunities for that."

Scientist, Russia

When dissatisfaction with the living environment did emerge, an internal move within the region often resolved the issue. Generally, unhappiness with the home occurs in the early phase, while living in temporary quarters or a hastily acquired home. Among ICT respondents, 35 percent completely agreed with the statement "The quality of my home is sufficient", and 45 percent agreed with it for the most part. Living conditions or living environment in particular did not pose an actual obstacle to committing to a place. When people become accustomed to the environment and learn to function in it, they often find it pleasant and relaxing. Small-town living can also be combined with economic wellbeing, especially when living in the suburbs of bigger cities or surrounding communities.

"My salary went down significantly when I moved to Finland, but this house is much cheaper than it would be in England, and food too is more affordable. In fact, my economic wellbeing increased, because here we don't need a car. In England I drove a hundred kilometres to work every day, and even had to use additional time to avoid rush hour. Now I cycle to work in ten minutes."

ICT expert, United Kingdom

Although Finnish urban areas are growing and the Helsinki metropolitan area can offer distinctly big city-like characteristics, cleanness, lack of pollution and safety continue to be Finland's strong points when measured on the international scale. Sixty-three percent of ICT professionals completely agreed with the statement "My living environment is safe" and 33 percent agreed for the most part (n=547). For people who come from unstable conditions, the fact that Finland is safe means a lot, as many respondents who originally came from former Soviet areas emphasised.

"Security… because of my background, because of where I come from. The security of everyday life, safety at night, a safe place to live, and a safe and stable society are all really important. Every time I go back home on holiday, weeks in advance I have to start thinking about it, preparing myself not to keep my wallet here [points to back pocket] or dress the way I do here, and things like that."

Scientist from the former Soviet Union

"It's so stable here that I never have to worry about anyone trying to kill me or cause trouble. The situation is so stable that you really hardly have to think about things like, what if the army interferes, or there's some kind of collapse."

Scientist from the former Soviet Union

Security, which is reflected in stable working conditions, emerged as a strength, and even as a pull factor, also among the officials and academic managers interviewed for this study. Female scientists in particular – even from relatively stable nations – stated that Finland's strength lies in gender equality, which translates to safety and a relative absence of street and workplace harassment. Respondents felt that it was a special luxury to be able to be out when it was dark, or in out-of-the-way areas. When discussing the country's safety, they referred not only to the instability of their countries of origin, but also to the threat of international terrorism. The question is how Finland can distinguish itself among hundreds of city regions with its safety or the high quality of its services, which are not special as such, but because of the backdrop that they create for living and working.

"I don't really like big cities. Small ones like Kemi and Oulu are OK; friendly and safe... Well, all the towns are safe when you compare them to Russia."

ICT expert, Russia

On the other hand, the spaciousness and quality of living are not always of a particularly high level, considering the target group of skilled professionals who are a relatively well-off demographic group. Some from countries such as the United States, Australia and others expressed surprise at the small size of homes in such a sparsely populated country. Living expenses are also relatively high in the centres of the larger cities and in Helsinki, even in international terms. This can be a problem for people – and not just those who come from countries with a lower standard of living.

"Living is also kind of a problem. We had much more living space in the States compared to here, you have to adjust to that – but we knew that and we have to adapt to the change. It's not just the size of the homes; it's surprising somehow that in a country this sparsely populated, people live in such cramped, expensive quarters. We were shocked about the prices, because living here is almost as expensive as in Boston, but the homes are smaller."

Spouse, United States

"We had problems finding a home with a garden at a reasonable price. The price of real estate in Helsinki is close to the level of Paris and London."

ICT expert, France

The home and the immediate living environment as such were not a problem area in the adaptation process, and cultural issues did not come up either. The factors that rendered the physical environment somewhat less interesting – though not exceedingly so – were the slightly boring and plain style of Finnish urban architecture.

In terms of living environment, the collision of cultures occurred mostly when people were looking for a new home. Finnish landlords are not always very willing to rent to foreigners, which can make it difficult to find an apartment. It also gives a negative image of Finns' attitudes toward foreigners and reduces the chances, when first moving to the country, of finding an apartment that meets expectations. Many people are faced with this problem even when their employer agrees to act as guarantor for their first home. On the other hand, when people settle for an apartment they are not happy with and want to change to a new one soon after moving, this creates additional work for the employer and causes stress for the new immigrant, who is probably already engaged in several other adapting processes. As far as living, respondents were satisfied with the developed environment, but the urban architecture or the diversity of homes received no accolades. Some Eastern European respondents felt that the environment was more reminiscent of the cities of the old Eastern Block than other European countries, and for this reason, felt somewhat familiar.

In a broader sense, adapting to a living environment is tied to geography and climate. Although some respondents viewed the changing of the seasons as positive changes in the environment, many from more southern climates talked about the depressing impact of the dark autumns and winters as they faced their third winter in Finland. Respondents found themselves gaining a greater understanding of the local culture when they themselves experienced the growing melancholy that Finnish people tend to as autumn wears along. On the other hand were feelings of oppression and a desire to leave that was sometimes exacerbated by this natural phenomenon.

"Oh yes, of course, the climate, I forgot about that, sorry, now that the winter is almost over – but it is too long. In the beginning of the winter I thought that I could take it, but by the end I became almost desperate. But there's nothing you can do about the climate, I guess."

Scientist from Central Europe, interviewed in April

"I am going to leave in three to five years because of the weather."

ICT expert, France

Overall, the smoothly functioning, safe living environment helped commit respondents, even though the long, lightless winter acted as something of a deterrent to the commitment of some respondents who were used to a different climate. Nevertheless, climate is less of a barrier to immigration than is often touted in public discourse. Canada and Sweden, for example, are tempting destinations for a great many immigrants, even though their climate is very similar to Finland. The natural environment, forests and hiking paths and trails also represented an important way to relax for many respondents, much as for Finns themselves.

Nevertheless, the physical environment has more of an impact on deciding to stay on in a particular area, rather than being a deciding factor in selecting it in the first place. The quality of physical surroundings has a direct relationship with personal physical and psychological wellbeing. For example, the importance of nature, parks and even individual elements of the natural world in stress relief and recovery is substantial. The recovery can be about getting over the fatigue of long-term time investment at work or stress in a physiological, psychological or even functional sense (Ulrich 1984; Kaplan & Kaplan 1989). It is good to remember, however, that people accustomed to living in cities do not necessarily find nature and forests pleasant and invigorating; instead, they can even seem threatening and frightening.

9.2 Increasingly international urban areas

Global innovators adapt easily, and the respondents in this study too generally found the services in Finnish urban areas to be satisfactory. The question "What could the urban area offer or do to improve its attractiveness and make it easier for foreigners to settle there?" did not elicit many answers. One issue respondents underlined was the importance of the availability of English-language information about both private and public services. A particular wish was for it to be possible to conduct financial transactions (bill payment, bank services etc.) in English. This has in fact occurred in various urban centres, and respondents who were using those services several years ago reported that, on the basis of comments heard from other foreigners or through their own recent experiences, the situation had improved. Topographically, Finnish culture is actively becoming more and more international. Other desires with regard to services required more thought, indicating that the need for those improvements was not very acute – as far as services, areas seen as needing possible improvement included grocery stores selling ethnic food, language skills among bus drivers, the overall service culture and quality and friendliness of service, and the availability of various free-time activities and banking services in English. More than to remarkable problem areas, this points more to a lack of shortcomings.

Other services offered by Finnish urban areas seemed to meet respondents' needs, very well even. Libraries, running tracks, local transportation and other services provided by society were often cited as organised and of a good quality (Figure 10). Spouses were often somewhat less satisfied with services than their employed partners. The homogeneity of Finnish culture and a certain appreciation of simplicity are also manifested in the selections that stores offer.

"Finland is not a consumer or media culture. It's really difficult to find a new model of something, or fashionable clothing, maybe because there is so little competition. The "country" mentality of many Finns gives you the impression that they'd rather be living in the woods, picking berries and swimming in lakes. Not that it would not be a pleasant experience, but living in a European capital I do expect certain products and services to be available."

ICT expert, Britain

Indeed, Finland is not a likely destination for urban city dwellers, and is more appreciated by people who value small-town living and peace and quiet. Many international studies support this view regarding the insignificance of various cultural services or urban nightlife among the factors that make an urban area attractive (see, for example, Castells & Himanen 2001). In our study, the availability of cultural services and nightlife had the lowest ranking as 'very' or 'relatively important' factors in choosing a location and living environment. Most respondents felt that in terms of nightlife, there were enough pubs, restaurants and nightclubs, or even too many. The foremost problem they mentioned was Finnish drinking culture, which really lets loose in the above social arenas.

"I knew that alcoholism was a problem, but Finnish people really do not seem to know that you can also drink to enjoy something, not just to become completely inebriated."

ICT expert, United Kingdom

As a whole, though, the services available in urban areas did not seem to be viewed as problematic by foreign experts. They may have seemed slightly reduced and simple compared to the world's big cities, but they did function well and met respondents' needs. The lack of available English-language services caused greater problems, though such services continue to proliferate. The availability of Russian-language services even received praise, indicating yet another way in which Finnish cities are starting to look and feel more international. It should be noted, however, the operational environment, i.e. "what happens there", is closely tied to another, possibly more critical element of personal wellbeing: the shaping of the social environment. The power that services and the physical environment have to bind people to a place comes from the multiple meanings that are intertwined with them. For example, opportunities for free-time and other activities encourage commitment by way of operational and social factors associated therein – apart from relaxation and self-actualisation, they also support social interaction and the formation of social networks. Ability to participate in desired activities or the presence of nightlife are not necessarily in themselves enough to firmly anchor an individual expert to a particular urban centre, but the social interaction that occurs as their side-effect does help to bind people (see Gehl 1987).

To exaggerate slightly, the assessment of Finland in the "what happens there" category is that nothing much does. Instead of nightlife and street beat, people are able to enjoy a peaceful environment and outdoor activities. Neither benefit is a stand-alone reason to move to the country, but as Finland strives to construct its appeal, the advantages it can be said to offer do include characteristics that derive from such national traits as an unhurried pace of life, a pleasant environment and trust – mixed in with an international atmosphere and high-level professional opportunities. Many respondents found this equation to be ideal as an alternative to the combination of a hectic work pace and an even more hectic life in a big city, which many had personally experienced.

9.3 Lattetowns 'and local culture

Social environment, here, is divided into social interaction and local culture. Each plays a different role in adapting and committing to a place. Social interaction was already discussed in connection with work environment, but its role in people's private lives is possibly even greater – particularly in the adjustment of the spouses of skilled immigrants. It is not, however, limited to interaction between individuals, but is also reflected in the majority population's attitudes toward foreigners.

The 'spirit' of a place, or "genius loci", can be viewed as the external image of a particular place's identity. Practice and spoken word often refer to identity as 'atmosphere'. This means the "spiritual atmosphere" or "vibe" that the region emanates or that one senses when operating in the environment. Atmosphere is a highly subjective concept, but different countries and regions do have their own, unique atmospheres and the images that they reflect. An area's atmosphere is not an actual pull factor, though it does inhibit flow to regions by eliminating places that people consider unsuitable for themselves. An accepting atmosphere that is open to outsiders is thought of as positive and easy to adjust to.

This type of atmosphere is usually linked to larger university towns and international hubs of innovation. Academic institutions and international corporations are thought of as natural "recycling mechanisms" of different individuals – through their operations, they can shape an atmosphere toward openness. The impact of an atmosphere created by friends and people with similar interests is significant when deciding where to live. 'People with similar interests' does not necessarily refer to people who a skilled immigrant already knows, but in general to people who share similar interests and preferences (see Ritsilä 2000). An atmosphere can act as a barrier to moving, when those outside the region think that it can significantly influence their quality of life. An atmosphere that feels like a barrier usually deviates from the lifestyle or ideals of an expert in some crucial way. It may be an excessively hectic big-city culture or an introverted, watchful small-town culture. The two opposites usually share a perceived difficulty of forming social relationships.

In the experience of foreign skilled workers, the same reserve characterises both Finland's general atmosphere and its people. It does not exhibit itself as overt racism or hostility, but more as passivity in interaction between people and as the exclusion of strangers outside of existing communities. Only 11 percent of respondents completely agreed that the atmosphere in their living environment was open and the people easy to approach (Figure 11). Nor are conditions for the formation of new multicultural communities or *global social spaces* particularly favourable, because of the small number of foreigners. It is also complicated by a local culture whose special Finnish feature is the combination of high technology and "small-town living". All of the special characteristics of Finnish working life and society discussed above are crystallised in this combination.

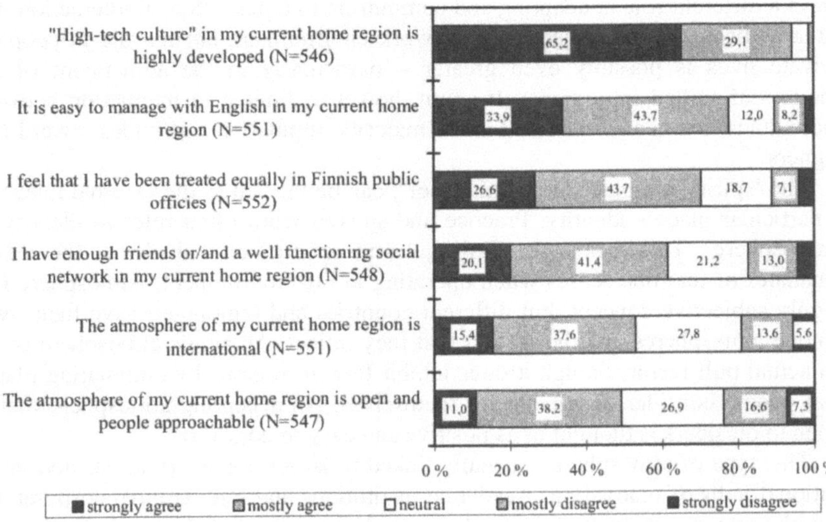

Figure 11. Satisfaction with social environment and local culture – ICT field. (source: Raunio 2003)

The social environment in Finland is quite friendly, but it can remain closed to foreigners because of a reserved culture of interaction and communication. As many foreigners reported, it can be difficult to approach Finns just to chat – spontaneous everyday communication can be quite limited. One must be proactive to make contacts; Finns, with their respect for the individual and for privacy, often wait for a hint from the other party before interaction can begin.

Approximately 60 percent of respondents completely or mostly agreed with the statement that they had enough friends in the area where they presently lived (Figure 11). Some 40 percent were dissatisfied with their present situation, and considering the international nature of their work environments, the figure is high. Once they made Finnish friends, foreigners considered them "good and trustworthy friends". This probably refers to the lack of hierarchy in Finnish society – friendship is "real" and not merely associated with a particular area of life or a way of social interaction (see Tropenaars & Hampden-Turner 1998).

"People are extremely nice both at work and outside of work. Difficult to approach, but afterwards very nice and friendly. People have very few prejudices and they are open to other nationalities and cultures. The near-universal ability to speak English makes communicating easier."

ICT expert, United States

Table 10. Nationality of friends, and plans for the future (cross tabulated) – ICT field. (N= 551) %

Nationality of friends/ *Plans for the future*	*Mostly Finnish*	*Mostly foreigners*	*Mostly the same nationality as myself*	*Finnish and foreign*	*Total*
I will remain in Finland permanently	45	17	15	24	25
I will return to my own country	17	25	23	20	21
I will move to another country	13	41	26	24	26
I have not yet thought about it	25	18	36	31	28
Total	100	100	100	100	100
N	89	118	80	264	551

Problems in the formation of social relationships are exacerbated by the lack of Finnish-language skills among foreign experts, the small scale of immigrant communities outside of the Helsinki metropolitan area, and the Finnish culture of communicating and interacting. Compared with other countries, people are required to make more of an effort to create arenas for meeting people, because the conditions for creating such a culture are traditionally – and continue to this day to be – relatively weak.

Many respondents reported attempting to learn Finnish but giving up because of the seeming impossibility of the task. On the other hand, many global experts and their spouses never even intend to learn the language. Twenty-three percent of respondents said that they spoke Finnish, but most of them had a Finnish spouse. One-quarter of respondents among bioscience experts reported being able to manage everyday matters with the Finnish that they knew. Those with a Finnish partner had easier access to social networks and were more naturally motivated to learn the language than foreign couples or single individuals.

The incentive to learn Finnish varied by workplace. Larger ICT corporations offered opportunities for language training, and some units required the ability to speak Finnish for social reasons to facilitate adjustment, and conversely also expected sufficient ability of Finns to communicate in English to ensure smooth operations in work tasks. The working language in those units was English. Scientists who worked in academic departments assessed the university-provided language training as poor because of large class sizes, class times or long distance from the workplace. Living environments were characterised as places where "everyone" spoke English and responded in English to foreigners' attempts to communicate in Finnish. Thus, the incentive to learn Finnish is weak in society as a whole, even away from the official English communication culture of the workplace.

Earlier studies (for example, Forsander 2002b; Paananen 1999) have supported the interpretation that Finns continue to expect foreigners to remain in their own social niche, without language skills, but preferably as an English-speaking guest of the country who, completely uncritical, is full of admiration for Finnish society. It is difficult to transition to an immigrant with plans to remain permanently and become Finnish. People admire foreigners who try to learn Finnish and become part of society "by converting their identity toward Finnishness", but it is not especially encouraged, not to mention automatically expected.

"At work, if you speak in English to someone, they'll respond in English, but naturally when they address other Finns, they do it in Finnish, and in this way you miss out on a lot of information. So, sometimes you don't know that there's a meeting or something, because naturally people are talking about it in their own language. In my opinion this amounts to a kind of glass ceiling, because as you advance in this career, at some point you are expected to teach, and if the courses are in Finnish, of course you won't be able to teach. And so you can't move ahead beyond that. This is really a problem."

Eastern European bioscience researcher

Apart from a few exceptions, respondents did not express a desire to become a permanent and full-fledged part of "Finnishness", but did want greater opportunities to feel like an equal member of the community. Inability to speak Finnish also restricts people's ability to interact socially in society. In the workplace, the consequence of frequently remaining on the outside of informal flows of information poses difficulties in career advancement.

Very seldom or only occasionally had anyone experienced racism or overt prejudice. None of the respondents had personally experienced violence, but had heard stories. Some had been a target of verbal harassment, though only incidentally. Some had experienced discrimination, but not everyone was certain that it was a case of conscious discrimination or a situation that they had experienced as discriminatory because of being a foreigner. In working life and elsewhere in society, skin colour was a factor that influenced discrimination.

Canadian research makes a distinction between visible and invisible immigrants and minorities. Visible foreigners experience more frequent and are more frequently targets of discrimination, regardless of their legal status (Breton et al. 1990; Pohjanpää et al. 2003). The findings of the present study support this view, even though there were relatively few experiences of overt racism among respondents. Seventy-three percent of Northern European respondents felt that the treatment they had received in public institutions was either completely or mostly equal, but among Chinese respondents, only 45 felt the same (Figure 11).

"No real experience with xenophobia, just isolated occurrences that I've heard about. Experiences with public organisations have been very encouraging, and the tax office in particular was very helpful. I have heard that some people with darker skin have come across problems in the bureaucracy, but compared with other countries it seems minimal. And I can't say how much of it is real discrimination and what is just perceived as discrimination. I have some experience with Italy, and I would say that things are better in Finland. I don't mean, however, that discrimination doesn't exist."

ICT expert, United States

"I have to say, regarding discrimination against foreigners in Finland, that if it exists, I have not experienced it. Except a number of times in bars when we're speaking Russian, someone will walk up and say 'you're Russian, aren't you?' And this historical stuff is a sensitive area. But in general things are fine."

Scientist from the former Soviet Union

"Selective racism" reflects Finnish attitudes about foreigners. Numerous earlier studies have found more negative attitudes toward darker-skinned foreigners compared with those who externally resemble Finns more, and our study corroborated this. The phenomenon seemed to apply to all wakes of life, in both work and private life. Finns and foreigners said that people who look distinctly different and particularly those with darker skin are more likely to experience discrimination in private life and in public institutions. As a whole, respondents thought that there was relatively little direct discriminatory or racist behaviour toward foreign experts in Finnish society.

Two phenomena stand out in Finnish local culture and give it its unique flavour: "small-town living" and the availability and applicability of high technology. The latter is often associated with a generally well-functioning society. In the social landscape, "small-town living" takes many shapes: Finnish society is characterised by a uniformity of lifestyles; people are fairly quiet and withdrawing but basically friendly; working life is not excessively competitive; the appreciation of families is manifested in both working life and on a societal level; and the environment is characterised by the proximity of nature – the congestion of big cities is often hard to find even in Helsinki. When this is joined with the lack of competitiveness or hectic lifestyles that describe many Anglo-Saxon cultures, and when one adds to this long vacations and a flexible working life that favours families, the whole that is formed provides a possibility for a lifestyle that trumps any of its individual components.

The Finnish lifestyle is relatively far removed from the hectic flows of the global economy, and indeed, most respondents did not view Finnish urban areas as particularly international (Figure 11). It is nonetheless these very factors that made Finland an interesting choice for some of the respondents. It is not easy to derive a competitive advantage out of external factors such as the good quality and safety of the living environment when faced with the competition of other urban centres.

"Finns are very honest and hard working. I think that the Finnish way of life is terrific and I am trying to adopt it and its practices in my own life. Finns become your friends because they want to, not because the can use you somehow. Finland is a safe and beautiful land and it feels like home. I don't ever want to leave."

ICT expert, United States

Basic Finnish values and the corresponding societal traits came across clearly enough. Most of the characteristics that shape this phenomenon are rooted in the welfare society ideology and in Finnish culture itself. Respondents particularly highlighted the trust placed in social operators and individuals. Here was a general trust in officials, even though people did not always understand the ways in which they operate or even though their actions were considered anti-foreigner to some extent. Trust can be seen as a valuable resource not only in the relationships between individuals but also in a business sense. In the corporate world, relationships between people play an ever-greater role, and so does trust in general. Associating trust with a particular society and community creates the image of a safe operating environment.

For a skilled worker operating in the global competitive culture, this kind of environment can offer an opportunity to apply his or her talents while at the same time enjoying a peaceful pace in other areas of life. This can even take the form of assimilation, which usually refers to people from elsewhere adopting the local culture and identity even more emphatically than locals.

"Actually, I like the quietness of social life and that it's OK to not constantly be part of the conversation and engage in small talk. In Latin cultures it's exhausting when, if you enjoy solitude, it is perceived as a problem, and people ask 'what's wrong' if you are not constantly participating in conversation and in social engagements."

Biotechnology expert, France

The "small-town living" and high-tech everyday of the Finnish environment can be said to flavour all of the social and workplace phenomena that make Finland, on the one hand, an interesting choice, but on the other hand, one that is not easy to approach. For the most part, it is easy to operate, but getting beneath the culture's superficial veneer is more challenging. Once one understands the gist of Finnish culture, it is easier to also understand its manifestations in the surrounding culture more broadly. The feeling of being an outsider in both the work community and in society as a whole consists of many components, and being an outsider clearly marginalises or even propels individuals away from marginalising environments. The point is that several cultural and societal qualities are interwoven with local physical and functional environments, providing the unique combination of living environment with specific local flavour. Still, in terms of attractiveness, without doubt social environment plays a major role while functional and physical environments function primarily as platforms for this social action

10 From national fortress to global networks

It is time to sum up the conclusions and the morale of our findings. What are the pivotal points we should learn from all this, in order to more profoundly understand the dynamic of global talent migration and to build more functional and equal societies in the global age? The main message consists of two parts. The first part emphasises that the long-lasting tradition of protection in our national system should be intentionally broken down in many parts, and we should focus on building more open platforms for global networks, in order to connect with the global pool of talent. Innovation environments, if not the labour market as a whole, should be connected to global brain circulation and mobile labour. This means a more significant role for regional development practices, in collaboration with national policies, to connect regions with global resources using sophisticated tools. The second part reminds that sophisticated micro-level analyses are needed in order to recognise the dynamics behind these processes and policy making.

For two decades, we have been talking about the global economy and the information economy. In the meantime, many other trendy concepts have also been invented to describe society and economy. It is the authors' claim, however, that the shift toward a globalising knowledge economy is the core dynamic of this phenomenon – the global operating environment and knowledge as part of the production process. All subsequent interpretations of "the creative class", "attention economy" or "network society" and so forth strive to explain this phenomenon with such an essential impact on our society and economy (Glaeser & Saiz 2003; Florida 2004; Nonaka & Takeuchi 1995; Cooke 1998; Davenport & Beck 2001; Castells 1996). All of the different interpretations share a view of high-quality human capital as the key resource for any society, region or organisation operating in the global environment. These interpretations reveal the need for new policies able to deal with the movement of human capital in a global environment.

Our focus, the case of Finland, offers an illuminative example how things change along with a new viewpoint when the world is seen through the individuals' eyes. Why would one of the most competitive nations in the world – the ideal model of the universal welfare state and simultaneous pinnacle of highly evolved information societies – not seem attractive to skilled global experts, who are looking for the best possible professional and life opportunities? Factors that prevent people from coming to and chase them away from Finland have their foundations in two deeply rooted phenomena that are intertwined, both of which often erode tolerance of "exceptions": the institutions of the nation-state and local culture.

The nation-state is still the basic form of society, developed to serve national, local inhabitants and operators in accordance with the ideology of a given nation-state. The culture and institutions of the nation-state interact to form a dynamic founded on supporting long-standing members of society and official citizens and excluding non-citizens and new-comers outside most social operations. In addressing the issue, it is not enough to merely change official institutions or practices (including work permits, the citizenship process etc.); it is also necessary to refashion society's informal practices, value systems and conceptions. Part of the answer lies in the view of Richard Florida, who concurs that talent does indeed drive growth, but attracting human capital is also an issue of tolerance; of openness and low barriers for the entry of talent (Florida 2004, 53). In our interpretation, openness and low barriers should be seen in their broadest sense and as applied to all relevant dimensions of society – not just in legislation, but also in public services, organisational practices of employers and behaviour of individuals. It is only a slight exaggeration to say that intolerance diminishes attractiveness the most, not just in the case of Finland, but in general.

In the informal culture of the highly homogenous Finland, being a non-citizen is frequently interpreted through ethnicity: the less one resembles the local population ethnically, the less 'Finnish' one is. The concept also introduces the many emotions and irrational arguments that play a part in making distinctions. The extent to which non-Finnish and local inhabitants stand on the same starting line, in hiring practices, for example, is primarily determined by the attitudes and practices of employers. In public services, too, the issue has to do with the attitudes of the service providers as well as the regulatory background and thinking behind such services. A society designed for "Finnish" or other "local people" cannot expect to be able to utilise and reward the skills of "non-locals", even when the economy is seen as global and "non-local". Society itself, not only the economy, must adapt its attitudes and practices, if we are to link to the global talent pool.

When labour and talent flow through the nation-states' machineries, we are dealing with labour market encounters between people, different value systems and cultures, and new ways of operating. It is not possible to treat expertise as a separate article in the same way as other resources. Individuals who possess creativity and knowledge come equipped with their own value systems and cultures. We get the whole expert with all of his or her human characteristics and social connections. When we talk about being attractive to experts, at issue is not just the mobility of resources, but also the encounter between different social value systems and social relationships. As labour markets become supranational and expertise arrives in the form of individuals, merely knowing how to operate in a global business environment is not enough; also the human aspects of the environment need to be recognised.

Intensifying globalisation links organisations more and more intimately with worldwide networks of capital, expertise and culture – geographical locations are just stops along the flow of capital and people. But although the role of nation-states has changed rapidly, it is in no way disappearing; on the contrary. The nation-states and the supra-national institutions in which the government participates, including the European Union, impose powerful controls over the movement of capital and people. Creating a 'global society' that can operate successfully in the global operating environment does not mean the disappearance of local or national character. Rather, global society requires that the environment accept difference. It also requires the ability to function as part of a global network, be it the transnational labour market, legislation or business operations in general. The skilled expert will, in his or her turn, evaluate the surrounding society, and when necessary, seek a new place in which to operate and invest his or her expertise. All societies have their special characteristics, and the intention is not to give them up, but rather, to adjust their business and human climates to respond to the requirements of the globalising labour market of experts.

The migration of experts is steered by factors that can be related to globalisation as well as to mechanisms that are specifically national. The changing operating conditions in organisations, discussed above, and the factors that affect international migration – including national and EU regulatory controls – all affect the lives of experts working and living aboard. Although initially they change location as apart of globally operating businesses or through social relationships, the local brand of the new location, with all of its attractive, retaining and deterring characteristics will influence the choices that individuals make in the future – whether to stay or go, and the images that they will walk away with. In several countries, state structures are changing as we speak – a commitment to help retain transnationally operating individuals should be expected of a society that wants to renew itself and expects these individuals to contribute their expertise to benefit the society in question.

What does it take to link to the global talent pool? The push and pull factors discussed in this book are examined from a 'Finland-specific' perspective, evaluating how Finnish culture and its institutional embodiments, the welfare state and official practices, affect the quality of living and working environments in which these experts operate. This way, we can identify the special factors, both competitive advantages as well as handicaps, that help to distinguish Finnish work environments, urban regions and the country as a whole from the other options that are available to global experts. When creating regional policy in a global context, one's position in relation to others in the same field, as well as region-specific features must be recognised. In the global field of choices, it is possible to examine and evaluate the different elements that make a particular urban area or country attractive or unattractive, and thus recognise the extent to which it is realistic to try to attract or retain selected target groups (Raunio 2001; 2002). The field of choices may serve as a tool for forming policy, as it works as a "focusing device" that helps to recognise the strengths and weaknesses of the region in terms of attractiveness.

10.1 Elements of attraction

Pulling, pushing, preventing and retaining forces that create the attractiveness of a certain place in global field of choices have two main dimensions: the *experienced environment*, meaning the present place of residence, and the *imagined environment*, referring to the opportunities that emerge and the *attainability* of these possibilities. Positive experiences anchor people once they have arrived, and appealing images look attractive to the outside. These Finland-specific features of four forces creating attractiveness that we described in detail earlier in this volume are summed up in Figure 12.

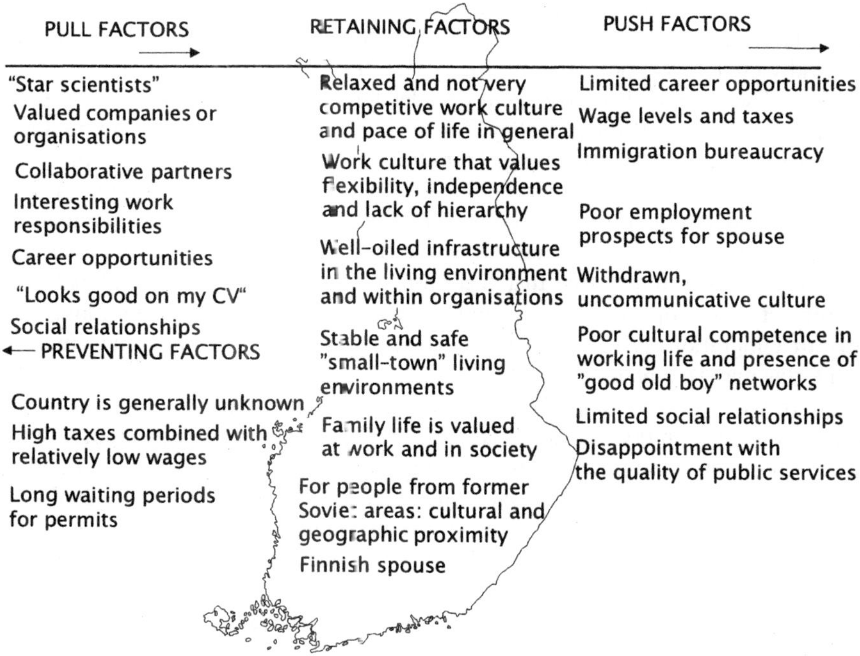

Figure 12. Finland as is appears on the global experts' field of choices.

However, in order to define the tool set needed for the "regional policies of the global age", it is necessary to link the key messages of this book to more generic "elements of attraction". Elements of attractiveness provide the content for the pushing, pulling, deterring and retaining forces of a place. Using a generic concept, it is possible to create a framework for making policy and doing further research on the subject. First, as already noted, in the global field regional qualities must be seen in the context of national *culture* and especially a *social system*, which make up the base for society's institutions. Second, in the image-based reality of information society, road signs with powerful and clear imagery communicate effectively about the existence of a particular place and the opportunities it can offer even outside the physical borders of a particular place (Raunio 2001). General *images* of places and the particular *brands* of particular actors located in that place may be distinguished from one another. Images may be good or bad, strong or weak, but a brand always contains certain ingredients that have a clear added value for the viewer.

In the Finnish case, brands were clearly connected to globally renowned companies or individual scientists or groups of scientists – in other words, to other global operators, instead of a particular nation-state or city region. These are the first fibres that connect a nation-state to the global operating environment, also at the individual level, potentially lifting it to the target group's global field of choices. The regions that have spent decades tending to such fibres, namely parts of the United States (Silicon Valley, Boston), United Kingdom (London, Oxford) or Germany (Baden-Wurttemberg, Frankfurt), already occupy a visible place on the global field of choices, whereas Finland, a new country of immigration with new knowledge regions , is only on the ascendant. At this stage of development, it is not enough to merely create an "attractive environment" or to promote tolerance – right now, it is imperative that the country become linked to the global economic network. For a nation-state and its operators, which, following a long history of emigration, have linked their economy to the global operating environment, this may be a natural first step.

Thus, when general lack of knowledge (weak image) fosters doubt about a particular country's ability to offer meaningful professional and career opportunities, or a high-quality living environment, strong brands may offer a solution. Internationally well-known businesses and trusted teams of scientists and individual academic stars do help to erode suspicions that are rooted in ignorance. The fact that a flourishing, global corporation or a top team of scientists have chosen Finland as its location seems to promise a generally well-functioning society. Often the mere fact that a business is located in a particular region is enough to make people assume that a company that offers such interesting work opportunities and an employee base of such high-quality expertise could not possibly be located in a region with a low quality of life – particularly when the organisation's own employees are able to confirm this assumption. Star scientists and the accompanying teams of researchers have a similar effect, evoking images of a globally high level of expertise or even of a global scientific "hot spot". In order to create attractive images, credible linkages to respected operators are critical. As the economic and social development marches on, it is probable that perceptions and images of a given region and its operators mix and become linked to one another in the eyes of global experts weighing their options on their field of choices.

From the standpoint of an individual person, global companies or teams of scientists in one's own field can offer a safe and familiar operating environment – the first platform or landing pad – in an otherwise unfamiliar social environment. 'Safe and familiar', in this context, mainly refers to the multiplicity inherent in the career and lifestyle choices that the global economy offers. It is nevertheless an environment that individuals recognise well enough as their "own" to believe that they can become a successful participant in it.

As indicated, globally rather unknown Finnish regions enter the global network primarily through its star scientists and internationally renowned organisations. Nevertheless, in the long term, also the quality of the living environment as a mirror of its society and the culture of the region will play greater roles. Work environments and living environments may be evaluated through four sub-categories, as is in the following conceptualisation of attractiveness that has emerged from our empirical data.

The main work environment-related factor that attracted foreign experts to Finland and retained them was the actual *content* of the work; interesting and challenging job responsibilities. The attractiveness of job responsibilities varied depending on the type of creative innovation environment. Interesting work and the opportunity to build a career also made the experts tolerate difficulties in adapting to their environment to some extent.

Career and work opportunities, being hired and advancing in ones career make up the second key element of attractiveness. The simple precondition is that employers are willing and able to hire foreign workers. What is significant to a foreign expert in the work and career opportunities on offer may not be as significant for the domestic workforce. Such considerations include an employer's competence in hiring and treating equally all employees regardless of national or ethnic origin. Indications of this kind of competence are to be found in an organisation's culturally sensitive and multicultural management style and its organisational structure. Career and work opportunities form the foundation in the development of an attractive, creative innovation environment.

Career advancement and recruitment of foreign experts are closely connected to third element of an attractive work environment: organisational *culture*. Respondents saw the *Finnish work culture* as relaxed, non-hierarchical and respectful of individuals, which many considered a highly positive factor. Similar qualities have characterised expert organisations around the world for decades, but the Finnish culture's lack of hierarchy highlighted this impression. Also the family-oriented work environment stemming from the country's social system, i.e. a calm pace at work and the opportunity to achieve a balance in combining work and private life help to anchor experts to Finland. Attitudes toward the demands of family life and children are flexible and positive, making it possible to combine family and career. These aspects mirror the local culture and social system and lend a specifically Finnish veneer to the work environment.

However, a downside is the lack of a multicultural work environments and international work culture (English as working and socialising language etc.) that would provide wider opportunities for foreign experts. The career and professional opportunities that Finland offers can attract and anchor experts, but some of the factors that emerged in our study push people away. In particular, Finland's relatively limited professional and career opportunities were an obvious problem for a small country. The already limited job opportunities for foreign experts are limited even more by language skill- and work culture-related restrictions on the part of both employers and foreign employees. Also, respondents viewed their advancement opportunities within organisations as somewhat worse than those of their Finnish colleagues; i.e. they considered both their horizontal career development outside of their present employer as well as vertical advancement within the current organisation as poorer than that of Finns. Both phenomena are largely a result of the Finnish job market's inexperience with foreign employees.

The fourth key element of an attractive work environment is the work communities themselves: the professional and social qualities of the individuals who form the community. Interpretations of the Finnish culture of communication proved to be a negative side of work *communities* and caused difficulties in the integration of foreign experts to local work communities. A related and significant problem came in the form of poor employment prospects for spouses, a consequence of spouses' lack of language skills, problems with the applicability of professional experience and education, and, again, attitudes among Finnish employers regarding the recruitment of foreign workers.

Apart from the work environment, which is currently the dominant factor affecting the relocation of experts, it is also important to examine the quality of the living environment. While not crucial in making the initial decision to move to a region in the case of Finland, a high-quality living environment may encourage experts to remain in the country. Simply put, the quality of the living environment is a combination of four elements; physical, social, economic and functional (Linnamaa 1999).

The functional milieu consists of the quality and array of public and private services. These include basic services and infrastructure as well as luxury services (including events, free-time opportunities etc.), and in the global case, also the availability of services in the most common immigrant languages. The array of available services makes a difference, as does the way in which they are distributed, how well they function from the perspective of foreigners, and how the service structure reflects onto the surrounding environment. In terms of functional milieu, the factors that anchored respondents and that, in part, stemmed from Finland's small scale, were society's functionality, reliability and safety. Most services were found to work well, whether public or private, although the array was not always found to be rich, nor were service providers always accustomed to international clients. In addition, respondents expressed trust in officials and individuals, a factor that to some extent diminishes stress and improves quality of life. Safety and security translate to a predictable environment that allows people to move about whenever and wherever without fear. From the standpoint of a functional milieu, an immigration policy that assists in the recruitment and retention of foreign experts is critical. For example, the long duration of the work permit application process is a factor that inhibits immigration.

However, more interestingly, what may be an unquestioned strength from a national perspective may be a weakness from the point of view of a globally mobile individual expert. Surprisingly, the factors that in some cases pushed people away from Finland included disappointment with the level of health care and the school system: both systems have been valued to be of the highest quality in the world according to international comparative studies. However, national systems and individual persons have different criteria for evaluation. In some cases, the expectations placed on public services were too high, so disappointments occurred when using the system. Dissatisfaction with the school system is frequently connected to wanting to bring up one's children in one's own culture, in a more international culture, or in a cultural atmosphere of less 'free' upbringing. In this case, the issue is two-fold, touching upon not only the equalising impact of the welfare state but also the deeper cultural traits present in Finnish society. It is not so much a question of quality as it is of the availability of different high-quality alternatives. The bottom line is that a system built for one homogenous group cannot offer high-quality services for a diverse set of groups.

The *social environment* consists of customs of human interaction, language, values, local cultural norms and chosen lifestyle. For globally mobile workers, the international flair and multiculturalism of a place, the openness of its people and their ability to tolerate difference, as well as the presence of familiar social networks are important aspects of an attractive place. Social relationships are the personal or professional relationships that experts have with people and communities in their area. An extremely important factor that bound people to Finland was a Finnish spouse. Most respondents who were planning to stay in Finland permanently were married to or cohabited with a Finn. On the other hand, professional contacts were often what brought people to Finland in the first place. Conversely, a central factor propelling people away form Finland was the difficulty of forming social relationships. Although it is always challenging to form relationships in a strange, new country, in Finland the problem has to do with the smallness of immigrant communities, the specific Finnish brand of human interaction, and Finns' lack of experience with foreigners. Thus, the social dimension plays an extremely important part in the competition for talent. Although it is a complex and deeply rooted phenomenon and often extremely difficult to change, we ignore it at our peril.

The *economic environment* is the standard of living that can be attained in the region and the economic foundation that it offers for the future. In welfare states, the economic environment is clearly connected to a social system that promotes equality and emphasises income distribution. In the case of Finland, this translates to rather low salaries and high taxes, which together amount to a fairly low level of economic wellbeing when compared with liberal market economies. Together, Finnish wages, taxes and a rather low cost of living, especially outside of the capital region, combine to create a fairly competitive level of economic wellbeing, when compared with many other international opportunities. However, this can become a push factor at certain life stages, when the attainment of wealth is seen as most important.

Physical environment and quality of the living environment describe the developed environment, meaning the array of living opportunities and environments, and the natural environment, such as flora and climate. For many, Finland's seasonal changes and nature represented a pull factor, whereas the cold and dark winters made life difficult and had a negative impact on mood, thus pushing people away. On the other hand, "small-town" living environments primarily had a positive effect and encouraged respondents to stay. Typically, they considered their living environments as close to nature, safe and peaceful, and particularly those who lived outside of Helsinki expressed appreciation for short work commutes and opportunities for the enjoyment of nature, while working in cutting-edge high-tech companies.

It is essential to note both positives and negatives, as we target our development initiatives to support the establishment of a "human aspect" in innovation environments through the elements described above. Especially professional communities and work environments play a central role in generating appeal – when they appear sufficiently good and attractive, they may motivate experts to relocate to a certain region, even in the absence of any pressing need to leave the present region. By combining the human aspect, i.e. key elements of living and working environments, with a business-oriented innovation environment, we can strengthen the global attractiveness of a place. Since innovation refers to a technical process and creativity to a personal trait (an essential ingredient in the innovation process), the aim should be the *creative innovation environment*.

A creative innovation environment can be summarised as a combination of work and living environments that offers possibilities for realising and developing oneself through challenging work responsibilities, while being a part of a successful whole of experts and organisations. From the point of view of regional development, it combines elements of business and human environments to provide a sustainable way to utilise and support human intelligence as a source of wealth in a particular geographic location. Experts prefer operating environments that are interesting and challenging and that open up potential, future opportunities. Such operating environments feature, for example, a high-quality management and work culture that understands multiculturalism. Successful, well-respected, expertise-intensive companies, as well as the research, development and educational institutions that support them are at the core of creative innovation environments. A core of creative innovation environment may well be a single research team with a global network, but in order to be globally attractive, a rather plentiful overall job market for talent is often also desirable. These innovation environments allow individuals to develop and utilise their expertise through formal and informal networks, institutions and organisations. Creative innovation environments can also be seen as the "human" manifestation of the innovative environment in that they emphasise perspectives that extend beyond the merely technical or economic. The 'specifically Finnish' characteristics described above offer a good principle for understanding how to recognise the most important national and regional elements of attractiveness

10.2 Policies for creative innovation environments in the global age

Globalisation is not an independent phenomenon – it is more like a framework that enables an ever-broader distribution of people, goods, influence and capital, as well as a certain level of homogenisation. Globalisation is frequently described as a flow that sweeps over nation-states and renders them insignificant. But as a process, globalisation is regulated in a number of ways, and while the significance of national boundaries does undergo changes, there is no indication that they are being obliterated in the process. National regulation and supranational mechanisms, such as the European Union, form a counterpoint to the mobility of people and capital across national borders.

In the affluent West, the role of nation-states can even seem highlighted, as they strive to regulate globalisation's effects. There is no sign of the dissolution of national borders that is so often mentioned in globalisation discourse. To the contrary, in controlling globalisation, the role of the public sector has become more prominent. The local operating environment's characteristics, including safety, social services, a balance between taxation and wage levels, all determined by national institutions, can be decisive when individuals or corporations decide whether to relocate to a particular area. Immigration regulations and those related to the status of immigrants, and the national institutions that implement the rules, are central from the standpoint of a globally mobile workforce. Despite the important role of regions are creators of attractive environments, national factors such as these play a significant role in regulating the mobility of the global workforce, in the good and the bad, and they are significant to how we utilise the innovation potential of the global economy's experts.

A competitive economy and highly evolved information society must continue to develop policies that promote stronger innovation environments, but with a broader, more human-oriented and global focus. This is especially true when the aim is to offer an attractive point of convergence for global experts. Adding a human and global aspect to regional and national innovation environments would require support for organisations' attempts to attract expertise to the region, and convergence with the globally functional labour market of experts. The following policy adjustments are needed in welfare states to compete for global talent:

- *Innovation policies* should focus also on the capability of organisations to utilise multicultural expertise, recruit globally and offer professional rewards in return. This means policies and services that focus on improving the ability of employers to hire and convert existing expertise on the global job market, for example, through investing in diversity management, corporate culture and global recruiting.
- *Immigration policies* should be integrated with the global labour market by eliminating institutional obstacles to labour mobility, by redefining the relations between individuals and the social system, and by decreasing the exclusionary impact of other national institutions that restrict the lives and mobility of individuals. This requires turning the national culture's official "us and them" polar opposites toward a broader, more inclusive "us", which is not based on nationality or ethnicity, but on working together (immigration practices, service eligibility, basis for taxation, equal status with citizens etc.).
- *Integrated institutional decision making* is needed to implement policies that are not based on a particular sector of the national system, but rather combines the requirements of individual knowledge holders and the global economy. Labour, immigration, innovation and regional policies should be integrated to come up with the powerful tools needed to adjust current innovation environments.

The formation and implementation of these policies should take place at the regional level in order to adjust them to specific local and regional needs. Policy makers should acknowledge the fact that most foreign experts sought out positions that interested them and that just happened to be located in a particular region and a particular city. They did not choose Finland, for example, because of itself, nor did Finland choose them. Instead, the global job market presented them with an opportunity to develop in their area of expertise in an interesting job. Nevertheless, national or regional politics can influence attractiveness even when it is not rooted in national or regional characteristics per se, but on high-quality professional opportunities and innovation environments. Policies do not aim to profoundly transform the social system, institutions or culture, but to add some ingredients that provide them with the ability to function smoothly when faced with individuals who are both globally mobile and a crucial asset for regional and national economies.

In terms of business climate, it is possible to enhance the attractiveness of innovation environments through regional and national policies by supporting the birth and development of high-quality organisations that attract people from beyond national borders. Although the development of attractive organisations, such as Nokia, can be viewed as lucky coincidences, we can create a situation where such lucky coincidences can occur. For example, the welfare state's equal opportunities have been the foundation of educational policy and have ensured the availability of a well-educated workforce in Finland. In addition, many national and regional policy measures have helped promote the ICT and biotech industries discussed here. Similarly, the human aspects of innovation environments should be strengthened to develop "creative innovation environments" through social innovations.

The production of innovation benefits from both mobility and the commitment of global experts to an area. In order to support "brain circulation", investment in high-level expertise among innovation producers is not enough; also needed are carefully crafted immigration policy measures that incorporate an overall development perspective. Immigrant experts broaden the existing expertise base and introduce new forms of innovation. Further, some immigrant groups evolve into grassroots sub-cultures, which produce innovations that arise specifically from their otherness and from the fusion of cultures. Immigrants and ethnic minorities enhance the cultural diversity of innovative environments, and when correctly utilised, this has been shown not only to increase business opportunities globally, but also to produce innovation in the very collision of different viewpoints and ways of thinking.

The current operating environment requires sensitivity and readiness for change. It would be expedient for the public sector and its collaborators to consider shifting from sector-specific and operation area-specific administrative practices toward process management that takes entire phenomena as a starting point. The international mobility of labour and the global "brain circulation" of experts requires a process management approach, since the issues that come up range from image creation to taxation practices, from work permit practices to work environments, and even to the way that the welfare state is structured. In part, managing this process would supply the necessary preconditions that engage a knowledge-driven society in the creation of new products, instead of becoming a banana republic that merely produces the basic fodder that information societies consume (see Naumanen 2004).

The elimination of institutional barriers, "opening the doors" of national immigration and labour policies, and the development of urban areas need to be viewed as practical measures for treating people as a strategic resource. It would be beneficial to move away from bureaucratic and expense-focused administration to practices that primarily aim to reinforce human talent and skills. As we move toward the global information society, measures to address the availability of foreign experts are being taken, for example, in the form of a national discussion about an active immigration policy, as well as in targeted, urban-area projects for attracting specific experts. Regional need assessments and development strategies are useful in attracting expert workforce, but national development measures are needed as well. We would benefit from looking at the phenomenon from a holistic perspective.

The modification of present regulatory practices would lower the barriers that stand in the way of available experts, so that instead of inhibiting, they would enable. The most clear-cut example of this is immigration policy, which, if wisely implemented, can broaden the skill base of organisations and meet the job market's labour needs. The expertise within the borders of a single country is not enough, as economic operating environments and job markets expand beyond national borders. *Migration management* must therefore develop mechanisms for addressing the demand for expert workers, while still adhering to the dictates of international agreements. This requires awareness and acknowledgement of the complex character of international migration movements, and the aim of open, international cooperation built upon that foundation. At best, flexible international brain circulation flows bring added value to organisations, to the countries that receive immigrants, to immigrants themselves, and to their countries of origin.

At a practical level, the new significance of labour market demand in the development of immigration policy is manifested in the streamlining of practices related to work permits, and in proposals for managing the immigration of workers (Tanner 2003). Different countries have employed an array of approaches. *The point system* addresses qualities that the labour market is looking for, including applicants' professional competence, age and language skills. Using characteristics that are useful to the labour market as immigration criteria minimises the potential costs of immigration to society. Point systems that rate immigrants based on their 'labour market characteristics' are in use in countries including Canada, New Zealand, Switzerland, Australia and the United States. The spirit of the Finnish Aliens Act, revised in 2004, is also headed toward a policy of encouraging the immigration of skilled experts. This is indicated by the government programme for immigration policy that was submitted in 2005. The impact of these first steps toward openness remains to be seen, once they are transformed into practical operating methods and new attitudes among officials. Attitude changes and new institutional practices could have a significant impact on the attainment of such openness.

The tendency of individuals to act as 'gatekeepers of the system' is frequently based in their personal histories and in functioning as an established part of an organisation and its operations. Indeed, certain types of attitude climates become cemented in decision-making machineries through individuals, who mould operating methods and structures to serve their own attitudes. In such cases, a general attitude change will not necessarily change the attitudes ingrained in existing structures, operating methods and culture. The attitudes of the individuals who operate in key immigration oversight organisations – the companies that recruit workers and the authorities and agencies that handle immigration – are therefore critical to immigration policy. It is they who handle the practical implementation of various policies, reflecting their own attitude climate in their operating methods. Eventually, these become society's institutionalised attitudes. To change attitudes or culture, we also need to have operating methods that promote an understanding of the importance of human capital outside our own national borders.

Culture, too, is a changeable phenomenon. In fact, it is a continuously changing entity. Harrison (2000) suggests that whereas culture is the mother, institutions are the children: they adapt and mirror the culture to support existing culture. The pattern can also be reversed: by changing the institutions, it is also possible to change culture. The very establishment and status of nation-states was brought forth with the help of institutions and bureaucratic operating methods. The development of a culture of open, global societies can be promoted through the concrete measures described above. When there is local understanding of mutual dependence in the production of wellbeing, being foreign is not seen as a threat, but as a resource and an opportunity.

Discourses in many ways similar societies may be diverse as the case in the Nordic countries indicates. While Denmark has clearly been closing its doors to immigrants for some time, in Sweden and Finland, there is growing tolerance. Tolerance is partly a result of implemented policies that minimise the view that different groups are in opposite camps. Like Finland, also Swedish government, after a long, silent period, awakened at the beginning of the new millennium to ponder whether hiring skilled experts from abroad also improves the situation of foreigners who already live in the country. Recruiting experts would not just raise the profile of foreigners in general, but would also educate employers to hire workers from a more multicultural pool. In 2001, an immigration initiative by Sweden's liberal *Folkpartiet* proposed that professionals in fields where there is a demand for labour be granted temporary residence permits while they look for work. In the event that a job is found, a foreigner's status is to be converted to 'true' immigrant and a residence permit for working granted.

It may be that official attitudes in Finland have become more tolerant, but general attitudes toward immigration and immigrants represent one of the main barriers to the implementation of a more active immigration policy. For example, the Finnish Business and Policy Forum (EVA) has studied the Finnish attitude climate for nearly two decades, and during that time has not detected any notable change in the attitudes of the majority of the population toward greater tolerance. Immigrants continue to be seen as more of a security threat than an economic resource. Such attitudes are now rooted in institutional structures, further slowing down change.

Immigrants and immigration policy give rise to many emotions that are bound up with national identity and self-image. Any discussion of the issue of the country's attraction to immigrants seems to invite two kinds of reactions in the public sphere. *Nationalistic discourse* frightens people by proliferating images of "everyone" rushing to Finland in the event that borders are opened more to immigration. "Everyone" would want to come and live off of the plentiful social benefits that the gullible Finns would then pay for. On the other hand, the *self-pitiers* lament that no-one would move to Finland anyway, because the place is an arctic tax hell with an unintelligible language and a morose people, who drink too much and hate foreigners. The extremes of these viewpoints appeal to nationalistic, exclusionary forms of thinking for which no equivalent can be found in the reality and lives of the foreign experts interviewed for this book. When we undertake to consider new development policies, we must distinguish between reality, discourse and interpretations.

To come at a realistic idea of the interrelationship between outside world, immigration and the local dimension, it is necessary to move toward a more reasonable level and move away from a discourse that yanks on the emotional chain and appeals to national stereotypes. Nordic welfare state distributes the common good more equally than many other countries. Nevertheless, immigrant experts do not really benefit from social benefits, especially income transfers. Either they are not eligible or do not need them. But immigrants help secure these services to others by paying what are high taxes by international standards out of their – by international standards – modest wages. To simplify, this equation stops many from moving to Finland or staying on a more permanent basis.

This is not to say that the welfare state has no role to play in the retention of foreign experts. The Nordic welfare state has been very successful in preventing extreme forms of poverty and making society more equal. Welfare state policies have also resulted in a high-quality infrastructure and highly evolved information societies. These factors combine to make Finland a safe and well-functioning society, where people can enjoy luxuries such as efficient public transportation and safety at night. In this way, as a direct result of the services it provides, the welfare state plays an indirect role in the retention of foreign experts.

The European Union's immigration policy is slowly evolving toward uniformity. National immigration policies continue to be critical in regulating immigration, and will be for a long time to come. EU nations have widely differing traditions with immigration, and each country has its own relationships with immigrants' countries of origin. EU cooperation on immigration policy becomes important in determining attitudes and new models, which are culled from the immigration policies of EU member countries. Finland has learned from other European countries that there are many different ways of managing or not managing immigration, with different consequences. If national institutions are wise, they will learn lessons from the experiences of others – the most important one being that immigration and (many) immigrants are permanent and cannot suppressed, nor is it worth it to try, because they will merely find new channels of entry. Sensible immigration management – a few examples are provided here – permits mobility in a way that benefits everyone – the countries that receive immigrants and the ones that yield them, as well as the immigrants themselves. Calling for "immigration policy, not politics", or remaining in a state of indecision that political operators use to try and shirk their responsibilities to shift them to the officials will only enrich the grey economy and leave immigrants vulnerable to violations and abuse. We do need to control immigration, but the way that we do it is critical.

Migration flows periodically change their character. Countries of emigration turn into immigration receiving countries, and immigrants themselves look different depending on the country and the point in time. From the end of World War II until the 1980s, countries in Europe's periphery lost manual workers, whereas today they are immigration receiving countries. Immigration continues, but it has changed. Young people, students and various experts move to other countries in search of jobs and to gain new experiences. Also, the share of transnational commuters and different forms of brain circulation are growing. People do not have to emigrate, but they seek the change.

Even though competitive economies reach out to immigrant labour and experts, what they get are individuals with all their needs. Work only takes up so many hours of the day, and once it is over, the immigrant is no longer just an economic "production factor", but a member of society who requires society's services. No nation has ever succeeded in obtaining "plain" workforçe – they also get the families and all the needs that families have in society.

It should be noted that the current wellbeing of advanced economies comes from reaping the benefits of the record-making development era of the previous decades. Being too enamoured of one's own success will make today's heroes into tomorrow's losers. The global economy evolves an accelerating pace, and that means that planning, preparedness and development are an everyday norm. Old structures and old operating methods must not obscure the dynamic of the new operating environment. As we come up with strategies to attract experts globally, it is time to switch our focus from the protection of national systems toward connectivity with global talent and society.

References

Aallas, E. (1997). Salailtua ulkomaalaispolitiikkaa. YYA-pimeästä hämärän EU:n rajamaille. In Järvinen, T. & Kortelainen, A. (Ed.) Muukalaiset. Juridiikasta ja asenteista kansojen kohdatessa. Helsinki: Edita. Pp.113-116.

Ahonen, P. (2002). Kaukana Euroopan sosiaalipolitiikan "Rooma" ja "Maastricht". Avoimen koordinointimetodin näkökulma. Janus Vol. 10, No 1, Pp.38–54.

Akande, W. (2001). Ireland: A Nation in Transition. San Jose: iUniverse.com.

Alanen, A. Venäjänkieliset asukkaat lisääntyvä vähemmistö. Kuntapuntari 2/2007. Statistics Finland. Pp. 17-21.

Alitolppa-Niitamo, A. (2004). The Icebreakers. Somali-Speaking Youth in Metropolitan Helsinki with a Focus on the Context of Formal Education. Series D 42/2004. Helsinki: Population Research Institute.

Ali-Yrkkö, J., Hermans, R., Hyytinen, A., Lindström. M., Paija, L., Pajarinen, M and Ylä-Anttila, P. (2004). Suomi ja Eurooppa kansainvälisessä työnjaossa – analyysi toimialojen ja klustereiden kilpailukyvystä. Publications of Prime Minister's Office, Edita, Helsinki.

Ali-Yrkkö, J., Joronen, T. and Ylä-Anttila (2002). Finland in the world economy – the era of liberalization In. Forsander, A. (Ed.) Immigration and Economy in the Globalization Process The Case of Finland. Sitra Reports series 20. Vantaa: Tummavuoren kirjapaino. Pp. 66-80.

Ali-Yrkkö, J., Koivisto, J. V., Lampinen, M. and Ylä-Anttila, P. (2000). Suomalaisyritysten kansainvälistyminen. In M.-L. Trux (Ed.) Aukeavat ovet – kulttuurien moninaisuus Suomen elinkeinoelämässä. Helsinki: WSOY. Pp.85–115.

Ali-Yrkkö, J., Lindström. M., Pajarinen, M and Ylä-Anttila, P. (2004). Suomen asema globaalissa kilpailussa – yritysten sijaintipäätöksiin vaikuttavat tekijät. The Research Institute of the Finnish Economy (Etla). Discussion papers No. 927, Helsinki.

Allardt, E. (1988). The Agrarian, the Industrial, and the Information Society. University of Helsinki, Department of sociology, working papers 42.

Apap, J. (2003). Shaping Europe's Migration Policy. A Comparative Analysis on Member States "Green Card" Legislation: A comparison of strategies in Germany, Sweden, the Netherlands and the UK. Paper presented at the EU Migration Policy Workshop, 21.–22.11.2003, Higher Institute for Labour Studies (HIVA), Katholieke Universiteit Leuven.

Auriol, L. and Sexton, J. (2002). Human Resources in Science and Technology: Measurement Issues and International Mobility. In OECD: International mobility of highly skilled. Paris: OECD Proceedings. Pp.13–38.

Baldwin-Edwards, M. (2004). Immigrants and the Welfare State in Europe. In Massey, D.S & Taylor, J.E. (Eds.) International Migration: Prospects and Policies in a Global Market. Oxford: Oxford University press. Pp. 318-334.

Balzat, M. and Hanusch, H. (2004). Recent Trends in the Research on National Innovation Systems. Journal of Evolutionary Economics. Vol 14, Pp. 197-210.

Barré, R., Hernández, V., Meyer, J-P. and Vinck, D. (2003). Scientific Diasporas. Paris: Institut de recherche pour le développement (IRD)

Bartlett, C. A. & Ghosal, S. (1992). Managing Across Borders. The Transnational Solution. London: Century Business.

Bassett-Jones, N. (2005). The Paradox of Diversity Management, Creativity and Innovation. Creativity and Innovation management. Vol. 14, No. 2. Pp. 169-175.

Bayer, A. (2002). Report on the main findings of the empirical research conducted in the framework of the project" Should I Stay or Should I Go" (unpublished) Should I Stay or Should I Go –project report.

BBC News 16.6.2003. Italy in "fire on migrants" row. http://www.bbc.co.uk (30.10.2003).

BBC News 23.10.2003. Italy's asylum seekers lose hope. http://www.bbc.co.uk (30.10.2003).

Berger, P. and Luckmann, T. ([1966] 1991). The Social Construction of Reality. A Treatise in the Sociology of Knowledge. Harmondsworth: Penguin Books.

Bergholm, T. (2003). SAK:n historia. http:// www.sak.fi /(23.10.2003).

Bergström, O. (2001). Externalisation of Employees: Thinking about Going Somewhere else. International Journal of Human Resource Management Vol. 12, No.3. Pp. 373–388.

Blomberg-Kroll, H. (1999). Kosta vad det kosta vill? Attitydmönster och attitydförändringar hos befolkning och eliter beträffande välfärdservicen i nedskärningarnas tid. Institutionen för socialpolitik. Åbo: Åbo Akademi.

Boyatzias, R. E. and Kolb, D. A. (2000). Performance, Learning and Development as Modes of Growth and Adaptation throughout Our Lives and Careers. In Peiperl, M., Arthur, M., Goffee, R. & Morris, T. (Eds.) Career Frontiers. New conceptions of working lives. New York: Oxford University Press. Pp. 76–98.

Breheny, M. (1999). (Ed.) The People: Where will they Work? Report of TCPA Research into the changing geography of employment. London. TCPA.

Breton, R., Isajiw, W., Kalbach, W. E. and Reitz, J. G. (1990). Ethnic Identity and Equality: Varieties of Experience in a Canadian City. Toronto: University of Toronto Press.

Brooks, D. (2000). Bobos in Paradise. The New Upper Class and How They got There. New York: Simon & Schuster.

Brown, A. D. (1999). The Six Dimensions of Leadership. Essex: Random House.

Building Ireland's Knowledge Economy (2004). The Irish action plan for promoting of R&D investments to 2010. (http://www.entemp.ie/publications /enterprise/2004/knowledgeeconomy.pdf.) (24.2.2006)

Burda, M. (2003). Humankapital und Arbeitsmarktinstitutionen bei gleichgewichtiger Arbeitslosigkeit. Bildung - Wirtschaftswissenschaftliches Seminar Ottobeuren, Mohr Siebeck, Tubingen.

Carmon, N. (1996). Immigration and Integration in Post-industrial Societies: Quantitative and Qualitative Analyses. In Carmon, N. (Ed.) Immigration and Integration in Post-Industrial Societies. London: MacMillan. Pp. 13–29.

Cartwright, R. (2002). Managing Diversity. Oxford: A Wiley company.

Casey, C. (2002). Critical Analysis of Organisations. Theory, Practice, Revitalization. Sage publications, London.

Castells, M. and Himanen, P. (2001). The Information Society and the Welfare State: The Finnish Model. Oxford University Press.

Castells, M. (1997). The Information Age: Economy, Society and Culture. Volume II The Power of Identity. Blackwell, London.

Castells, M. (1996). The Information Age: Economy, Society and Culture. Volume 1. The Rise of the Network Society. London: Blackwell.

Central Chamber of Commerce (2003). Suomalaiset yritykset haluavat edistää vastuullista tuontikauppaa. http://www.kauppakamari.fi / (15.3.04).

China Daily (2002). (http://www1.chinadaily.com.cn/news/cb/2002-06-13/73688 .html) 14.6.2002.

Coddan (2003). Income tax – Rates and Allowances. (www.ukincorp.co.uk/) (3.3.2004).

Cohen, R. and Kennedy, P. (2000). Global Sociology. Basingstoke: MacMillan Press.

Cooke, P., Uranga, M.G. and Etxebarria, G. (1998). Regional Systems of Innovation: an Evolutionary perspective. Environment and Planning A, Vol. 30. Pp. 1563-1584.

Cooke. P. (2004). The Role of Research in Regional Innovation Systems: New Models Meeting Knowledge Economy Demands. International Journal of Technology Management, Vol, 28 nos.2/4/5/6. Pp. 507-533.

Council of Europe (2003). Puheenjohtajan päätelmät. Brysselin Eurooppaneuvosto 16. ja 17. lokakuuta 2003.

Cross, M. and Waldinger, R. (1999). Economic Integration and Labour Market Change. In J. Hjarnö (Ed.) From Metropolis to Cosmopolis. Proceedings of the Second International Metropolis Conference. Copenhagen, September 25–27, 1997. Esbjerg: South Jutland University Press. Pp. 29–93.

Cummings, S. and Lambert T. (1998). Immigration Restrictions and the American Worker: An examination of competing interpretations. Population Research and Policy Review 17. Pp. 497–520.

Dahlén, T. (2001). Hantera kulturkrockar: hur ett transnationellt yrke växer fram och hålls ihop. In Flera fält i ett. Socialantropologer om translokala fältstudier ed. by Ulf Hannerz. Stockholm: Carlssons Bokförlag.

Daft, R. L. (2001). Organization Theory and Design. Seventh edition. Cincinnati: South-Western, Thomson Learning.

Davenport, T.H. and Beck, J.C. (2001) The Attention Economy. Understanding the New Currency of Business. Boston. Harvard Business School Press.

Deeprose, D. (2002). Global HR. Oxford,: Wiley Company.

DETE (2007). New Employment Permits Schemes. (http://www.entemp.ie/ labour /workpermits /guidelines.htm) (12.6.2007)

Dierickx, I and Cool, K. (1989). Asset Stock Accumulation and Sustainability of Competitive Advantage. Management Science, Vol. 35. No: 12, Pp. 1504-1511.

Downey, L. (2003). Creating Ireland's Innovation Society: The Next Strategic Step. Dublin. HEA & Forfas.

Dustmann, C. (2003). The Impact of EU Enlargement on Migration Flows. Home office online report 25/03.

EC (European Commission) (2000). Komission tiedonanto neuvostolle ja Euroopan parlamentille. Yhteisön maahanmuuttopolitiikka. KOM (2000) 757 lopullinen. Bryssel 22.11.2000.

(The) Economist (2005). European Migration. The Brain-drain Cycle. The Economist, Dec. 10th 2005. Pp. 33-35.

Ekholm, P. (2003). Tiivistyvä ja hajautuva Euroopan unioni. Helsinki: Edita.

El Periódico de Catalunya (2003). Las víctimas del naufragio de la patera en Câdiz se elevan a 34. El Periódico – edición impresa, 3.11.2003.

Esping-Anderssen, G. (1990). The Three Worlds of Welfare Capitalism. Cambridge: Polity Press.

European Commission (2003a). Komission tiedonanto neuvostolle, Euroopan parlamentille, Euroopan talous- ja sosiaalikomitealle ja alueiden komitealle. Maahanmuutto, kotouttaminen ja työllisyys. KOM(2003) 336 lopullinen. Bryssel 3.6.2003.

European Commission (2003b). Third European Report on Science & Technology Indicators. Towards a Knowledge –based Economy. Directorate General for Research. Brussels.

Expert Group on Future Skill needs (EGFSN) (2005). Skill Needs in the Irish Economy: The Role of Migration

Faist, T. (2000). The Volume and Dynamics of International Migration and Transnational Social Spaces. Oxford. Oxford University Press.

Findlay A., Li, F., Jowett, A. and Skeldon, R. (1996). Skilled international migration and the global city: a study of expatriates in Hong Kong. Transactions of the Institute of British Geographers, New Series 21. Pp.49 – 61

Finnish Tax Administration (2007). Foreign employee in Olkiluoto (www.tax.fi)

Flood, R.L. and Romm, N.R.A. (1996). Diversity Management. Triple Loop Learning. Wiley, London.

Florida, R. (2002). The Rise of the Creative Class. And How it's Transforming Work, Leisure, Community and Everyday Life. Basic Books, NY.

Florida, R. (2004a). America's Looming Creativity Crisis. Harvard Business Review, October 2004. Pp..122-134.

Florida, R. (2004b). Creative Class War. How the GOP's anti-elitism could ruin America's Economy. Washington Monthly January/February 2004.

Florida, R. (2005). The Flight of the Creative Class. The New Global Competition for Talent. NY: HarperCollins publisher.

Florida, R. and Tinagli, I. (2004). Europe in the Creative Age. Demos.

Forsander, A. (2000) Työvoiman tarve ja maahanmuuttopolitiikka. Millä ehdoin maahanmuuttajien osaaminen on vastaus työvoiman kysyntään? In M.-L. Trux (Ed.): Aukeavat ovet. Kulttuurien moninaisuus Suomen elinkeinoelämässä. Helsinki: WSOY. Pp. 143–202.

Forsander, A. (2002a). Glocalizing Capital and Labour – Old Structures, New Challenges. In Forsander, A. (Ed.) Immigration and Economy in the Globalisation process. The Case Finland. Sitra-report series 20, Helsinki. Pp. 81-118.

Forsander, A. (2002b). Luottamuksen ehdot. Maahanmuuttajat 1990-luvun suomalaisilla työmarkkinoilla. Väestöliitto, Helsinki.

Forsander, A. (2004). Social Capital in the Context of Immigration and Diversity; Economic Participatioin in the Nordic Welfare States. JIMI/RIMI, Vol. 5. No. 2. Pp. 207-227.

Friedman, T.L. (1999). The Lexus and the Olive Tree. Understanding the Globalization. NY, Anchor Books.

Fryer, P. (1984). Staying Power: The History of Black People in Britain. Pluto press.

Geddes, A. (2003). The Politics of Migration and Immigration in Europe. London: Sage.

Gehl, J. (1987). Life Between Buildings: Using Public Space. NY; VRN.

German Embassy, Washington DC (2004). Survey of German Tax Laws. http://www.germany-info.org/relaunch/business/taxes/german_tax_rates (3.3.2004).

Glaeser, E.L. and Saiz, A. (2003). The Rise of the Skilled City. Harvard Institute of Economic Research Discussion Paper No. 2025 FRB Philadelphia Working Paper No. 04-2.

Gordon, A. (1995). The Work of Corporate Culture: Diversity Management. Social Text 44, Vol. 13; No. 3. Pp. 3-30.

Ghosh, B. (2000). New International Regime for Orderly Movements of People: What will it Look Like? In Ghosh, B. (Ed.) Managing Migration. Time for a New International Regime. Oxford University Press. Pp. 220-248.

Government programme of Finland (2003). http://www.valtioneuvosto.fi /vn/liston/ (10.3.2004).

Granger, M. and Blomquist, G. (1999). Evaluating the Influence of Amenities on the Location of Manufacturing Establsihment in Urban Areas. Urban Studies, Vol. 36, No:11. Pp. 1859-1873.

Granger, M.D. (1993). Evaluating the influence of county-level amenities on the location of manufactruring establishments. Dissertation, UMI. Michigan; A Bell & Howell.

Granovetter, M. (1973). The Strenghth of the Weak Ties. American Journal of Sociology, Vol. 78, No:6. Pp. 1360-1380.

Green, A.E. (1997). A Question of Comprise? Case Study Evidence on the Location and Mobility Strategies of Dual Career Households. Regional Science Vol. 31, No. 7. Pp. 641-655.

Guellec, D. and Cervantes, M. (2002). International Mobility of Highly Skilled Workers. From Statistical Analysis to Policy Formulation. In OECD: International Mobility of Highly Skilled. OECD proceedings, France. Pp. 71-98.

Haikonen, J. & Kiljunen, P. (2003). Mitä mieltä suomalainen? Evan asennetutkimuksien kertomaa vuosilta 1984 – 2003. EVA -raportti. Taloustieto oy, Yliopistopaino, Helsinki.

Hakala, J.T. (2003). Luova prosessi tieteessä. Helsinki. Gaudeamus.

Hammar, T. (1990). Democracy and the Nation State. Aliens, Denizens and Citizens in a World of International Migration. Aldershot: Avebury.

Harris, N. (2002). Thinking the unthinkable. The immigration myth exposed. London: IB Tauris.

Harrison, L.E. (2000). Why culture matters? In Harrison, L.E. and Huntington, S.P. (Eds.) Culture Matters: How Values Shape Human Progress. New York: Basic books.

Helsinki by District 2004 (http://www.hel2.fi/tietokeskus/helsinki_alueittain_2004/index.html) 15.4.2005

Hirst, P.and Thompson, G. (1995). Globalisering – en myt? Internationell ekonomi och statlig styrning. Häften för kritiska studier 2/1995.

Hjerppe, R., Kari, S. and Lönnqvist, H. (2001). Johdanto. In Hjerppe, R., Kari, S. and Lönnqvist, H. (Eds.) Verokilpailu ja verotuksen kehittämistarpeet. VTT keskustelualoitteita 261. Discussion papers no:668. Helsinki: VTT. Pp. 1–4.

Hobsbawm, E. (1994). Nationalismi. Tampere; Vastapaino.

Hondagneu-Sotelo, P. (2001) Doméstica. Immigrant Workers Cleaning and Caring in the Shadows of Affluence. Berkeley: University of California Press.

Hämäläinen, M. (2001). Finnish Manager's Leadership Style – A Foreign Subordinate Perspective. Case Nokia Internet Communications. Unpublished pro gradu –thesis, Department of Management, Helsinki School of Economics and Business Administration.

ICI (Immigrant Council of Ireland) (2003). Labour Migration into Ireland. Study and Recommendations on Employment Permits, Working Conditions, Family Reunification and the Integration of Migration Workers in Ireland. Dublin: Future print.

Imbusch, K. (2001). EU Enlargement and Labour Immigration to Germany. No Massive Migration to be Expected. Economic Trends 6/2001. Pp. 93–97.

IMD (2001). The Competitiveness Yearbook. Switzerland, Lausanne.

IOM (International Organization for Migration) (2002). Selective Migration Flows from Albania to Italy, project code 988.CIT. Final Report.

Iredale, R. (2001). The Migration of Professionals: Theories and Typologies. International Migration Vol. 39 No. 5. Pp. 7–26.

(The) Irish labour market review. (2006). A FÁS Review of Irish Labour Market Trends and Policies. FÁS, Dublin.

(The) Irish labour market review. (2005). A FÁS Review of Irish Labour Market Trends and Policies. FÁS, Dublin.

Johnson, M. and Regets, J.M. (1998). International Mobility of Scientists and Engineers To the US- Brain Drain or Brain Circulation? NSF Issue Brief, June 2, Pp. 298-316.

Jokela, M. (1998). Episteemiset yhteisöt globaalien ympäristöongelmien äärellä. In Mykkänen, J. and Koskinen, I. (Eds.) Asiantuntemuksen politiikka – professiot ja julkisvalta Suomessa. Helsinki University Press. Helsinki. Pp.166-187.

Joly, D. (2000). Some Structural Effects of Migration on Receiving and Sending Countries. International Migration Vol. 38 (5). Pp. 25–39.

Joronen, T., Pajarinen, M. and Ylä-Anttila, P. (2000). Hansakaupasta hampurilaisketjuihin – historiallinen katsaus. In M.-L. Trux (Ed.): Aukeavat ovet. Kulttuurien moninaisuus Suomen elinkeinoelämässä. Helsinki: WSOY. Pp. 117–142.

Järjestöjen kannanotto ulkomaalaislain kokonaisuudistuksesta (2001).

Kangas, O. (1986). Luokkaintressit ja hyvinvointivaltio. Sisältöanalyyttinen tarkastelu suurimpien puolueiden ja etujärjestöjen sosiaalipoliittisista kannanotoista. Helsingin kauppakorkeakoulun julkaisuja D-84. Helsinki: Helsingin kauppakorkeakoulu.

Kaplan, R. and Kaplan, S. (1989). The Experience of Nature: A Psychological Perspective. New York: Cambridge University Press.

Kari, M., Laitinen-Kuikka, S. and Markwort, J. (2001). Sosiaaliturvajärjestelmät eri maissa. Suomen vakuutusalan koulutus ja kustannus Oy. Helsinki: Yliopistopaino.

Karisto, A., Takala, P. and Haapoja, I. (1998). Matkalla nykyaikaan. Elintason, elämäntavan ja sosiaalipolitiikan muutos Suomessa. Helsinki: WSOY.

Kaseva, H. and Vartia, P. (2002). Kohti eurooppalaista veroastetta. Suhdanne 2/2002. Pp. 82-87.

Keeley, B. (2007). Human Capital. How What You Know Shapes Your Life. OECD Insights. Paris. OECD.

Kelly, E. and Dobbin, F. (1998). How Affirmative Action Became Diversity Management. American Behavioral Scientist, Vol. 41, No. 7. Pp. 960-984.

Kets De Vries, M. F. R. (1994). Making a Giant Dance. Across the Board, Vol. 31, No. 9.

Kiander, J. (2001). EU:n itälaajeneminen ja suomalaiset työmarkkinat. Kansantaloudellinen aikakauskirja Vol. 97, No. 2, Pp. 296–314.

Kiander, J. (2004). Kiina ja Intia nousemassa talousmahtien kärkeen. Economic Trends 5/2004.

Kiljunen, K. (1999). Maailmantalouden hallinta. In S. Hassi, K. Kiljunen, S. Pietikäinen (Eds.): Maapallo haaste. Helsinki: Kustannusosakeyhtiö Otava.

Kinnunen, T. (2003). "If I can find a good job after graduation I may stay." Ulkomaalaisten tutkinto-opiskelijoiden integroituminen Suomeen. Occasional Paper 2b/ 2003. Helsinki: CIMO & Otus.

Knocke, W. & Herzberg, F. (2000). Mångfaldens barn söker sin plats. En studie om arbetsmarknadschanser för ungdomar med invandrarbakgrund. Stockholm: Svartvitts förlag.

Knocke, W. (1991). Women Immigrants – What is the "Problem"? Economic and Industrial Democracy. Vol. 12. Pp. 469–486.

Knocke, W. (1993). Kön, etnicitet och teknisk utveckling. In C.-U. Schierup & S. Paulson (Eds.) Arbetets etniska delning. Studier från en svensk fabrik. Stockholm: Carlssons förlag.

Kochan, T., Bezrukova, K., Ely, R., Jackson, S., Joshi, A., Jehn, K., Leonard, J., Levine, D. & Thomas, D. (2003). The effects of diversity on business performance: report of the diversity research network. Human resource management, Vol. 42, No 1. Pp. 3-21.

KOF index of Globalization (2007). http://globalization.kof.ethz.ch/ (1.6.2007)

Korkiasaari, J, (2000). Suomalaiset Ruotsissa 1940-luvulta 2000-luvulle. In Jouni Korkiasaari & Kari Tarkiainen (Eds.): Suomalaiset Ruotsissa. Suomalaisen siirtolaisuuden historia 3. Turku: Siirtolaisuusinstituutti. Pp. 133–496.

Korkiasaari, J. and Söderling, I. (1998) Finland: From a Country of Emigration into a Country of Immigration. In Söderling, I. (Ed.) A Changing Pattern of Migration in Finland and its Surroundings. Väestöntutkimuslaitoksen julkaisusarja D 32. Helsinki: Väestöliitto.

Koskinen, P. (2003). Uudet pelurit työntyvät gsm-markkinoille. Talouselämä 52/2003. 15.

Kotkin, P. (1992). How race, religion and identity determine success in the new global economy. Random House, NY.

Kotler, P. (1988). Marketing management: Analysis, planning, implementation and control. New Jersey: Prentice hall.

Kotler, P., Asplund, C. Rein, I. and Haider, D. (1999). Marketing places Europe. How to attract investments, industries, residents and visitors to cities, communities, regions and nations in Europe. Bolton. Prentice Hall.

Kujala, J. and Kuvaja, S. (2002). Sidosryhmät eettisen liiketoiminnan kirittäjinä. Helsinki: Talentum.

Kuptsch, C. and Pang, E.F. (2006). (Eds.) Competing for Global Talent. Geneva: International labor office (ILO).

Kurjenoja, J. (2003a). Lapsiperheiden verokurimus. Lapsiperheiden verotus, lapsilisät sekä päivähoito 11 Euroopan maassa. Verotietoa 37. Helsinki: Veronmaksajat.

Kurjenoja, J. (2003b). Kansainvälinen palkkaverovertailu 2003. Verotietoa 35. Helsinki: Veronmaksajat.

Kuznetsov, Y. (2006). (Ed.) Diaspora Networks and the International Migration of Skills. How Countries Can Draw on Their Talent Aboard? WBI Development studies, The World Bank, Washington DC.

Laari, O. (1997). Suomi ja inkerinsuomalaiset – etnisyys velvoittaa? Tiede & Edistys 4, Pp. 302–316.

Lash, S. (2002). Critique of Information. Sage Publications, London.

Lepola, O. (2000). Ulkomaalaisesta suomenmaalaiseksi. Monikulttuurisuus, kansalaisuus ja suomalaisuus 1990-luvun maahanmuuttopoliittisessa keskustelussa. Helsinki: Suomalaisen Kirjallisuuden Seura.

Lewis, R.D. (2002). When Cultures Collide. Managing Successfully Across Cultures. London: Nicholas Bearley Publishing.

Liebig, T.(2007). The Labour Market Integration of Immigrants in Denmark.OECD Social Employment and Migration Working Papers 50, OECD Directorate for Employment, Labour and Social Affairs.

Light, I. and Gold, S.J. (2000). Ethnic Economies. NY. Academic Press.

Linnamaa. R. (1999). Kaupunkiseudun kilpailukyvyn rakenteelliset ja dynaamiset elementit. In Sotarauta, M. (Ed.) Kaupunkiseutujen kilpailukyky ja johtaminen tietoyhteiskunnassa. ACTA 106, Helsinki; Suomen kuntaliitto. Pp. 18-40.

Luo, Y.-L. and Wang, W.-J. (2002) High-Skill Migration and Chinese Taipei's Industrial Development. In International Mobility of Highly Skilled. Paris: OECD Proceedings. Pp. 253–270.

Lutz, H. (1993). Migrant Women, Racism and the Dutch Labour Market. In Wrench, J. and Solomos, J. (Eds.) Racism and Migration in Western Europe. Oxford: Berg. Pp. 129–142.

Maffesoli, M. (1996). The Time of the Tribes. The Decline of Individualism in Mass Society. London. Sage Publications.

Malecki, E.J. and Bradbury, S.L. (1992). R&D Facilities and Professional Labour: Labour force Dynamics in High Technology. Regional Studies Vol. 26, No. 2. Pp. 23-136.

Martin, P. and Widgren, J. (2002). International Migration: Facing the Challenge. Population Bulletin Vol. 57, No. 1. Pp. 1–43.

Martin, P. (2002). Policies for Admitting Highly-skilled Workers into the United States. In OECD: International Mobility of Highly skilled. OECD proceedings, France. Pp. 271-290.

Massey, D. S., Arango, J., Hugo, G., Kouaouci, A., Pellegrino, A. and Taylor, J. E. (1993). Theories of International Migration: A Rewiew and Appraisal. Population and Development Review 19 No. 3. Pp. 431–466.

Massey, D.S. and Espinosa, K.E.(1997). What's Driving Mexico-U.S. Migration? A Theoretical, Empirical and Policy Analysis. The American Journal of Sociology Vol. 02, no.4. Pp.939-999.

Mattusch, N. (2004). EURES adviser, Employment office of Freiburg, Germany. Personal announcement In "Can we manage without competence abroad?"- seminar 23.3.2004, Turku, Finland.

McMullen [Fitzpatrick, I. and Ruiz, R.] (2007). How Emerging Economies Are Winning at Pay. (http://www.haygroup.com/downloads/ww/workspan-_How_Emerging_Economies_Are_Winning_at_Pay_March_2008.pdf)

Menz, G. (2002). Patterns in EU Labour Immigration Policy: National Initiatives and European Responses. Journal of Ethnic and Migration Studies Vol. 28, No. 4. Pp. 723–742.

Mercrer (2005). IT Pay around the World Survey 2005 – country rankings.

Mishra, R. (1981). Society and Social Policy: Theoretical Perspectives on Welfare. 2nd edition. London.

Ministry of Interior (2006). Suurten kaupunkiseutujen politiikkakokonaisuus. Alueiden kehittäminen 35/2006. Helsinki. Ministrof Interior.

Myrskylä, P. (2003). Maahanmuuttajat hivuttautuvat työmarkkinoille. Hyvinvointikatsaus 3/2003. Pp. 32–37.

Naumanen, M. (2004) TEKBARO. Teknologiabarometri kansalaisten asenteista ja kansakunnan suuntautumisesta tietoon perustuvaan yhteiskuntaan. (http: //www.tek.fi /teknologia/ tulevaisuus/ teknologiabarometri.pdf) (15.3.04).

Necef, M. (2000). Den danske debat om invandrere og fl ygninge 1964– 2000 – synspunkter i og på forskningen.Den jydske historiker. No. 89 juni 2000. 133–159.

NIFU/STEP (2005). Report on Science & Technology. Inicators for Norway. Oslo: The Research Council of Norway.

Noki, S. and Kovanen. K. (2008). Maahanmuutto- ja innovaatiopolitiikat kansainvälisessä osaajakilpailussa. Tarkastelussa Suomi, Irlanti, Isosta-Britannia, Kanada, Saksa ja Yhdysvallat. Opetusministeriön julkaisuja 2008:18. Ministry of Education

Nonaka, I. and Takeuchi, H. (1995). The Knowledge-creating Company. Oxford University Press.

Nordfors, R. (2001). Kansainvälisen koulun perustaminen Espooseen. Loppuraportti. Espoo: Espoon kaupunki (unpublished).

Nordström, L. (1991). Den ekonomiska integrationen. In Wilhelm Agrell (Ed.): Nationell säkerhet utan gränser. Stockholm: Allmänna förlaget.

OECD Factbook (2007): Economic, Environmental and Social Statistics. Paris: OECD

OECD (2006). Migration database. (www.oecd.org, migration data)

O'Neill, D; Nolan, B and Williams, J. (2002). Evaluating the Impact of a National Minimum Wage: Evidence from a New Survey of Firms in Ireland. Department of Economics Working Paper N117/09/02, Other Publications by External Agencies No. 20, 46 p.

Ojala, J and Lamberg, J-A. (2001). Douglass C. North ja uusi institutionaalinen taloustiede. In Riukulehto, S. (Ed.) Järkäleitä ja kulmakiviä. Instituutiot yhteiskunnassa. University of Vaasa, Levon institute, publication 96, Vaasa. Pp. 66-85.

Paananen, S. (1993). Työvoimaa rajan takaa. Työpoliittinen tutkimus 54. Helsinki: Työministeriö.

Paananen, S. (1999). Suomalaisuuden armoilla. Ulkomaalaisten työnhakijoiden luokittelu. Helsinki: Tilastokeskus.

Pettersson, R. F. (2003). Missä viipyvät Suomen nobelistit? Tieteessä tapahtuu 1/2003. Pp. 4–9.

Pierson, C. (1998) Beyond the Welfare State? The New Political Economy of Welfare. 2nd edition. Cambridge: Polity Press.

Piore, M. J. (1979). Birds of Passage. Migrant Labor and Industrial Societies. Cambridge: Cambridge University Press.

Pohjanpää, K., Paananen, S. and Nieminen, M. (2003). Maahanmuuttajien elinolot. Venäläisten, virolaisten, somalialaisten ja vietnamilaisten elämää Suomessa 2002. Elinolot 2003:1. Helsinki: Tilastokeskus.

Porter, M. (1989). Competitive Advantage of the Nations. Free press.

Portes, A. (1997). Globalization from Below: The Rise of Transnational Communities. WPTC-98-01. Princeton: Princeton University.

Portes, A. (1999). Conclusion: Towards a New World – the Origins and Effects of Transnational Activities. Ethnic and Racial Studies Vol. 22, No. 2. Pp. 463–477.

Prasad, P., Elmes, A.J., Mills, M.B. and Prasad, A. (1997). Managing the Organizational Melting Pot: Dilemmas of Workplace Diversity. Sage, London.

Rahikainen, M. (2001). "Naiset näkyvät Suomessa tekevän vaikka mitä". In M. Rahikainen and T. Räisänen (Eds.) "Työllä ei oo kukkaan rikastunna". Naisten töitä ja toimeentulokeinoja 1800- ja 1900-luvulla. Tietolipas 176. Helsinki: SKS. Pp.17–35.

Rakennetyöttömyyden purkaminen. Projektin raportti (2003). Työhallinnon julkaisu nro 321. Helsinki: Työministeriö.

Raunio, M. (2001). Osaajat valintojen kentällä. Helsingin, Tampereen, Turun, Jyväskylän, Porin ja Seinäjoen seutujen vetovoimaisuus virtaavassa maailmassa. Sente-julkaisuja 11/2001. Tampere: Tampereen yliopisto. Alueellisen kehittämisen tutkimusyksikkö.

Raunio, M. (2002a). Image of Finland Divided among Foreign ICT Professionals. Economic Trends 2/2002, Pp 21-28.

Raunio, M. (2002b). Suomi globaalitalouden osaajien valintojen kentällä. Ulkomaalaisten huippuosaajien mielikuvat ja todellisuudet suomalaisessa työ- ja kaupunkiympäristössä. Sente-publications 15, University of Tampre.

Raunio. M. (2003). Should I Stay or Should I Go? Images and realities of Foreign ICT professionals in Finnish work and living environments (English Summary). Sente- Working papers. University of Tampere.

Raunio, M. (2007). Creative Regions and Globalizing Socaial Capital: Connecting foreign ICT Experts to Finnish Innovation Environments. In Cooke, P. and Schwartz, D. (Eds.). Creative Regions. Technology, Culture and Knowledge Entrepreneurship. Regions and Cities, London. Routledge. Pp.40-62.

Reich, R.B. (1995). Rajaton maailma. Yritysten ja kansallisvaltioiden uudet pelisäännöt. Helsinki: Sitra.

Report by Aliens Act working group (Ulkomaalaislakityöryhmän mietintö) (2001) Sisäasiainministeriön julkaisusarja 12:2001.Helsinki. Ministry of the Interior.

Rio, C. M. (2000). "This Job Has No End": African American Domestic Workers and Class Becoming. In J. K. Gibson- Graham & S. A. Resnick & R. D. Wolff (Eds.) Class and Its Others. University of Minnesota Press: Minneapolis. Pp. 23–46.

Ritsilä, J. (2000). Mobility of the highly educated labour force. University of Jyväskylä, Faculty of Economics. Working paper 214.

RKP (2003). Ruotsalaisen kansanpuolueen puolueohjelma. http://www.sfp.fi /page/8/ 23.html (15.3.04).

Rogerson, C.M. (2000). Knowledge-based or Smart Regions in South-Africa. Paper presented in Urban Futures Conference 14th of July 2000, Johannesburg, South-Africa.

Rogerson, J.R. (1999).Quality of Life and City Competitiveness. Urban Studies, Vol.36. No.5-6. Pp. 969-985.

Rollason, N. (2002). International Mobility of Highly Skilled Workers: The UK Perspective. In OECD: International Mobility of Highly skilled. OECD proceedings, France. Pp. 327-340.

Roseveare, D. and Jorgensen, M. (2004). Migration and integration of immigrants in Denmark. Economics department working papers No. 386. OECD, ECO/WKP 20004/9.

Rouvinen, P. (2004). Competitiveness in the New Economy. The Research Institute of the Finnish Economy (Etla). Discussion papers No. 786, Helsinki.

Ruhs, M. (2006). Ireland: A Crash Course in Immigration Policy. Country profile prepared for the Migration Policy Institute, Washington

Rutanen, P. (2003). Kiinan dynamiikan taustalla tie aktiiviseksi osallistujaksi. Economic Trends 6/2003. Pp. 58-61.

SAK (Central organisation of Finnish trade unions) (1998a). Neljännes virolaisista haluaisi työskennellä Suomessa. Tiedote, 15.6.1998.

SAK (Central organisation of Finnish trade unions) (1998b). Suomalaiset tukevat Viron EU-jäsenyyttä – Virolaisten tuloa Suomeen töihin pelätään. Tiedote, 15.6.1998.

SAK (Central organisation of Finnish trade unions) (2000a) SAK:n osastopäällikkö Eero Heinäluoma: Itälaajeneminen merkitsee suurta muutosta työmarkkinoilla. Tiedote,4.9.2000.

SAK (Central organisation of Finnish trade unions) (2000b) Jopa 400 000 virolaista tulisi Suomeen töihin. Tiedote, 4.9.2000.

SAK (Central organisation of Finnish trade unions) (2001a) Työmarkkinoilla varauduttava EU:n laajenemiseen. Tiedote, 21.9.2001.

Salt, J., Clarke, J. and Schmidt, S. (2000). Patterns and Trends in International Migration in Western Europe. Eurostat Theme 3 Population and social conditions. Luxembourg: Eurostat.

Sarvimäki, Matti (2003). Euroopan unionin itälaajentuminen ja maahanmuutto Suomeen. VATT-tutkimuksia 98. Helsinki: Valtion taloudellinen tutkimuskeskus.

Sassen, S. (1999). Guests and Aliens. New York: The New Press.

Sassen, S. (1998). Globalization and Its Discontents. Essays on the new mobility of people and money. New York: The New Press.

Sassen, S. (1991). The Global City. New York, London, Tokyo. Princeton: Princeton University Press.

Saxenian, A. (2006). New Argonauts. Regional Advantage in a Global Economy. Cambridge, Harvard University press.

Saxenian, A (2002). Local and Global Networks of Immigrant Professionals in Silicon Valley: Public Policy Institute of California. San Francisco, California.

Saxenian, A. (1999). Silicon Valley's new Immigrant Entrepreneurs. PPIC, San Francisco, California.

Saxenian, A. (1994). Regional Advantage: Culture and Competition in Silicon Valley and Route 128. Harvard University press.

Saxenian, A. (1989). Regional Networks and Resurgence of Silicon Valley. Working paper no:497, Institute of Urban and Regional Development. University of California, Berkeley.

Schein, E.H. (1992). Organizational Culture and Leadership. 2nd edition. SF. Jossey-Bass Publishers.

Schienstock, G., Kautonen, M. and Koski, P. (2004). Escaping Path Dependency: The Case of Tampere, Finland. In Cooke, P. Heidenreich, M. and Braczyk, H-J.(eds.) Regional Innovation Systems. The Role of Governance in a Globalized World. 2nd edition. Routledge, London. Pp. 127-153.

Schienstock, G. and Kuusi, O. (1999). (Eds.)Transformation Towards a Learning Economy. The Challenge of the Finnish Innovation Systems. Sitra 213, Helsinki.

Science and technology policy council of Finland. (2003). Alueiden elinvoima syntyy innovaatioista. Osaaminen, erikoistuminen ja verkottuminen ratkaisevat menestyksen kansainvälisessä kilpailussa. Helsinki: TEKES.

Sennett, R. (2002). Työn uusi järjestys. Miten kapitalismi kuluttaa ihmisen luonnetta. Tampere: Vastapaino.

Siebert, H. (1999). The World Economy. London & New York: Routledge.

Silverman, M. (1991). Citizenship and the nationstate in France. Ethnic and Racial Studies Volume 14 Number 3. Pp. 333–350.

Singer, A. and Massey, D.S. (1999). The Social Process of Undocumented Border Crossing among Mexican Migrants. International Migration Review Vol. 32, No. 3. Pp. 561-592.

Sklair, L. (2001). The Transnational Capitalist Class. Oxford: Blackwell.

SOMERA-toimikunnan mietintö (2002). Komiteanmietintö 2002:4. Helsinki: Sosiaali-ja terveysministeriö.

SOPEMI (2006a). Trends in International Migration. Annual Report. 2006 Edition. Paris: OECD

SOPEMI (2006b). International Migration and Denmark. Sopemi report to OECD 2006. The Danish ministry of refugee, immigration and integration affairs.

SOPEMI (2004). Trends in International Migration. Annual Report. 2004 Edition. Paris: OECD.

SOPEMI (2003). Trends in International Migration. Annual Report. 2003 Edition. Paris: OECD.

SOPEMI (2001). Trends in International Migration. Annual Report. 2001 Edition. Paris: OECD

Sorainen, O. (2001). Työlupajärjestelmästä ennustettava, nopea ja joustava. Teollisuustieto 18/2001, Työelämä-liite. Teollisuus & Työnantajat .

Stalker, P. (2000). Workers Without Frontiers. The Impact of Globalization on International Migration. London: Lynne Rienner Publishers.

Statistics Finland (2005). Statistical Yearbook of Finland. Official Statistics of Finland. Statistics Finland. Helsinki. Multiprint.

Statistics Finland (2002). Foreigners and international migration. Population 2002:8, Helsinki.

Steinbock, D. (2004). Finnish Born Globals Face Extra-ordinary Challenges. Economic Trends 3/2004. Pp. 15-18.

Sthåle, P. and Grönroos, M. (1999). Knowledge Management – Tietopääoma yrityksen kilpailutekijänä. Ekonomia-series. WSOY. Porvoo.

Stora Enso (2003). Annual Report. http:// search.storaenso.com/2003/ (15.3.04).

Strandell, A. (1998). Asukasbarometri 1998. Asukaskysely suomalaisista asuinympäristöistä. Ministry of Environment, Finnish Environment 343. Helsinki.

Straubhaar, T. (2000). Why Do We Need a General Agreement on Movements of People (GAMP)? In Gosh, B. (Ed.) Managing Migration. Time for a New International Regime. Oxford University Press. Pp. 110-127.

Survey of German Tax laws (2004). www.germany.info/relaunch/business/taxes/ german_tax_rates.html (23.5.2005)

Tanner, A. (2003). Siirtolaisuus, valtio ja politiikka: Kanadan, Sveitsin ja Uuden-Seelannin työvoiman maahanmuutto ja politiikka 1975–2001. Ulkomaalaisviraston julkaisuja 4. Helsinki: Ulkomaalaisvirasto.

Tattari, V. (1989). Kaupunkien kehittämisstrategioita ja –keinoja OECD -maissa. Selvitysraportti, Suomen kaupunkiliitto. Sanomalehti Oy, Lahti.

The Times (2003) Where the Good Jobs Are Going? The Times, August 18, 2003. www.time.com/time/magazine/article/ 0,9171,1101030804-471198,00.html (15.10.2003).

Third European Report on Science & Technology Indicators (2003). ftp://ftp.cordis.lu/pub/indicators/docs/3rd_report.pdf (15.3.04).

Thunö, M. (2003). Channels of entry and preferred destinations: The circumvention of Denmark by Chinese immigrants. International Migration, Vol. 41, No. 3. Pp. 99-130.

Tilastokeskus (2003). Ulkomaalaiset ja siirtolaisuus 2002. Foreigners and international migration 2001. Väestö 2003:8. Helsinki: Statistics Finland.

Torvi, K. and Kiljunen, P. (2005). Onnellisuuden vaikea yhtälö. EVA:n kansallinen arvo- ja asennetutkimus 2005. EVA –raportti. Taloustieto Oy. Helsinki. Yliopistopaino.

Trompenaars, F. and Hampden-Turner, C. (1998). Riding the Waves of Culture. Understanding Diversity in Global Business. New York: Mc Graw Hill.

Trompenaars, F. (1993). Riding the Waves of Culture: Understanding Cultural Diversity in Business (First Edition) London: Nicholas Brealey.

Trux, M.-L. (2000). Monimuotoinen työyhteisö. In M.-L. Trux (Ed.) Aukeavat ovet – kulttuurien moninaisuus Suomen elinkeinoelämässä. Helsinki: WSOY. Pp. 261–216.

TT (Teollisuus ja työnantajat): (2002). Globalisaatio ja Suomen elinkeinoelämä.

Törmälä, K. (1998). Nokian Oulun yksiköiden ekspatrioottien kulttuurinen sopeutuminen 1990-luvulla. Unpublished pro gradu-thesis. Taideaineiden ja antropologian laitos. University of Oulu 1998.

Ulrich, R.S. (1984). Aesthetic and Emotional Influences of Vegetation. A Review of the Scientific Literature. Swedish council for building research. Document D 22:1985, Stockholm.

Valtiovarainministeriö (2001). Talouspolitiikan lähivuosien haasteista. Valtiovarainministeriön talouspolitiikan strategia –ryhmän muistio.

Van Steenbergen, B. (1994). The Condition of Citizenship: an Introduction. In B. van Steenbergen (Ed.) The Condition of Citizenship. London: Sage. Pp. 66–75.

Vartia, P. and Ylä-Anttila, P. (2003). Kansantalous 2028. Helsinki: ETLA & Taloustieto.

Vertovec, S. and Cohen, R. (1999). Introduction. In Vertovec, S. & Cohen, R. (Eds.) Migration, Diasporas and Transnationalism. Cheltenham: An Elgar Reference Collection. xiii–xxviii.

Sustainable Cities for the 21st Century. Brisbane: Longman. Pp.252-285.

Virdee, Satnam (1999). England: Racism, Anti-racism and Changing Position of Racialised Groups in Economic Relations. In Dale, G. & Cole, M. (Eds.) The European Union and Migrant Labour. Oxford: Berg. Pp. 69–90.

Virtanen, P. (2003a). Koulutetun työvoiman kansainvälinen liikkuvuus. Empiirinen tutkimus akavalaisten muuttoaikeista ulkomaille. Pro gradu -thesis, Department of Economics, University of Helsinki.

Virtanen, V. (2003b) Valta- ja vastavirtaan. Selvitys maassamuuttajien elinoloista, uuteen kiinnittymisestä ja arvotaustasta Suomessa. Sisäasiainministeriön julkaisu 14/2003.

Wallerstein, I. (1974) The Modern World System. New York: Academic Press.

Werner, H. (2002). The Current "Green Card" Initiative for Foreign IT Specialists in Germany. In OECD: International Mobility of Highly Skilled. OECD proceedings, Paris, OECD. Pp. 321-326

Widgren, J. and Martin. P. (2002). Managing Migration: The Role of Economic Instruments International Migration Vol. 40, No. 5., Pp. 213–229

Wikhall, M. (2002). Culture as Attraction – Migration Decisions of Highly Educated in a Swedish context. In ERSA – From industry to advanced services. European Regional Science Association's International conference 2002. Book of Abstracts. Pp. 203.

Wiklund, T. (1995). Det tilljorda landskapet. En undersökning av förutsättiningarna for urban kultur in Norden. Göteborg: Bokfoörlaget Korpen.

Willoghby, K. (1995) The Local Milleux of Knowledge-based Industries: What Can We Learn from a Regional Analysis of Commercial Biotechnology. In Brotchie, J., Batty, M., Blakely, E., Hall, P. and Newton, P. (Eds.) Cities in Competition. Productive and Helsinki: Ministry of Interior..

Wrench, J. (1991) Gatekeepers in the Urban Labour Market: Constraining or Constrained? In Cross, M. & Payne, G. (Eds.) Work and the Enterprise Culture. Explorations in Sociology No. 38. London: The Falmer Press.

Zuboff, S. (1987). In the Age of the Smart Machine: The Future of Work and Power. Basic Books.

APPENDIX 1

Materials and methods

Phase-by-phase method of the implementation of the research

Preliminary research, scientific literature and documentary materials

The present study made extensive use of current reports, official documents and media reports from both Finland and abroad. The materials were compiled from various databases and from Finnish and international internet news summaries. Intensive media tracking was also carried out from the end of 2001 until spring 2004.

Selection process of the target group and the preliminary interviews

The data derived from interviews and survey questionnaires was collected in four major urban centres – places where most of the foreign experts work. In Finland, both foreigners and skilled workers are concentrated in the biggest cities. The areas included in the study were the capital city-region (in practise, Helsinki and Espoo), Turku city-region including Salo (the ICT cluster of Salo is connected with the urban region of Turku), Tampere city-region and Oulu city-region.

In each region, expertise-focused companies and university departments with foreign workers in positions demanding a high level of expertise were selected. ICT respondents worked in companies and biotech respondents mostly in academic research units and departments. Some biotech respondents were also selected in the internet survey, but their share was small (less than 2 percent).

In order to provide background and sharpen the perspectives used in the study, also people who were in charge of recruiting and adjusting of foreign workers were interviewed. These included corporate human resources employees and supervisors, the managers of the units that were hiring, as well as relocation consultants who help newly-arrived foreign experts in a number of practical matters, from transportation to their new home to dealing with the tax office, and even shopping. Also interviewed were local and government officials who work with immigration issues. The intention of the interviews was to gather information from the standpoint of the organisations with regard to foreign experts, and to understand the recruiting and assimilation processes at a practical level. The professionals involved in assimilation and immigration matters and the recruiters were asked in some parts to consider some of the same questions that were presented to the target group. The objective was to reveal possible differences in viewpoint or conflicts in the interpretations of employers, employees and the officials regarding the reasons that had brought the respondents to Finland, as well as new immigrants' experiences with Finnish working and living environments. Among employers, no obvious conflicts arose in the interpretations they offered. More obviously differing viewpoints emerged among officials, and these can be said to reflect the opinions of "official Finland." These differences in viewpoint are visible in the parts of the book that deal with immigration policy.

In practice, representatives of the public sector – locally and nationally – had so far had little experience with issues having to do with foreign experts. This points to the newness of the trend in the context of Finnish urban development and of developing the attractiveness of Finland and its labour market.

As mentioned in the Foreword, part of the research for this book was conducted as part of the "Regional Brain Gain" initiative, coordinated by Synocus Oy (Inc.). At the end of 2002, the project collected basic personnel data, including the number of foreign employees in the organisation, from 40 different organisations.

The survey in the "Should I Stay or Should I Go" study

As part of Mika Raunio's[12] (2002) "Should I Stay or Should I Go?" study in 2001–2002, an internet survey was conducted to discover foreign experts' valuations and assessments of their life in Finland. The goal of 30–100 responses from each urban area was reached. The questionnaire was delivered electronically to the actual target group via company human resource departments. Of the delivered questionnaires, 556 were returned, which represents a response rate of about 40 percent – low, but nevertheless meeting validity requirements. The single-delivery method contributed to the low response rate; repeat requests to return the questionnaire were not made, and such requests can boost the response rate by as much as 20 percent. In addition, the survey was rather long, which further lowered the rate of response. In the case of companies, the same target group was also being asked to participate in other, internal surveys. The majority of the responses, as seen in Table 2, came from the Helsinki metropolitan area. This reflects the concentration of expertise-intensive fields, immigrants and foreign experts in the area of the capitol.

Interviews with foreign experts in Finland

The experiences and views of the target group – ICT and biotech experts – were evaluated through thematic interviews. For ICT experts, the interviews were extended to spouses as well, because relocation usually involves the whole family. The themes and final questions of the interviews were developed using information obtained from earlier phases of the study.

---

12 "Should I Stay or Should I Go" -project was headed by professor Markku Sotarauta, Research Unit for Urban and Regional Development Studies (SENTE), University of Tampere, Finland.

ICT respondents were selected from people who had voluntarily signed up to participate in an internet survey. This group encompassed different countries of origin, age groups and genders. To reach spouses, the target group itself was utilised, as were various associations and contact persons who collaborated with foreign spouses either through work or a civic group.

Table 1. Responses to targeted internet survey, by city.

City of residence	*Responses*
Helsinki	216
Espoo	156
Tampere	66
Turku/Salo	45
Oulu	35
Others	38
Total	*556*

At universities, the selection of respondents was done directly, according to name, through personnel logs. University administrations do not collect information about the nationality of their employees, so this "hands-on" method was the only systematic way to reach the target group. The target group received an interview request via e-mail, and all who agreed were subsequently interviewed.

The most international area of academic research is the natural sciences, especially biotechnology. The University of Helsinki's biosciences units employ the greatest number of foreigners of all Finnish universities (in 2003, 116 of the 400 scientists working in its institutes were of foreign origin). The total numbers of scientists, including the share of foreign scientists, were much lower in other biotech units included in the study, namely universities in Tampere and Oulu. University scientists and instructors frequently have an official employment contract and thus constitute members of the public sector; however, in this context we will use the terms official and public sector to denote other *officials* who are excluded from our target group.

The duration of the interviews was generally 45 to 90 minutes and most were recorded and transcribed. ICT respondents were interviewed by Mika Raunio and Agnes Bayer, and the biotech experts were interviewed by Annika Forsander and Perttu Salmenhaara. Edina Rudner also interviewed the foreign spouses of ICT experts in order to expand the scope of the study to include the viewpoints of the families of experts, because family members play a significant role in the wellbeing and choices that experts make. Among the interviewers, Bayer and Rudner were of an immigrant background, which may have helped to disarm respondents from trying to present a uniformly positive front. Many respondents value the interviewer's ability to, even marginally, share his or her own experience with immigration. While the interviews with experts showed no clear sign of "keeping up appearances", their viewpoints did differ from those of their families, and the interviews with spouses were therefore justified. Most interviews were conducted in English, with the exception of 15 interviews that occurred in Finnish or Hungarian.

Table 2. Number of experts and spouses interviewed, by city.

City of residence	*Experts*	*Spouses*	*Total*
Helsinki and Espoo	28	9	37
Tampere	21	8	29
Turku/Salo	16	7	23
Oulu	16	8	24
Total	*81*	*32*	*113*

Table 3. Interview structure used in thematic interviews of foreign experts.

<table>
<tr>
<td>Occupational factors<ul><li>Job description</li><li>Working methods (autonomy vs. control)</li><li>Equivalency of job description and qualifications</li><li>Incentives</li><li>Motivation and opportunities for professional development</li><li>Satisfaction with work and reasons for it</li><li>Atmosphere of work environment</li><li>Interviewee's opinion of measures Finnish decision-makers should take to attract more foreign expertise to the field</li></ul></td>
<td>Images and background factors of immigration<ul><li>Decision to move – how the decision was made, what factors affected it (role of values in making choices: career, spouse's career, image of living environment, other)</li><li>Role of social relationships – what was the source of the information that led to the decision to move</li><li>Impact that the source of information or discussions with various people had on the decision (significance of the source of information)</li><li>Opportunities – respondent's past and present opportunities and desire for moving</li></ul></td>
</tr>
<tr>
<td>Future<ul><li>Producing the ideal: where to live and what to do, if free to choose</li></ul></td>
<td>Place of residence<ul><li>Social services and quality of living environment</li><li>Use of public services</li></ul></td>
</tr>
</table>

▪ What will the interviewee's life look like in five years, if s/he is free to choose (place of residence, work) ▪ How much faith the interviewee has that the ideal will/will not become a reality	▪ Opinion on the quality and significance of services in choosing a place of residence ▪ Social relationships: contact with group of one's own nationality, contact with close connections in the country of origin, contact with the transnational community in Finland, contact with the surrounding environment, and methods of free-time use